SOLAR INTERIORS

SOLAR INTERIORS

Energy-Efficient Spaces Designed for Comfort

Katherine Panchyk

VNR **VAN NOSTRAND REINHOLD COMPANY**
NEW YORK   CINCINNATI   TORONTO   LONDON   MELBOURNE

Copyright © 1984 by Van Nostrand Reinhold Company Inc.
Library of Congress Catalog Card Number 82-25914
ISBN 0-442-28786-0

Printed in the United States of America

Designed by Paul Chevannes

All photographs and illustrations by the author unless otherwise noted.

Published by Van Nostrand Reinhold Company Inc.
135 West 50th Street
New York, New York 10020

Van Nostrand Reinhold Company Limited
Molly Millars Lane
Wokingham, Berkshire RG11 2PY, England

Van Nostrand Reinhold
480 La Trobe Street
Melbourne, Victoria 3000, Australia

Macmillan of Canada
Division of Gage Publishing Limited
164 Commander Boulevard
Agincourt, Ontario M1S 3C7, Canada

16 15 14 13 12 11 10 9 8 7 6 5 4 3 2 1

Library of Congress Cataloging in Publication Data

Panchyk, Katherine
  Solar interiors.

  Bibliography: p. 157
  Includes index.
  1. Solar heating. 2. Solar air conditioning.
3. Buildings—Environmental engineering. I. Title.
TH7413.P33 1983   747'.8869   82-25914
ISBN 0-442-28786-0

CONTENTS

To my family

ACKNOWLEDGMENTS

I would like to express my sincere appreciation to the following people for their help and advice:

Barbara Ravage, editor at Van Nostrand Reinhold, for guiding me through the production of this manuscript; Robert, Richard, and Diana, for their cooperation and encouragement; Joong Lee and George Baker, structural engineers, for advice on the structural feasibility of the retrofits; Thomas Wieschenberg, Robert Panchyk, and Robert Stidolph, my photographers, for their great photos; The Homesworth Corporation, American German Industries, and Pella/Rolscreen Company for contributing photos of their products; and all the people who allowed their homes to be photographed and Con Edison for permission to use a photograph of their Westchester Conservation House.

INTRODUCTION

There is a disturbing gap between the field of solar energy and that of interior design, almost as though one had nothing to do with the other. Yet there is a direct relationship between the natural elements and the interior environment, both of which affect human comfort within. This book sets out to explore and define this relationship between the exterior and interior in order to arrive at total *nature-sensitive* interiors.

Since interiors serve as environments for individuals, the first step is to study human reactions to indoor surroundings. This analysis of human thermal responses reveals several concepts, some of which are little known but all of which may aid the design of a comfortable environment for occupants of a space.

The second step involves a survey of the numerous materials available for use in an interior today. A close look at the properties of these materials shows how they function as part of human shelter in the form of insulation from adverse external forces, storage of heat from the sun's energy, or as a cooling influence. An additional function of these materials, having to do solely with human thermal responses to them, is pointed out to facilitate appropriate material selection in planning interiors.

A breakdown of specific design techniques follows. Methods for natural daylighting design, maximum utilization of artificial illumination, use and storage of heat from the sun, natural ventilation, heat circulation in a space, window treatment including shading, insulating, and heat collecting, floor and wall treatment, fabric selection, and furniture arrangement are all explored.

The individual aspects of design then come together in the final step, which demonstrates total designs responding to various combinations of external influences. Because intended spatial function and internal and external influences differ, every space is unique and every corresponding design solution therefore unique as well. Total design solutions illustrate how we can most fully benefit from exposures having desirable natural influences, as well as overcome the problems of those exposures with adverse natural influences; design alone can alter undesired effects and achieve optimum interior environments. Each design solution recognizes the influence of outdoor conditions upon the interior and fulfills the function for which it was intended. Finally, every solution acknowledges the sensitivity of human beings to their interior surroundings.

Chapter 1

THE HUMAN BODY AS A HEATING AND COOLING SYSTEM

MAN IS THE MOST INTELLIGENT OF CREATURES, BUT like all living things he is highly sensitive to his physical surroundings, so much so that both natural and man-made environments have a great impact on his productivity and well-being. A 1951 study done by Ellsworth Huntington in *Principles of Human Geography* on man and climate shows that adverse weather conditions diminish health and productivity in human beings. In much the same way, a deficient interior environment can have unfavorable psychological and physiological effects on individuals. For this reason, before attempting to design or redesign a man-made environment, we need to explore the human responses to it.

Although some reactions of a human being to a given physical setting may be labeled psychological, there are often physiological bases for such behavior. For instance, although working in an office without windows can have a negative psychological effect on an individual, his low spirits may well be due in part to the physical and physiological effects of poor lighting and inadequate ventilation.

Passive solar architecture and interiors respond to the elements of nature. This same responsiveness can be applied to the individuals who will experience these buildings and spaces. In this way, a harmony can be established among the three basic components of environmental design: *nature, building,* and *man.* The design of the *building* will evolve based on the two elements that made it necessary—*nature* and *man.*

The next three chapters are devoted to how human beings respond to the environment surrounding them. What makes individuals comfortable? What in their interior environment makes them uncomfortable? Very often, occupants of a space may have feelings of discomfort but cannot pinpoint the cause.

A number of physical conditions and design elements affect the quality of living within an interior; some are obvious, others are rather subtle. A complete study of human responses to the man-made environment can reveal the causes of discomfort and thus eliminate them with appropriate design solutions.

Human Thermal Comfort: The Comfort Zone

Individuals judge their own thermal comfort in an interior space by sensations of heat or cold. When neither excessive heat nor cold is felt, the interior is judged to be thermally comfortable. This condition indicates that the space is within an individual's *comfort zone.* The comfort zone can therefore be defined as a thermal condition within which little or no effort is needed for the human body to adjust to the surrounding environmental conditions.

Effective Temperature

The temperature a person feels results from the temperature of the air as well as the relative humidity and the movement of air within a space. Since these three thermal elements are interrelated, a change in one can often be compensated by an adjustment in another. A rise in air temperature, for instance, can be comfortable when com-

1

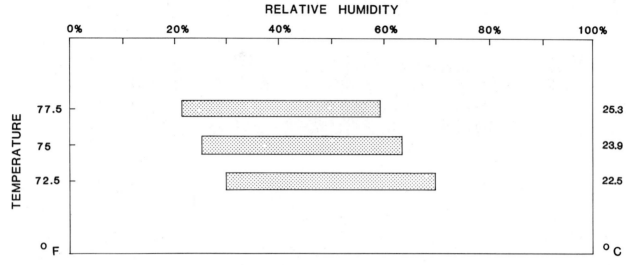

RELATIVE HUMIDITY

TEMPERATURE

°F   °C

1-1. New comfort-effective temperatures of 73° to 77°F ET (22.8° to 25°C ET) as determined by the ASHRAE in its 1982 Handbook of Fundamentals *for lightly clothed sedentary* individuals, where average room-surface temperatures are equal to room-air temperatures and where air movement is less than 40 feet per minute.

bined with increased air movement. On the other hand, the comfort temperature is lower in a space having a high percentage of relative humidity.

American scientists have developed the term *effective temperature* to denote the combined effects of air temperature, relative humidity, and air motion. For example, an effective temperature of 70 (70 ET) is a combination of 70°F (21°C), 50 percent relative humidity, and relatively still air moving at a rate of only 15–25 feet per minute (4.6–7.6 m/min.). The chart in figure 1-1 shows the latest range of effective temperatures that are considered to be within the comfort zone by the ASHRAE (American Society of Heating, Refrigerating and Airconditioning Engineers) in the 1982 *Handbook of Fundamentals*.

Factors Affecting the Comfort Zone

Because such factors as age, sex, activity level, type of clothing, and climatic origin all influence a person's comfort level, effective comfort zone temperatures assume certain things about an individual: he or she will be considered an average person at seated rest, wearing ordinary indoor clothing. Also applicable will be the climate someone is normally familiar with; for instance, people from tropical climates will generally be comfortable at temperatures as much as 30°F (16.7°C) higher than those from a cold climate would be. Individuals performing a physical activity are comfortable at significantly lower temperatures than those at rest. Because of variations in metabolism, people above forty years of age generally prefer warmer temperatures than those below that age. Women tend to require slightly higher temperatures than men.

The rising cost of fuel in recent years has prompted many people to try adjusting to comfort at lower indoor temperatures, sometimes by wearing warmer clothing. This change in indoor wear, however, is not reflected in figure 1-1 on interior comfort-effective temperatures.

The Body as a Heat Generator: The British Thermal Unit

The human body can be compared to a heat-generating plant in which the fuel burned is food. Only 20 percent of the energy derived from the oxidation of foods is directly used by the body; the remaining 80 percent is released as heat. The heat produced by the human body is expressed in terms of *British thermal units* (calories). A British thermal unit, or Btu, is the amount of heat needed to raise the temperature of one pound of water one degree Fahrenheit. (A calorie is the amount of heat needed to raise one gram of water one degree Centigrade.) This same unit is used to measure heat gain from the sun, mechanical equipment, and appliances. The amount of heat generated by the body can vary greatly, depending on the type of activity one is involved in. A seated person at rest generates approximately 400 Btu/hour (100.8 kcal/hr.), whereas one engaged in heavy exercise can generate up to 2,500 Btu/hour (630 kcal/hr.).

Heat Transfer to and from the Body

In order to maintain equilibrium, the human body gives off heat to the surrounding environment. Heat is transferred to and from the body in four basic ways: *radiation, conduction, convection,* and *evaporation.*

Radiation

The two basic types of radiation are visible radiation such as solar radiation, and thermal, or invisible radiation such as that produced by a hot radiator. Visible radiation is a high-temperature, short-wave energy that passes through the atmosphere as a ray or a beam. Upon striking an object, a portion of the visible radiation is absorbed as heat while the rest is reflected as light. Thermal radiation is a lower-temperature, longer-wavelength radiation of heat that can be given off by any object. In an interior environment,

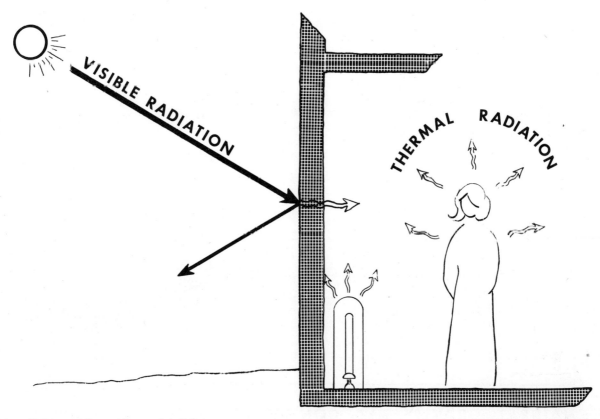

1-2. *Visible and thermal types of radiation.*

thermal radiation is the type that occurs most frequently.

All objects radiate thermal energy to the surrounding environment. When an object is warmer than surrounding objects and surfaces, a net radiant heat loss from the object results. When, on the other hand, its surroundings are warmer, the result is a net radiant heat gain. In the same way, the human body radiates its heat to surfaces and objects within a space, resulting in a net radiant heat loss from the body. When, however, a person stands close to a source of radiant heat such as a radiator, this hot surface radiates its heat toward the body, resulting in a net radiant heat gain by the body. Excessive radiant body-heat loss or gain in an interior results in an adverse thermal environment for an individual.

Conduction

Conductive heat transfer occurs when two objects of different temperatures are in contact with each other. The direction of heat flow is from the warmer to the cooler object, and the rate of heat transfer depends on the type of contact made. The heat loss of the human body by conduction is significant only when contact is made with a surface or object colder than the human body. While air is always in contact with the human body, its insulating quality makes human conductive heat loss to the surrounding air insignificant in an interior environment.

Convection

Heat can be transferred by motion or convection of an element. Forced convection occurs when air is warmed and then ducted from one location to another. Convective heat transfer can also occur naturally when warm air, lighter than cold air, rises, causing cooler air to replace it. This natural gravity convection of air sets up a circulation of heat within a space. When a source of heat is present in a space, the natural gravity convection of air becomes stronger, and heat is transferred from the surface of the heat source at a rapid rate. An individual exposed to air movement experiences cooling by convection. In an interior with relatively still air conditions, cold drafts along the floor induced by natural gravity air convection can cause air movement of approximately 15–25 feet/minute (4.6–7.6 m/min.), causing convective cooling of the body.

Evaporation

Evaporation of moisture from a surface causes cooling of that surface. The faster the rate of evaporation, the faster the rate of cooling. The rate of moisture evaporation is controlled by the moisture content of the air. The relative humidity, therefore, determines the effectiveness of cooling by evaporation.

The cooling of an object is facilitated when moisture is present upon its surface. Evaporative cooling of the human body can occur naturally under hot environmental conditions when the sweat that forms upon the skin's surface evaporates.

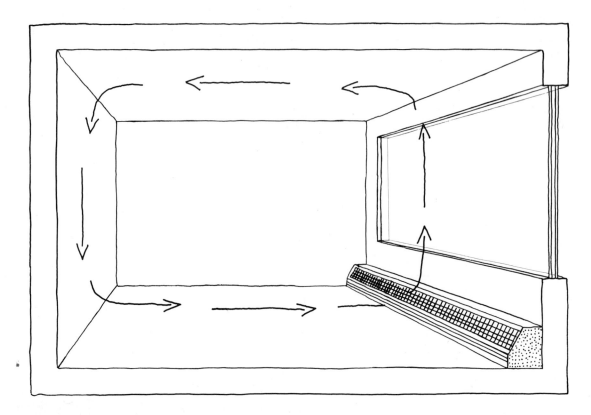

NATURAL GRAVITY AIR CONVECTION

1-3. When a source of heat is introduced into a space, the warmed air rises and induces air circulation within.

Significance of Radiation, Convection, and Evaporation in Heat Transfer from the Body

Of the four types of heat transfer, radiation, convection, and evaporation are most significant in moving heat from the body in an interior space.

It is estimated that for standard indoor conditions, a person at rest generating 400 Btu/hour (100.8 kcal/hr.) at 74°F (23.3°C) and 50 percent relative humidity loses 25 percent of total body heat through evaporation, 25 percent through convection, and 50 percent through radiation to surrounding objects and surfaces. The relationship of these losses varies depending on the surrounding environmental conditions and skin temperature. However, loss through radiation from the body is most significant, and therefore its control may be helpful in efforts to adjust to lower temperatures. In order to achieve thermal comfort it is helpful to know some common causes of body heat gain or loss.

Sources of Heat Gain by the Body
1. Digestion of food
2. Physical activity
3. Tensing of muscles or involuntary physical activity (shivering)
4. Absorption of radiant heat from the sun, or glowing or nonglowing hot objects
5. Air temperatures warmer than skin temperature
6. Contact with warmer objects

Sources of Heat Loss from the Body
1. Radiation to colder objects and surfaces
2. Conduction to air below skin temperature
3. Conduction through contact with colder objects
4. Evaporation through breathing and sweating
5. Air convection

Human Body Adjustment to Cold and Warm Temperatures

Our adjustment to lower indoor air temperatures involves more than simply increasing layers of clothing. The human body itself, through a biological process, is able to adapt to warmer or cooler temperatures. Although normal inner body temperature is 98.6°F (37°C), skin temperature can vary significantly. The average skin temperature of a person at rest at room temperature ranges from 86° to 97°F (30° to 36.1°C). The body regulates the temperature at the surface of the skin in response to the surrounding environmental conditions.

When indoor air temperature rises above an individual's comfort zone, the body's circulatory system responds as a heat convecting medium. In order to dissipate heat from deeper body tissues, the superficial veins begin to dilate, carrying the body's interior heat via the blood to the surface of the skin. This action causes the skin temperature to rise, which in turn increases the heat loss from the skin by radiation and convection to the surrounding environment.

After the veins have dilated to a maximum (therefore making the heat loss through the skin as great as it can be), sweating becomes the body's tool to dissipate heat through evaporative cooling of the skin.

When indoor temperatures drop below the comfort zone, the superficial veins constrict while deeper veins dilate. This brings blood away from the skin surface and moves it to the internal organs to retain body heat. In this way, a minimum of body heat is transferred to the skin, lowering the skin temperature and in turn decreasing heat loss from it.

Influence of Humidity Levels on Comfort

The amount of moisture the air can hold is determined by its temperature. Cold air can hold significantly less moisture than warm air. *Relative humidity* is the ratio of moisture present in the air to the maximum the air is able to hold at a given temperature. For example, air at 40°F (4.4°C) and 100 percent relative humidity contains considerably less moisture than air at 85°F (29.4°C) and 100 percent relative humidity.

Humidity affects human comfort most acutely in warmer temperatures, when evaporative cooling becomes a major means of body heat dissipation. The rate of evaporation of moisture from the surface of the skin determines its rate of cooling, and both of these are dependent on the saturation of air with moisture.

When air is highly saturated with moisture, the rate of evaporation is slow; dry conditions, on the other hand, facilitate evaporation. It is for this reason that people living in extremely hot and dry climates are able to maintain more effective body heat regulation than those in hot and humid climates. According to John E. Flynn and Arthur W. Segil in *Architectural Interior Systems,* some maximum temperature and humidity combinations at which the body is still able to maintain thermal equilibrium are:

88°F (31°C)　　—100 percent relative humidity
99.5°F (37.5°C)—51 percent relative humidity
113°F (45°C)　　—18 percent relative humidity

Although humidity plays an important role in human thermal equilibrium in warm temperatures (those above the comfort zone), its effects as a source of heat loss from the body become less significant as environmental temperatures cool. At indoor temperatures of 65°F (18.3°C) and 45 percent relative humidity, a person at rest generating 400 Btu/hour (100.8 kcal/hr.) loses only about 70 Btu's (17.6 kcal), or 18 percent of total body heat generated, through evaporation. This indicates that the wintertime thermal effects of indoor humidity levels on the body are minimal. Nevertheless, some researchers advocate humidifying indoor air as a means of increasing comfort at lower temperatures, even though this theory holds true only under extremely dry conditions. In most residences, activities such as cooking, laundering, and bathing, combined with transpiration of houseplants, generally add enough moisture to the indoor air to maintain relative humidities of at least 30 to 35 percent. Increasing the relative humidity much beyond this may result in severe condensation on windows and within exterior wall framing.

Humidifiers

Although many people feel that dry air is unhealthy, there is little medical evidence confirming the health benefits of humidifying indoor air. Other than minor discomforts, the health of people who work in buildings with humidified air and of those who work in buildings with drier air does not vary significantly.

Not only are the health benefits of humidifiers doubtful, but sometimes the humidifiers themselves are the cause of respiratory problems. Organisms that thrive in humidifiers have been linked to an allergic lung disease. Outbreaks of what is called "humidifier fever" have been reported among groups of workers in buildings with humidified air. Symptoms include shortness of breath, cough, and fever. Typically, symptoms disappear on the weekend and reappear on Mondays, when the worker returns to an office filled with contaminated air.

Such minor discomforts caused by low indoor relative humidity as dry skin can be prevented with oils and moisturizers. When excessively dry indoor conditions cause discomfort to people with sinus problems or a propensity for nosebleeds, humidification may be desired. Since organisms thrive in water at or slightly above room temperature, humidifying devices using water at these temperatures require the most maintenance. Weekly cleaning of humidifiers and daily washing of cool-mist vaporizers is recommended. Health problems associated with humidifying devices do not apply to steam vaporizers because of the germicidal effect of boiling water.

Effect of Air Movement on the Body

In addition to temperature and humidity levels, movement of air is an important factor in the health and comfort of individuals in an interior environment. Air can be moved by mechanical systems through ducts or fans, by natural gravity convection, or through drafts created by open windows. The velocity and the path of the moving air have an important relationship to individuals in both summer and winter.

Air motion transfers heat from the body and causes accelerated evaporation of moisture from the skin. The temperature at which an individual can be comfortable in the summer increases as indoor air velocities rise above 25 feet/minute (7.62 m/min.). The velocity of indoor air at or above room temperature can be as high as 200 feet/minute (60.96 m/min.) without any complaints of excessive draft or disruption of task activities. The chart in figure 1-4 shows how increased air movement can compensate for uncomfortable temperature or humidity levels. Certain combinations of wind speed, temperature, and relative humidity can create near comfort conditions for a person at seated rest.

Several factors influence the effectiveness of natural ventilation in an interior. The main determinant of outside airflow into a space is the position of window openings

TEMPERATURE & HUMIDITY		AIR VELOCITY	
76°F (24.4°C)	50% RH	15–25 ft./min.	(4.5–7.8 m/min.)
75°F (23.9°C)	80% RH ⎫	100 ft./min.	(30 m/min.)
80°F (26.7°C)	30% RH ⎭		
82°F (27.8°C)	30% RH ⎫	200 ft./min.	(60 m/min.)
75°F (23.9°C)	100% RH ⎭		

1-4.   *Air movement as compensation for uncomfortable temperature or humidity.*

with respect to prevailing summer winds. A wintertime priority may be to seal windows and insulate cold exposures, but free airflow through the house becomes important during warmer seasons. Although summer and winter considerations often conflict, good planning and efficiently sealed and insulated openings can serve both summer and winter interests. Techniques such as triple glazing, heavy drapery, and thermal shades or shutters can minimize heat loss at windows during the winter, yet provide the opportunity for summertime ventilation (see chapter 10), when a natural airflow through the interior assures comfort and reduces the need for mechanical cooling.

Although the cooling of the body is not commonly desired in winter, air movement is nevertheless essential for the proper distribution of heat within a space. Air circulation, whether from a hot-air distribution system or through natural gravity convection, affects individuals within a space. The type of heating system as well as the layout and design of the interior determine how air currents are created within. Since occupants are closest to floor surfaces, cold downdrafts at windows and along the floor can make them chilly even at optimum environmental temperatures. Chapter 10 suggests methods of heat circulation and prevention of drafts.

Air Quality and Indoor Pollution

A combination of temperature, relative humidity, and air movement that falls within the comfort zone provides an ideal thermal environment for an individual. An important nonthermal element, air quality, has equal significance in the overall health and comfort of individuals in their interior environment.

The term *air quality* is often associated with outdoor air. When the natural air currents are diminished and polluted air is trapped above an urban area, the air quality is reported to be unhealthy. In much the same way, the lack of air movement or fresh air changes in an interior can cause the used air to become overly polluted, resulting in unhealthy indoor air quality.

In large commercial buildings, the number of necessary fresh-air changes is calculated and then supplied by mechanical ventilating systems. Air change standards vary with the type of occupancy, density, and use of space. In private homes air infiltration is often the only means of wintertime ventilation.

Air Infiltration

The main problem with relying on infiltration of outdoor air is that it does not supply a constant rate of fresh air.

The infiltration rate of a structure varies with its construction and outdoor wind velocities. The highest infiltration occurs on the windward side of a building, usually the north or west exposure in cold climates. This type of uncontrolled ventilating system is highly wasteful of energy. Rooms with large window areas often receive excessive outdoor air, while centrally located spaces such as kitchens and bathrooms may remain underventilated.

Outdoor wind velocity is not the only element that affects air infiltration rates. In homes with open vertical spaces such as stairways, internal air-pressure changes caused by the outdoor-indoor temperature differential plus gravity convection also encourage infiltration of cold air. In wintertime, heated indoor air rises, pulling in cold outdoor air through cracks and around door and window frames. This upward air motion is called the *chimney effect,* as it is similar to the draft in a chimney. Chimney effects are strongest during the heating season, resulting in increased air-exchange rates.

In early spring and late fall, outside temperatures moderate and the chimney effect within becomes less significant. For this reason, a home with sealed windows may have adequate ventilation in the winter but poor air quality in the fall and spring. Once mild weather permits the opening of windows for ventilation, fresh air supply is no longer a problem.

Requirements for Fresh Air

In an average house, enough fresh air usually leaks in through cracks and around door and window frames to keep the home properly ventilated, providing at least one air change per hour. This exchange rate of 1.0 allows for the replacement each hour of the total volume of air inside by outdoor air. Minimum ventilation standards established in several European countries range from requirements of up to 4.0 air changes per hour in kitchens (France) down to a minimum of .3 air changes per hour for a living room (Poland). The air exchange rate most often recommended for living areas is 1.0.

Setting minimum ventilation standards for a private home can be difficult. William Shurcliff in his 1981 book *Super Insulated Houses and Double Envelope Houses* indicates that a rate as low as .2 air changes per hour may be acceptable in homes of small families where kitchen odors, moisture, and pollutants are minimal. However, a level of .5 to 1.0 air changes per hour is more acceptable for average families or in homes containing sources of indoor pollutants.

In an effort to reduce fuel consumption, individuals are

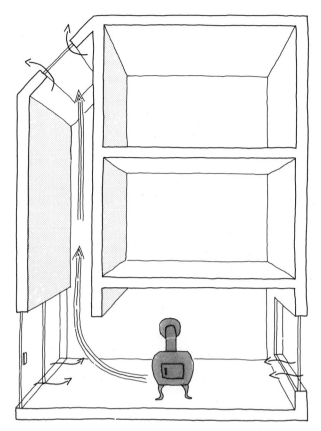

THE CHIMNEY EFFECT

1-5. In a heated space, open vertical shafts tend to create an upward draft, encouraging infiltration of cold outside air at the lower level and exfiltration of warmed room air at the top.

making their homes increasingly airtight, decreasing the air exchange rate to as little as .05 changes per hour. When incoming fresh air is reduced to this extreme, dangerous buildup of indoor pollutants may result. Some factors affecting potential indoor pollution ultimately determine the number of air changes a space needs.

Certain appliances or heating devices will cause more or less pollution. For instance, flueless heating devices and gas stoves give off carbon monoxide as a result of incomplete combustion. Carbon monoxide, an odorless gas, can deprive the body of oxygen, and for this reason it is toxic even at a concentration as low as .3 percent. Fireplaces and wood stoves that use room air for combustion may lower the oxygen content of room air. In highly sealed, well-insulated buildings, it is best to minimize the use of devices that add carbon monoxide or deplete oxygen supply within a space. Substituting pollution-free appliances such as electric stoves and retrofitting fireplaces to have outside air ducted into the fire chamber can be effective in eliminating this type of indoor pollution.

Building design and construction materials can often determine indoor pollution levels. Radon gas, a radioactive gas that seeps out of the soil and building materials such

as concrete and stone, is often present in unacceptable levels in well-sealed buildings. When seventeen energy-efficient homes in the United States and Canada were examined by the Lawrence Berkeley Laboratory in Berkeley, California, 35 percent of these homes were found to have excessive radon levels.

While virtually all naturally occurring materials emit radon, the gas is rapidly dissipated when outdoors. Indoors, however, adequate ventilation is necessary to dissipate the gas. The design of a building can encourage radon emission into a space. Underground and earth-sheltered structures may contain higher levels of radon gas than above-ground structures. Radon levels in basements, for example, are usually double what they are in living spaces due to seepage from the ground. Solar systems circulating room air through rocks that store heat from the sun may carry heavy concentrations of radon gas.

The seepage of radon into basements and underground living spaces can be curtailed by coating floor and wall surfaces with epoxy or other sealants.

Although increased ventilation can eliminate radon accumulation in a given space, such action may seem contradictory and wasteful of energy at a time when everyone is making efforts to insulate and seal buildings. Additional fresh air may not be necessary in many cases. When, however, increased fresh air is required, a heat exchanger can be installed to use the heat of the outgoing exhaust air to warm incoming cold air. A number of heat exchangers are available on the market. Some are sophisticated systems designed for commercial buildings, while others (like the Mitsubishi Lossnay Model VL-1500 MC) are low in cost and use only about 50 watts of electrical power.

Building insulation and interior materials also affect levels of indoor pollution. Plastic building insulation such as urea formaldehyde can give off fumes as it cures. Glues used in plywood and particle board also add fumes of this nature to a space. In well-sealed buildings accumulation of these fumes has caused respiratory and other health problems. To avoid excessive fumes, good-quality building insulation and proper installation are important considerations. Equal concern for quality should be given for interior product selection.

In addition to the above pollution sources, other variables such as personal habits, lifestyles, and occupant densities may influence the fresh-air requirements in a space.

For example, a person at rest needs approximately 16 cubic feet (.45 m^3) of air per hour, so the amount of fresh air needed will depend on the average number of people occupying a space. Also, strenuous activity will dramatically increase the quantity of air required. An individual walking at 4 miles (6.4 km) per hour requires almost five times as much air—79 cubic feet/hour (2.24 m^3/hr.) as a person at rest. Smoking, too, will have its influence, making necessary up to three times the number of air changes of an interior with no smoking. Finally, such activities as cooking and cleaning may increase the need for fresh air. Common household products often contain a variety of organic compounds that may be harmful. Kitchen odors and other unpleasant smells tend to linger in poorly ventilated spaces.

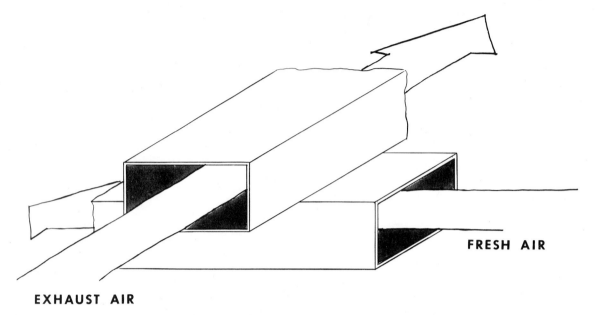

FRESH AIR

EXHAUST AIR

1-6. *Plate-type heat exchanger. Outgoing room air tempers fresh incoming air.*

Eliminating Indoor Pollution

The first step in dealing with an indoor pollution problem is recognizing its existence. After finding the source or sources of pollution, the next step is minimizing its effects by its elimination, treatment, or local or general ventilation of the space with the use of a heat exchanger.

In order to achieve human comfort it was necessary first to define it in chapter 1. We can now proceed to a more detailed study of human thermal behavior in chapters 2 and 3 to provide additional insight for creating comfortable interior environments.

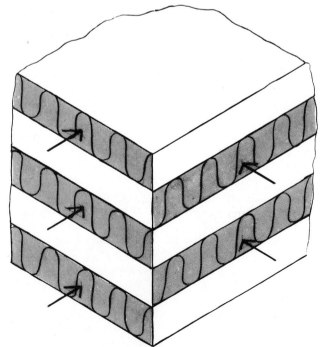

1-7. *Heat exchangers made with maximum contact surface area between the cold and warm air mass achieve increased efficiency. Model shown consists of several layers, increasing contact area.*

Chapter 2

THE SENSATION OF WARMTH OR COOLNESS

WHEN WE FEEL AN OBJECT, WE CAN USUALLY DEtermine whether it is hot or cold. If upon touching its surface we receive a warming sensation, we call it hot; when sensing coolness, we call it cold. In fact, "coolness" does not exist within human thermal experience; only heat does. Heat is generated by the random motion of molecules; the greater the motion, the greater the heat. The temperature at which no heat at all is generated and molecular motion stops completely is called *absolute zero*, which is $-459°F$ ($-273°C$). At any temperature greater than absolute zero, heat is generated.

Because we judge temperatures relative to our own skin temperature, that particular human skin temperature becomes the border between what we call hot and what we call cold.

The range of temperatures sensed by an individual is rather limited. As temperatures become hotter or colder than the human skin temperature, sensations increase until contact becomes painful to the touch. As temperatures rise or fall beyond this point, we become unable to distinguish between hot and cold. The temperatures that we are best able to sense fall between the two extremes of a very slight variation from skin temperature to a burning sensation from either excessive heat or cold. But there are inaccuracies even in this range. Since the human body regulates skin temperature to adjust to the surrounding environmental conditions, skin temperature can vary about $11°F$ ($6.1°C$), from 86° to 97°F (30° to 36.1°C). Because of this variation, an object at 90°F (32.2°C) can feel cool at times and warm at other times; objectively its temperature remains constant.

These subjective conclusions about temperatures of objects, surfaces, and the environmental air can be misleading and even contradictory. Because objects within an interior tend to be at room temperature, which in winter is approximately 25°F (13.9°C) below average skin temperature, human temperature sensations become an integral part of thermal comfort.

High-Temperature Heating Systems

Most conventional heating systems are based on high-temperature heat, with a small radiant surface area. For instance, 21 square feet (1.95 m²) of steam radiator surface (steam at 212°F, 100°C) or 7 linear feet (2.13 m) of hot water (210°F, 98.9°C) baseboard radiation is enough to heat a room, with an average heat loss of 5,000 Btu/hour (620 kcal/hr.). A forced hot-air system, with supply air at 140°F (60°C) and a delivery velocity of 500–750 feet/minute (152–229 m/min.), can heat a similar space with a 12-by-2½-inch (30 by 6.35 cm) register. In both systems the result is a high-temperature heat source confined to a small region of the room.

Two major problems arise in homes with high-temperature heating systems. First, because radiant heat transfer between the human body and its surrounding environment is a significant factor in the total thermal comfort of an individual, the optimum condition results when surfaces are neither far below nor high above room temperature. In most conventional systems, however, blasts of warm air or strong heat radiation occur at selected points within the room. To an individual coming in from bitter-cold outdoor temperatures, warming up near a hot fire or radiator may seem ideal, but in the long run, living conditions with high-temperature systems can be somewhat unpleasant. When seated near the heating device, one feels warm as the radiant heat from the surface of the heating device is transferred to the body; but when in areas of the room more remote from the radiator, its radiant influence decreases and the transfer of heat is reversed. Now the human body's heat radiates toward the surrounding surfaces, which in winter are often below room temperature. And because these transitions occur only through radiant heat transfers directly between the body and objects surrounding it, the indoor ambient air temperature may not be affected at all. For this reason, thermometers and thermostats will not record any temperature variation, yet occupants will feel discomfort.

A second problem with high-temperature heating systems is the uneven circulation of warmed air. As room air passes over a heating device, it is heated and rises through gravity air convection in an air motion that is the main carrier of heat through all parts of the house. Obstructions such as furniture, curtains, and interior partitions, however, may make this type of air circulation inefficient, as some areas remain overheated while others are uncomfortably cool.

Localized Radiant Heat

There are instances when a localized high-temperature heating device can be efficient in warming a person directly by radiation. Radiant heaters now on the market utilize localized heat transfer for energy conservation, but because they are designed to give off radiant heat, they are of little value in increasing the air temperature when placed in the center of the room. A person seated in front of the device, warmed through direct radiant heat transfer, can turn down the thermostat and benefit from the localized warmth so long as he remains seated at a task, or reading or watching television. Unless he remains in one place for a significant length of time, however, the device cannot be sufficiently utilized.

Low-Temperature Heating

Low-temperature heating of approximately 80°–100°F (26.7°–37.8°C) is highly compatible with solar interior spaces. Because passive solar systems involve the structure itself as a heat-collecting and storage element, walls, floors and ceilings themselves, functioning as heat-storage or "thermal mass," often become the radiant heating surfaces within. In general, the heat collected by thermal storage walls is at considerably lower temperatures than the heat in conventional heating systems. While solar storage materials usually range in temperature from as low as 75°–100°F (23.9°–37.8°C), conventional systems have temperatures between 140° and 212°F (60° and 100°C). The more evenly distributed lower-temperature passive solar system offers a comfortable, more uniform heat than the conventional system.

Tests conducted in 1978 by Sandia Laboratories in Los Alamos, New Mexico, show the thermal behavior of two basic types of passive solar heat-collecting surfaces. In both cases relatively low temperatures were recorded. A *Trombe wall* passive solar system, using a 16-inch-thick (40.6 cm) concrete block heat-storage wall with top and bottom vents, was observed. Temperature readings taken on a typical clear midwinter day with outside air temperature of 23°F (−5°C) were as follows:

Exterior wall surface temperature—93°–153°F (33.9°–67.2°C)
Interior wall surface temperature—84°–96°F (28.9°–35.6°C)
Air at the top vent—84°–132°F (28.9°–55.6°C)

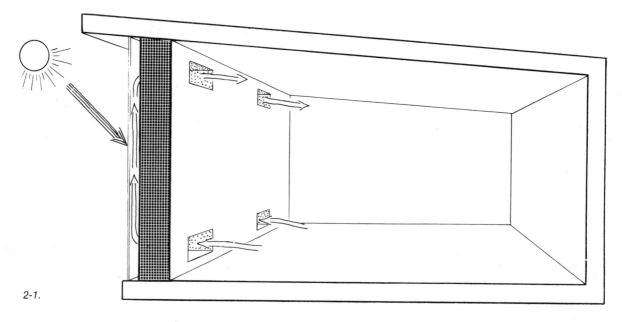

2-1.

TROMBE WALL (DAY)

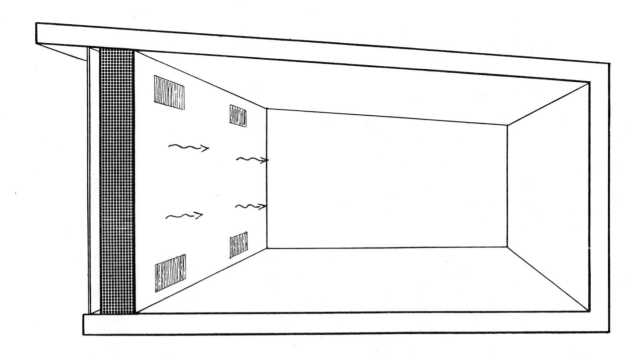

TROMBE WALL (NIGHT)

2-2.   *At night vents are closed and warm wall adds heat to space.*

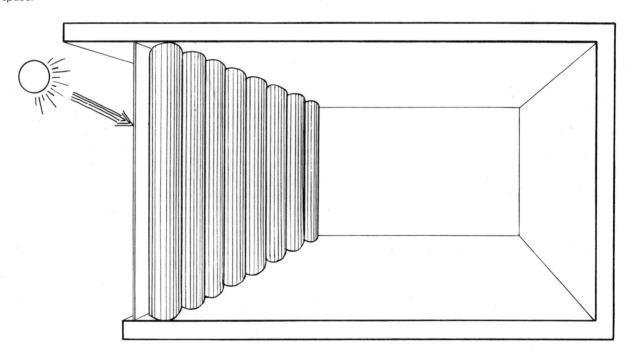

WATER WALL (DAY)

2-3.   *Water in tubes is warmed by the sun during the day.*

2-1.   *During the day, sun warms masonry wall; simultaneously, warmed air between wall and glass circulates into living space via upper and lower air vents.*

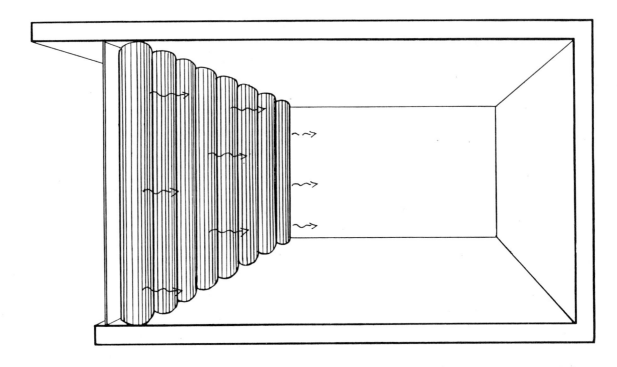

WATER WALL (NIGHT)

2-4.   *At night warm water adds heat to space.*

Although the temperatures of the exterior surface of the heat-collecting wall reached a high of 153°F (67.2°C), the interior surface remained below 100°F (37.8°C) to provide low-temperature radiant heat.

Temperatures were also recorded in a *water wall* system with 12-inch-diameter (30.5 cm) blackened fiberglass tubes used as heat storage. At mid-height, the water temperature within the tubes varied from 82° to 101°F (27.8° to 38.3°C). In water storage systems, however, stratification occurred when water convection currents within water storage containers caused warmed water to rise to the top. Water stratification of up to 32°F (17.8°C) was observed from the bottom of the tube to the top. Since stored solar heat is most useful near the floor, stratification, causing the highest temperatures to occur at the top of the water tubes, is undesired.

Until recently, electric heating was the traditional system capable of providing radiant ceilings for heating a space. In passive solar design, ceilings with heat-retention qualities can be used to store and radiate solar heat. A radiant ceiling can be warmed by solar radiation entering through a window and reflected up toward the ceiling, or the roof itself can become the radiant mass warmed by the sunlight upon its exterior surface. The roof pond system is an excellent example of the latter type of low-temperature radiant ceiling. The water ponds, 6–12 inches (5–30.5 cm) thick, are enclosed in plastic and supported by a metal deck roof. On a clear winter day, the sun warms the water to an average temperature of 75°F (23.9°C). Although this temperature is relatively cool, the great mass of warm water adds significant heat to the space and stabilizes indoor temperatures year round.

A low-temperature radiant heating effect can occur in any interior where the winter sun penetrates for considerable lengths of time (general south exposures). As the surfaces, objects, and furniture within the room warm up from direct sunlight, their surface temperatures increase, and occupants benefit from additional radiant heat transfer. Since most objects and surfaces within an average interior are not able to store heat from the sun, however, there is no long-lasting radiant effect. When an interior is designed with objects and surfaces that do have heat-storage capability, or when existing surfaces can be retrofitted (as described in chapter 6) to function as thermal mass, a longer-lasting radiant effect is possible.

The main objective of low-temperature heating is to create a comfortable heating system that may feel cool to the touch while gently adding Btu's to an interior space. The benefit of living in spaces with low-temperature heating stems from three major improvements over conventional high-temperature systems. For one, low-temperature radiant surfaces provide comfortable heating without blasts of hot air and strong air convection currents inducing drafts at floor level. Second, because of the large area of radiant surfaces, heat is added to a space more evenly than with smaller-area conventional heating systems. Furthermore, since one or more major room surface is warm, the body's heat loss through radiation, its highest form of loss, is consequently reduced.

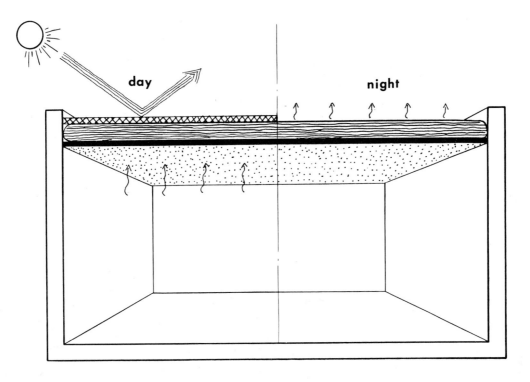

ROOF POND
(SUMMER)

2-5.   In summer, water absorbs heat from the room while the light-colored insulating cover reflects sunlight and insulates water from daytime heat. At night, covers are removed and water cools.

2-6.   In winter, sun warms water during the day. At night, insulating covers go on to prevent heat loss from water. Warm water radiates heat toward living space.

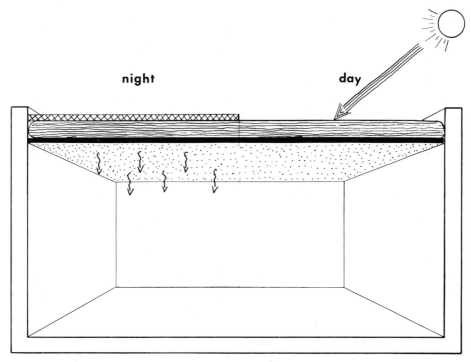

ROOF POND
(WINTER)

Temperature Sensations Due to Type of Contact and Material Conductances

Besides skin temperature variations, there are two other, more important, reasons why the human body is a poor judge of temperatures. The main factor that determines whether an object feels warm or cold is the *rate* at which heat is added to or taken away from the body. The two elements that control the rate of heat flow between the human body and an object are the conductance of a material and the type of contact it makes with the skin.

Conductive Transfers: Interior Contact Comfort

Individuals in an interior environment continuously experience *conductive heat transfers*. Picking up objects, sitting down, stepping on the floor, and lying on a bed all involve body contact with interior surfaces. When most surfaces and objects in an interior are compared to the human body, it is evident that at 98.6°F (37°C) the body is the heat generator, while at an average of 70°F (21°C), the objects within the room are a drain on body heat.

Materials and surfaces within the room all seem to be of different temperatures to the touch even though objectively they are all of constant temperature. Even in such a controlled environment as a refrigerator, certain objects are sensed as mildly cool while others can feel bitingly cold. The reason for this is not a difference in temperature, but a difference in the conductances of the various materials.

Since the conductance of a material determines the rate of heat flow from the skin upon contact, the higher the conductance value of a material, the faster it draws away body heat. For this reason, some materials can feel comfortable at room temperature, while others do not.

An example of this principle is a water bed. Although lying on an ordinary mattress produces no discomfort, an unheated water bed at 70°F (21°C) feels cold to lie on. Because the conductance of water is higher than that of most fabrics, it can remove the body's heat at a more rapid rate upon contact. This is why the water in a water bed must be heated to temperatures close to that of the human body if the bed is not to be experienced as cold.

Most furniture, however, is not heated to be comfortable for human contact. The "contact comfort" therefore depends solely on the kind of fabrics and materials selected in the design of an interior environment.

How Complete Is the Contact?

Material conductances work in conjunction with *contact* to complete a thermal sensation for an individual. A material having a given conductance can feel warmer or cooler depending on the type of contact the body is able to make with it. The more complete the contact, the more heat is removed from the body. A masonry floor with a smooth-surface finish therefore feels colder to the touch than one with a coarse surface. Smooth, silky fabrics feel colder than brushed, textured ones.

This principle holds true with any material used inside a home. Because of the wide range of materials and textures available for a modern interior, conductances and contact surfaces can vary widely.

A conflict may arise between the desired types of contact in summer and winter interiors. Although facilitating bodily heat loss through contact with furniture and surfaces is an advantage during the summer, conserving body heat with textures that surround and insulate the body is desirable during the winter.

Seasonal changeover from winter to summer textures is still customary in European interiors. During the summer, wool carpets are rolled up and stored, and summer fabrics are often draped over chairs and sofas. Although this is not always practical, interiors can be designed with a certain amount of flexibility for seasonal changeover.

Summer Contact Comfort

There are two basic qualities to look for in fabrics and materials selected for summer use.

1. Allowance for the cooling of the body through ventilation: Thin, loosely woven fabrics permit air circulation around the body and facilitate its ability to cool off. Cane, rattan, wicker, and linen are good examples of materials with airflow characteristics.

2. Noninsulating: Upon contact with the body, interior fabrics that are insulating by nature inevitably keep its heat from dissipating (figure 4-2 in chapter 4 lists the conductivity and resistivity of various fabrics). In summer interiors, smooth surfaces and thin natural fibers such as linen and cotton have the best properties for thermal comfort. Because smooth leathers and plastics have a tendency to stick to the skin, they are more comfortable when textured to minimize sticking.

Winter Contact Comfort

With all the cooling influences upon the body in a winter interior, an individual looks to "warm" furniture and insulating clothing to maintain comfort. A fabric is "warm" not because it is heated, but because it has a low conductance value, which acts to insulate the body from the negative thermal effects within. For winter "contact comfort," the following are recommended:

1. Materials with low conductances; they insulate best. One of the most highly insulating elements is air itself. Because of the insulating quality of air, any surface or fabric that traps air is a good insulator. Interior materials such as wood, cork, and brushed fabrics are low in conductance, whereas metals, glass, ceramics, and other masonry products have high conductances (see figure 4-2).

2. Shaggy or brushed fabrics and coarse textures; they trap more air than smooth, polished finishes. For this reason, highly textured surfaces low in conductance are appropriate for winter interiors. In a passive solar interior, where masonry surfaces are needed for thermal mass, throw rugs or pillows may be used where contact is most frequent.

It now becomes evident that the old tradition of winter and summer changeover of fabrics in a home is not based on aesthetics alone, but also on thermal principles of human comfort. Therefore, investigating the thermal properties of

2-7. *Smooth finish on wood floor feels cool to the touch.*

2-8. *Rough texture of grass mat reduces surface contact area, minimizing cool sensation upon contact. (Photo: Thomas Wieschenberg)*

2-9, 2-10. *Rattan and cane allow airflow for increased summertime contact comfort.*

(Photo: Thomas Wieschenberg)

interior materials is important in the preliminary stages of planning an interior environment (chapter 4 explores this further).

Sensation of Cold and Warm Surfaces Surrounding the Body Without Contact

In an effort to adjust to indoor conditions, the human body regulates the methods of heat loss from the skin. The proportion of body heat lost through each of the three major types of heat transfers—radiation, convection, and evaporation—changes with seasonal variations in an interior space.

Figure 2-11 shows that at indoor temperatures above 80°F (26.7°C), evaporation is the main source of body heat dissipation. As the temperature in a space drops below 80°F (26.7°C), convection and radiation take over as the

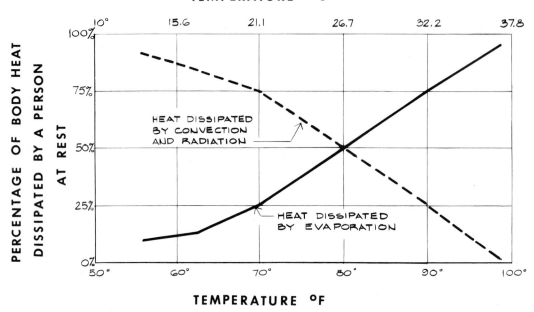

TEMPERATURE °C

2-11.   *How the human body regulates heat loss.*

chief methods of cooling the body. At 68°F (20°C), with an approximate relative humidity of 45 percent, over 81 percent of the total body heat generated by a person at rest is lost through convection and radiation. In most wintertime interiors, radiation, in fact, becomes the highest form of heat loss from the body.

The rate of radiation of heat from the body depends largely on the temperature difference between the skin and the surfaces surrounding the body. In a wintertime interior, however, a large portion of radiant heat lost by an individual is from the surface of his clothing. For this reason the radiant effects of cold surfaces and the corresponding loss from the body can vary according to the types of clothes worn by individuals. As body heat becomes well insulated by warm clothing, the surface temperature of clothing approaches room temperature, and radiant losses decrease.

Thermal Radiation Within a Space

Radiation is still one of the more mysterious types of heat transfer. Since it involves only the source and the object, surrounding air has little control over it.

Radiation from a source is always emitted perpendicular to its surface. The heat gain by the object is greatest when thermal waves are received perpendicular to its surface, and decreases as the angle of incidence becomes smaller.

Radiation of heat can be visible, in the form of light, or invisible, in the form of heat waves. Although light and heat are related, they occupy two ends of a spectrum. Light is a high-temperature, visible type of energy; heat is a lower-temperature, invisible form of the same energy. As the temperature of the energy decreases, it ceases to be visible, moving into the infrared range. It then is referred to as thermal radiation. Invisible to the eye, the path of thermal radiation is nevertheless detectable with special cameras.

A thermogram, the photographic representation of radiant heat transfer, is sometimes made to monitor heat loss from a house.

The Greenhouse Effect

Materials transparent to visible radiation are not necessarily transparent to thermal radiation. While visible solar radiation and high-temperature infrared radiation from the sun can pass through glass, lower-temperature thermal radiation cannot. It is this property of radiant energy that makes the capture of solar heat possible. Solar radiation passing through glass strikes objects inside and warms them. These objects, in turn, radiate heat energy in the thermal range, which can no longer pass through glass, and is captured within. This method of trapping heat, which commonly occurs in a sealed car on a sunny day, is called the *greenhouse effect,* and is the basis of all forms of solar heating.

Emissivity

Because all objects and surfaces in a living space are above absolute zero, they radiate heat continuously. But a "cold" surface in a room with a temperature of 60°F (15.6°C) radiates its heat at 60°F, while the human body radiates its heat at approximately 90°F (32.2°C); the temperature differential thus creates a net cooling effect on the warmer object (the human body) and a warming effect on the cooler object (the surface).

Three elements determine the amount of thermal energy radiated from a surface:

1. *The temperature of the radiating surface.* The warmer an object, the faster the rate of thermal radiation from its surface.

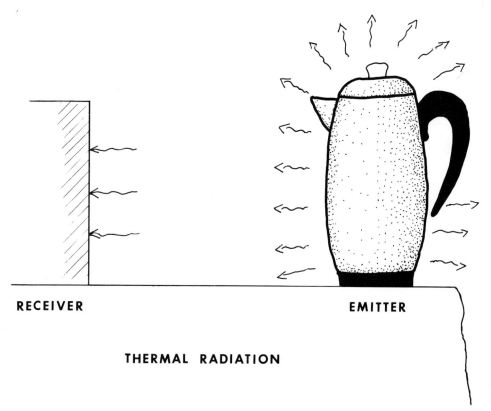

RECEIVER   EMITTER

THERMAL RADIATION

2-12.   *Thermal radiation is emitted perpendicular to the source's surface. Heat gain by the receiver is greatest when it* *can intercept the thermal waves given off by the coffee pot at a perpendicular angle.*

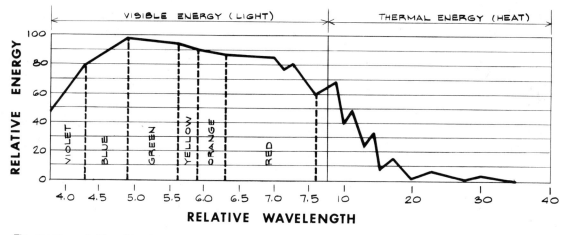

2-13.   *The spectrum: light and heat.*

2. *Surface finish.* Given the same temperature and volume, an object with a rough surface will radiate more heat than one with a smooth finish. A closeup view (figure 2-15) of an object's surface shows that for an equal size, the rough texture provides more surface area and can therefore radiate more heat. In tropical climates, textured finishes like stucco are used for efficient cooling by radiation.

3. *Heat-retention quality or emissivity of materials.* The molecular composition of a material determines how well it can radiate heat from its surface. Although most building materials are good emitters of thermal energy and give off most of their heat at a given temperature, polished or metallic materials are extremely poor emitters of radiant heat. The low emissivity of shiny metallic finishes makes them useful as a surface finish when heat loss must be kept to a minimum.

Reflectance

Although material reflectances most often apply to the reflection of visible solar radiation, invisible thermal radiation can be reflected as well. The reflection of visible radiation

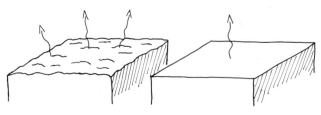

2-15. A rough surface increases the surface area, creating higher heat loss.

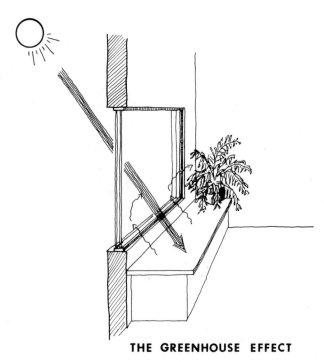

THE GREENHOUSE EFFECT

2-14. Visible solar radiation enters through glass and warms objects. Invisible thermal radiation given off by the warmed objects cannot pass through the glass, and so becomes trapped inside.

aluminized surfaces serve as heat barriers in building insulation, shading devices, and even specially developed thermal wear and blankets.

Emittance (E), which is a material's emissivity expressed as a decimal fraction, and its thermal reflectance, also expressed as a decimal fraction, are interrelated so that the sum of the two is always 1.0. Since most materials have negligible thermal reflectances, their emittance is high, usually around .9, allowing efficient heat dissipation. Metallic finishes, however, have the dual quality of high reflectance and low emittance, making them suitable for manipulation of radiant heat in a living space.

Figure 2-16 shows emittance, as well as the reflectance of solar and thermal radiation of various surface finishes.

In addition to being good reflectors of thermal energy, polished metallic surfaces also reflect large amounts of solar radiation. However, because of their low emissivity, they retain a significant amount of heat upon their surface. In warm climates, a metallic surface is therefore less efficient as an exterior finish than a white painted surface would be. Because of the high heat-retention quality of polished finishes, radiators with a smooth metallic surface are less efficient in giving off heat than ones with a rougher painted surface.

depends mostly on color, while thermal radiation does not respond to colors. The composition and surface density of a material is what determines its ability to reflect thermal radiation.

Most objects, regardless of their color, absorb much of the thermal energy they intercept. Highly polished metallic surfaces such as aluminum foil, on the other hand, can reflect large amounts of thermal radiation. Because of this,

2-16. Reflectance and emittance of various surfaces.

Material	Reflectance of Solar Radiation	Reflectance of Thermal Radiation	Emittance
Polished silver	.93	.98	.02
Aluminum foil		.95	.05
Polished aluminum	.85	.92	.08
Copper	.75	.85	.15
Chromium plate	.75	.85	.15
Galvanized steel		.75	.25
Aluminum paint	.45	.45	.55
White lead paint	.71	.11	.89
Red clay brick	.23–.30	.06	.94
Wood (pine)	.40	.05	.95
Limestone	.43	.05	.95
Black matte	.03	.05	.95

Changing Surface Temperatures

The most evident summer-to-winter thermal changes within a home involve the temperature and humidity of indoor air, but other more subtle changes take place as well. Extreme outdoor weather conditions can raise or lower the temperatures of surfaces within a space. The extent to which inside surface temperatures are affected by weather conditions depends on how well a surface is insulated.

The temperature gradient through an exterior wall shows the effect of outdoor temperature on inside surface temperatures. At an outdoor temperature of 0°F (−17.8°C) an 8-inch (20 cm) common brick wall's inside temperature drops to 50°F (10°C) when indoor air is at 70°F (21.1°C). Adding just one inch (2.5 cm) of cellular glass insulation changes the gradient significantly, raising the interior surface temperature by 10°F (5.6°C), to 60°F (15.6°C).

At the time many of the now-existing uninsulated homes were built, little attention was given to the effects of radiant heat transfers within. More recently, concern is growing about excessive heat loss and cold surfaces in a home. Adding insulation to existing wall cavities is the best way to reduce heat loss and to moderate surface temperatures. This is often difficult or impossible to accomplish, however. When insulating is impractical, wall treatment through interior design can successfully decrease interior surface temperature variations caused by the external elements (more about this in chapter 10).

Because of the strong influence of radiant heat transfers on the body, a small change in the average surface temperature in a room has a greater effect on individuals than the same change in the indoor environmental air temperature. If the comfort zone is established with an assumption that all surfaces within will remain at or near room temperature, occupant discomfort results when surface temperatures deviate from room temperature. As the gap between the indoor environmental air temperature and the average surface temperature widens, the established comfort zone is no longer valid.

The MRT (Mean Radiant Temperature)

Every room has average surface temperatures characteristic of its exposure, layout, and wall treatment. While objects, furniture, and interior partitions are most often at room temperature, window surfaces, exterior walls, slabs on grade, floors above unheated basements, and ceilings below the roof or unheated attics inevitably vary somewhat with outdoor weather conditions.

Many conditions influence the temperature of surfaces within a space:

Outdoor temperature and wind velocity. Outdoor temperature has a direct influence on surface temperatures within, as shown by temperature gradients through the wall. As the insulating value of the wall becomes greater, the effect of outdoor temperatures on interior surfaces decreases.

Because of "wind chill," the velocity of outdoor air also has an impact on surface temperatures. As wind speed increases, exterior surfaces of a building are cooled more rapidly, producing lower interior surface temperatures. Although wind infiltration is greatest on the windward side of a structure, the conductive cooling effect of the wind is greatest on sides of the building parallel to the direction of the wind.

Solar radiation on an exterior wall. Direct sunlight upon an exterior wall can raise its temperature significantly. The

2-17.   Insulation not only reduces heat loss but also raises indoor wall surface temperatures, creating a beneficial effect on human comfort.

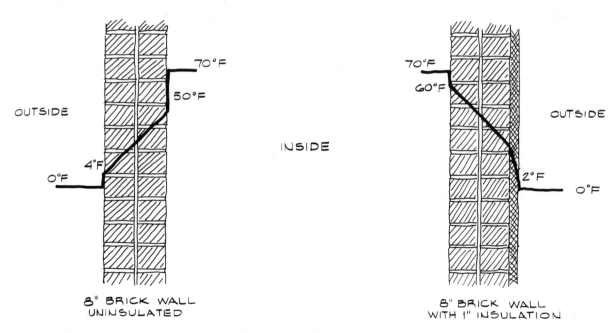

THERMAL GRADIENTS

extent of this solar-radiation surface temperature increase is determined by the color of the surface itself. Temperature measurements recorded under similar solar conditions showed a 30°F (16.7°C) difference between the temperatures of a surface with a dark finish and one with a light finish. Color is an effective and inexpensive way to increase desired heat gain or else reduce the buildup of unwanted heat upon surfaces receiving direct sun. When surface temperatures must be minimized, seasonal shading of surfaces with trees and surface vegetation can further reduce excessive surface temperatures.

Heat-generating equipment. Furnaces and other heat-producing devices below a living area can increase the floor temperature within that space. In the summer, rooms containing heat-generating equipment can be ventilated to reduce this effect.

Interior color finish. Surfaces in an interior absorb a varying amount of visible radiation, depending on their color. At low levels of illumination, the temperature variation due to color is slight. Temperature differences due to color become more pronounced when surfaces are exposed to intense visible light such as solar radiation, flames from a fireplace, or excessive electric lighting.

Lighting. While the heat from lightbulbs in residences is not very significant, it is in offices and public spaces where fixtures are spaced close together, the lighting creating a radiant ceiling effect.

Heat is emitted at a rate of 3.4 Btu/watt hour (.86 kcal/watt hr.) of electrical energy consumed. A 100-watt lightbulb, therefore, gives off 340 Btu's (85.7 kcal) each hour. A study made on the heating effect of internal lighting shows that the heat given off by a lighting system of 6 watts/square foot accounts for approximately 36 percent of the total cooling load of a building, and balances its heat losses when outdoor temperatures are 25°F (−3.9°C) or above. Added heat from lighting, plus its radiant effect on individuals, necessitates cooling of the space during most of the winter season.

As an energy-conserving measure, environmental designers use direct ventilating or water cooling systems to draw off some of the waste heat given off by lighting. The excess heat is ducted or piped to other areas of the building where the heat is needed, or exhausted to the outside when the heat cannot be utilized.

To increase the efficiency of heat removal from lighting, fixtures that trap much of the heat given off by the lamp are desirable. Polished aluminum reflectors reflect both visible light and thermal radiation into the room, and are useful in those spaces where heat from lights is desired. A white enamel coating on the reflector and louver surfaces, on the other hand, reflects mostly visible light into the space and absorbs much of the thermal radiation given off by the fixture. The localized heat absorbed by the lighting unit can be efficiently removed by direct cooling. Similarly, light-transmitting materials such as glass permit a high percentage of visible radiation to enter the space, while trapping most of the heat waves within the luminaire.

Although direct mechanical cooling of lighting fixtures in offices and commercial spaces is often necessary, design techniques can successfully minimize the thermal effects of lighting. Lowering illumination levels where task lighting can be substituted and using high-efficiency low-wattage fixtures results in significant reduction of both energy consumption and heat gain from lighting.

In order to calculate thermal effect on occupants of all the surfaces in a space, the average of all major surfaces must be taken. This average is called *mean radiant temperature* (MRT). Because large surfaces have a greater influence than small ones, the surface sizes are taken into account in establishing the MRT for any interior space,

$$MRT = \frac{A_1T_1 + A_2T_2 + A_3T_3 \text{ (etc.)}}{A_1 + A_2 + A_3 \text{ (etc.)}}$$

(A): area of each surface taken into consideration
(T): the corresponding surface temperature

Comfort is highest when the mean radiant temperature is very close to room temperature. When the temperature of even one surface, such as a window wall or radiant slab, is significantly higher or lower than that of the other surfaces, the MRT and human comfort are affected. For example, in a room of six surfaces of equal area, with five surfaces at room temperature, 70°F (21°C), and one surface at 60°F (15.7°C), the mean radiant temperature is as follows:

$$MRT = \frac{5[A(70)] + A(60)}{6A} = 68.3°F$$

Although the five interior surfaces are at comfort level, one cold surface lowers the MRT by approximately 2°F (1.1°C). Although 2°F does not seem like a drastic decrease in the mean radiant temperature, it has significant thermal implications for the people within a space.

The MRT in an interior space is believed to have a 40 percent greater effect on body heat loss than room air temperature. Consequently, a 1°F (.56°C) change in the MRT is equivalent to a 1.4°F (.78°C) change in the environmental air temperature. This implies that within a moderate range of indoor air temperatures (approximately 65°–75°F, or 18.3°–23.9°C) every 1°F (.56°C) increase in the average

MRT	AIR TEMPERATURE
67°F (19.4°C)	74.2°F (23.4°C)
68°F (20°C)	72.8°F (22.7°C)
69°F (20.6°C)	71.4°F (21.9°C)
70°F (21.1°C)	70°F (21.1°C)
71°F (21.7°C)	68.6°F (20.3°C)
72°F (22.2°C)	67.2°F (19.6°C)
73°F (22.8°C)	65.8°F (18.8°C)
74°F (23.3°C)	64.4°F (18°C)

2-18. *As the mean radiant temperature in a room varies, the air temperature in that room must also change to assure maximum comfort.*

surface temperatures above 70°F (21°C) allows a 1.4°F (.78°C) decrease in the air temperature, for the same feeling of comfort. Conversely, in the example above, the 2°F drop in the MRT must be compensated by a 2.8°F (1.56°C) increase in the room air temperature. According to this principle, all of the combinations in figure 2-18 provide equivalent comfort.

Controlling surface temperatures in a space facilitates energy conservation efforts by reducing heating or cooling requirements.

Summer Savings Using MRT

In large buildings, environmental designers have devised ways to cool off slabs and walls during summer nights by natural ventilation. Night air, channelled along the surface of structural elements within, lowers the mean radiant temperatures and the cooling requirements for the following day.

Nocturnal ventilation works equally well in single-family homes. Cool night airflow through open windows or forced ventilation of outdoor air cools interior surfaces during summer nights. The cooling capacity of surfaces, however, depends on their ability to absorb heat. Cooled masonry, or water walls, and concrete slabs can absorb significant heat from an interior space, resulting in effective radiant cooling. Since solar interiors most often have heat-absorbing materials within to soak in and store heat from the sun during the winter, these interiors have the potential for natural radiant cooling during the summer.

Because a natural radiant cooling system depends on night air for ventilation, it works effectively only in climates with relatively cool summer nights. To maximize the radiant cooling potential of surfaces, it is best to shade or insulate them from the hot summer sun.

Flexible insulation makes the roof-pond passive solar system adaptable for both winter heating and summer cooling (see figures 2-5, 2-6). In the winter operation, insulating covers are placed over the water at night to reduce heat loss from the warmed water. In the summer, covers stay on during the day and are removed at night to cool off the water. The next morning, water and ceiling temperatures are at their lowest point. As the temperature within rises during the day, the cooled radiant ceiling absorbs thermal radiation from people and from objects within the space.

Winter Savings Using MRT

In winter, surfaces warmed by the sun raise the mean radiant temperature, as in passive solar spaces, allowing a lower thermostat setting without adverse effects on individuals. Although any warmed surface is beneficial, warmed floor slabs are most advantageous, since they minimize the usual floor-to-ceiling temperature variations. The dual benefit of extra heat supply and warmed surfaces is the prime advantage of solar interiors.

Living spaces in attached housing offer similar benefits in mean radiant temperatures since they have fewer exterior surfaces than the single-family detached home. Because of moderate surface temperatures within attached housing, its occupants can more easily tolerate lower indoor air temperatures.

2-19. *Thermal mass cooled through night ventilation within a space becomes a heat sink for unwanted daytime heat that accumulates in an interior.*

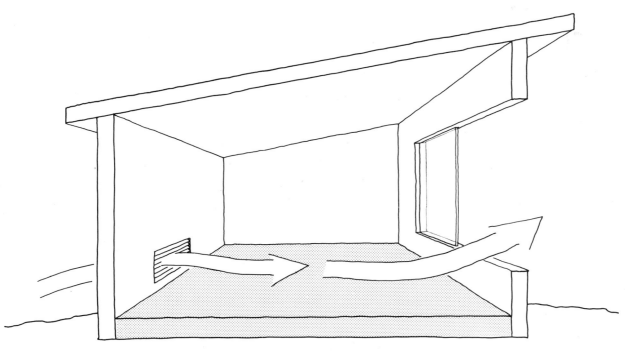

NIGHT AIRFLOW COOLS THERMAL MASS FLOOR

Day and Night MRT Variations

Interior comfort control through Heating, Ventilating and Air Conditioning (HVAC) systems becomes increasingly difficult with fluctuations in the mean radiant temperature. With uninsulated exterior walls, inside surface temperatures vary not only with seasons but also from day to night. Day and night variations can become a significant problem with any window area, especially when large south-facing glass is used in solar interiors. Although the daytime temperature of the glass is within the comfort range, its surface temperature cools considerably at night, causing excessive radiant heat loss from the individuals within. Nighttime insulating cover for glass surfaces increases the comfort of people within the space and makes direct passive solar systems more efficient. Because flexible insulation is an integral part of solar interiors (see chapter 8), it is important to design glass areas that permit easy installation of nighttime insulating cover.

Proximity of Cold Surfaces

Calculating MRT in a space helps in arriving at air temperature requirements for occupant comfort. The only factor the MRT does not take into account is the proximity of a particular surface to the individual. Calculations include surface temperatures and sizes, assuming that all surfaces of equal areas have equal influence upon individuals. In reality, due to the layout of human occupancy clusters or seating and sleeping areas, a person may be influenced by one particular surface more than by the other surrounding surfaces. Someone working next to a large window surface, for instance, is influenced by its temperature more than by the temperature of other surfaces farther away. Similarly, someone sleeping in a bed close to an exterior wall feels the thermal effects of that wall most acutely. Even the posture of the body with respect to a surface influences its total effect. For example, a person facing a cold surface in the standing position is chilled more than someone turned sideways to that surface would be. These person-to-surface reactions may cause discomfort to some while not affecting others. Because radiant heat exchange is more complete when a surface is nearby, its effects upon an individual are magnified.

The designer of the interior is the one who ultimately controls the thermal interaction of individuals in a space with the surrounding surfaces. Design actions such as *wall treatment* appropriate for walls of different exposures; *window treatment,* for efficient shading and insulation when necessary; *floor covering,* providing thermally efficient treatment when needed; and *furniture arrangement,* with optimum location of people within the room, are all factors in the total thermal comfort of individuals in their interior environment.

Chapter 3
HOW ACTIVITY LEVEL INFLUENCES THE BODY'S GENERATION OF HEAT

THE HUMAN BODY PRODUCES ENERGY FROM FOOD ingested by the process of metabolism. The rate of energy produced by the body depends on the type of activity performed. The more energy needed by the body to do mechanical work, the higher the metabolic rate becomes. Since the efficiency of the body to perform physical work is low, only 20 percent of the energy supplied by the metabolic process is used for activity; the rest is given off as "waste" heat. This waste heat varies widely with a person's level of physical activity, and can influence heating or cooling requirements within a space.

For the space itself, additional Btu's given off by people create internal heat gain and often make increasing demands on cooling and ventilating systems. For the individual, an increased level of physical activity alters the required comfort zone.

A person lying at rest generates the least amount of heat. This state is usually referred to as the basal metabolism. Sitting at rest increases heat production by 62 percent, while muscular tension, even without motion, further increases the metabolic rate. As activity levels rise, the heat generated by the body increases to a maximum of ten times the basal rate.

Figure 3-1 indicates the amount of heat energy produced by a man of average height and weight engaged in various types of physical activities. The corresponding comfort zone temperatures for each range of physical stress applies for individuals engaged in these activities for more than two hours.

The amount of heat generated by metabolism varies somewhat with each individual. Differences in age, sex, size, and body weight are all contributing factors in individual metabolic rates.

Deviations from the comfort zone can also affect metabolic rates. Conditions slightly below the comfort zone cause muscle activity that increases metabolic rates by 30 to 100 percent. At rest and under severely cold conditions, involuntary shivering may increase metabolism by two to three times the normal rate at rest. Similarly, upon exposure to environmental temperatures above the comfort zone, metabolism rises up to 30 percent.

Increases in the metabolic rate are greatest when cold or heat exposure is sudden. As an individual becomes accustomed to an environment, his metabolic rate levels off.

Planning Activity Areas for Thermal Balance

In previous chapters, individual thermal sensitivities are examined one by one to arrive at an understanding of what comprises total thermal confort. Most of the thermal interactions between an individual and the surrounding elements, however, are based on a person at rest generating 400 Btu/hour (100.8 kcal/hr.). Once a person is engaged in physical work, comfort requirements change.

Changes in air temperature as shown in figure 3-1, as well as in the fresh air supply, may be necessary with increased activity. Because of these required changes in the surrounding environment, activity levels need consideration in the design and planning of interior spaces. Fur-

ACTIVITY	METABOLIC HEAT		APPROXIMATE COMFORT ZONE (Depends on insulating value of covers used.)
	Btu/hr.	Kcal/hr.	
Sleeping—bed rest	250	(63)	
Sitting at rest	400	(101)	70°F +
Sitting—desk work	450–550	(113–139)	(21.1°C)
Standing—light work	550–650	(139–164)	65°–70°F
Normal circulation	600–750	(151–189)	(18.3°–21.1°C)
Moderate work and walking about	750–1,000	(189–252)	
Walking on level ground @ 2.5 mi./hr.	840–1,080	(212–272)	60°–65°F
Walking on level ground @ 4.5 mi./hr.	1,200–1,600	(302–403)	(15.6°–18.3°C)
Walking up a 10% slope @ 2.5 mi./hr.	1,360–1,920	(343–484)	
Heavy work: lifting, pulling, and pushing	1,500–2,000	(378–504)	55°–60°F
Very heavy exercise	1,500–2,500	(504–630)	(12.8°–15.6°C)

3-1.   *Activity levels can influence air temperature necessary to maintain comfort.*

thermore, because of the nature of an activity, certain design elements may be desirable, regardless of the amount of heat the activity generates. Optimum layout and orientation of interior spaces can facilitate maintenance of a suitable environmental condition for a given activity.

Types of Activities in an Interior Space

The daily schedule of an individual comprises a number of activities. The isolation of each activity and the space in which it is most likely to occur can give an indication of the environmental needs within that space, Maximum daylighting, natural ventilation, solar radiation or its absence within an interior are all options open to the designer. These design options are best accomplished by choosing exposures that offer the needed natural elements. When the orientation of an interior space is fixed, however, interior design techniques can compensate for unfavorable natural elements. Utilizing the various properties of interior materials for insulation, light reflection, and effective shading can result in a more desirable interior environment.

The heat given off by individuals within can significantly influence the heating requirements of a space. In many forms of shelter in history, the main source of heat was the bodies of the occupants themselves. Because houses today are larger, with greater heat loss, and individuals have higher standards of comfort, body heat has less effect on the overall thermal needs of a space. As a building's insulation value increases, however, internal heat gain from body heat, as well as from lights and appliances, can have greater importance.

In a space occupied by a large number of people, or by those whose activity levels are high, the Btu's given off by occupants become increasingly influential in the thermal balance of the space. The thermal needs of a room with an average heat loss of 5,000 Btu/hour (1,260 kcal/hr.), for example, can be balanced by ten people sitting at desk work. If the people within the space become more active, it becomes necessary to cool the space.

Activity levels in commercial and business interiors are often quite predictable. Anticipated activity and occupant densities can be estimated and used to size Heating, Ventilating and Air Conditioning (HVAC) systems that can handle these additional thermal loads. Interiors having excessive internal heat gain due to occupancy for most of the year can be oriented to keep additional heat gain from external elements to a minimum.

Within a residence, activities are not always predictable, and are dependent on personal habits, modes of living, and work schedules. In the planning and subdivision of interior spaces in a home, a designer can make certain assumptions about the types of activities that will be taking place within each space. Because most activities in a home are likely to be within the light to moderate range of physical stress, it is the *nature* of the activity, and not its level of stress, that becomes a deciding factor in the environmental requirements for the space.

Spaces within a residence can usually be divided into four categories: (1) *Living space,* one in which some type of activity takes place during much of the day and evening. These spaces should have optimum benefits of available natural elements. (2) *Support spaces,* such as kitchens and bathrooms, which are necessary but have sporadic occupancy. (3) *Low-usage spaces,* such as dining area, family room, den, or study that are sometimes underused in homes with multiple living spaces (bedrooms in daytime may fall into this category). (4) *Buffer spaces,* or rooms and areas unoccupied most of the time, such as closet, pantry, laundry room, basement, furnace rooms, and garages.

While Americans still dream of a spacious single-family detached home with more than one living space, the ideal home from the point of view of energy efficiency may be undergoing some shrinkage. As households become smaller and energy costs higher, demand is rising for smaller, more energy efficient homes. This implies a new task for the designer of interiors. Because the family room, study, or den may have to be eliminated, the concept of the *dual-function space* is evolving. For example, although space usage in each home differs, the dining room is used on the average only 15 percent of the time; combining it with

3-3.   Sunspace as living space.

a study, library, or den can dramatically increase its usefulness. In the same way, bedrooms unoccupied for most of the day can double as work or studio spaces, while children's bedrooms can serve as playrooms during the day.

Solar Greenhouse as Living Space

In some instances, a passive solar heating system can serve as a supplementary living space. A "solar greenhouse" attached to a home can be any enclosed space, terrace, or balcony that faces within 25° of true south, with clear access to winter sun. Whereas a traditional greenhouse is all glass, the solar type has glazing mostly on the south face with opaque materials on the other facades. Other features that distinguish a solar greenhouse from the standard type include double-insulated or thermopane glazing; all-solid exterior walls that are well insulated (slab and perimeter insulation is used); heat-absorbing materials (thermal mass) chosen particularly to soak in and store heat from the sun; and flexible insulation over glass surfaces to minimize nighttime heat loss.

Although this type of addition may be called a greenhouse, it does not have to serve as a year-round indoor vegetable garden. Under the "shrinkage" philosophy, a solar greenhouse can simply be a sunspace that is energy independent. The space can be used for a variety of activities—eating, working, relaxing.

The feature that distinguishes this type of additional living space from the traditional types is that it is not a drain on the home's energy consumption. On the contrary, on a clear winter day most solar greenhouses collect enough heat for their own thermal needs, plus additional heat for adjacent rooms. Because the temperature within a natural solar greenhouse without any auxiliary heat tends to fluctuate, however, it may not always be available for occupancy. On cold winter nights, for instance, it is most efficient to close off such a greenhouse space and allow its nighttime temperature to drop. During the night, it acts as a buffer between the adjacent living space and the cold night air.

Any space added or retrofitted to serve as a solar greenhouse becomes a net heat gain for the spaces adjacent to it. The extent of the energy benefit depends on the size and design features of both the greenhouse and the adjacent spaces. In an apartment, for instance, where overall heat loss is small, an attached solar balcony can contribute significantly to heating the interior spaces. Similarly, a well-insulated house can receive a considerable amount of its required heat from an attached sunspace. The area of sunspace glazing is generally two times its floor area. When intended as a major source of heating for adjacent spaces, the sunspace glazing area should be 20 to 50 percent of the total floor area of rooms to be heated, with materials such as water or masonry within to absorb and store incoming solar energy.

When converting an existing porch or exterior space to an enclosed solar greenhouse, one can often take advantage of existing heat-storage materials in the form of a concrete slab floor or a solid masonry wall. When the wall between the greenhouse and the adjoining interior spaces is solid masonry, without an air space or insulation, heat is transferred through the wall by conduction to supply radiant heat to adjacent areas. When water storage or a concrete or masonry floor is used as thermal mass, or heat storage, natural-gravity or forced air circulation is needed to supply heat to other interior spaces.

Even without heat storage capability, a solar greenhouse adds significant heat to a home. With no heat storage materials, however, day and night temperature fluctuations become considerably greater, making it excessively warm in the daytime and cold on winter nights.

In mild weather, a solar greenhouse addition becomes continuous living space, but in warm weather heat buildup in a greenhouse space can become a problem. For this reason, effective ventilation and shading of the greenhouse is necessary to keep its temperature within the comfort range. Vents at the top of the glazing, where most of the heat accumulates, can generate natural exhaust of hot air. Exterior shading devices and deciduous trees are also very effective in keeping heat gain to a minimum. Interior shading devices are useful, although somewhat less effective (more about this in chapter 8). Insulated shades provide the added benefit of reducing conductive heat gain in the summer and, in the winter, lowering nighttime heat loss. Flexible insulation can increase the efficiency of the solar greenhouse as a heating system, reducing heat loss through the glass by 80 to 90 percent.

While temperature fluctuations in a solar greenhouse make it less reliable as additional living space, its changing environment generates an awareness of outdoor climate that leads individuals within to live more in rhythm with nature.

The development of energy-independent spaces and "shrinkage" indicates a changing direction in the evolution of housing. Planning for shrinkage can eliminate unnecessary interior spaces, and along with them, the extra energy needed for their year-round maintenance.

Time of Occupancy

In planning indoor environments for various activities, the time and length of occupancy are important considerations. In public, office, and commercial spaces, time can make a dramatic change in both activity and occupant densities. Restaurants, theaters, or stores, for instance, have given time-spans of occupancy, with maximum densities at certain hours of the day.

In a home, time of occupancy is once again a factor of personal schedules. Occupancy and corresponding thermal requirements in a home can be determined only by the individuals residing there.

Thermostat settings should correspond to individual needs, depending on activity level and presence within the space. Homes unoccupied during the day can have temperatures of approximately 10°F below the comfort level during this period. Because activity levels of individuals in a dwelling are most often greater during the day than in the evening, lower daytime temperatures may be appropriate even when individuals are at home. Other factors, such as higher surface temperatures and entering solar radiation,

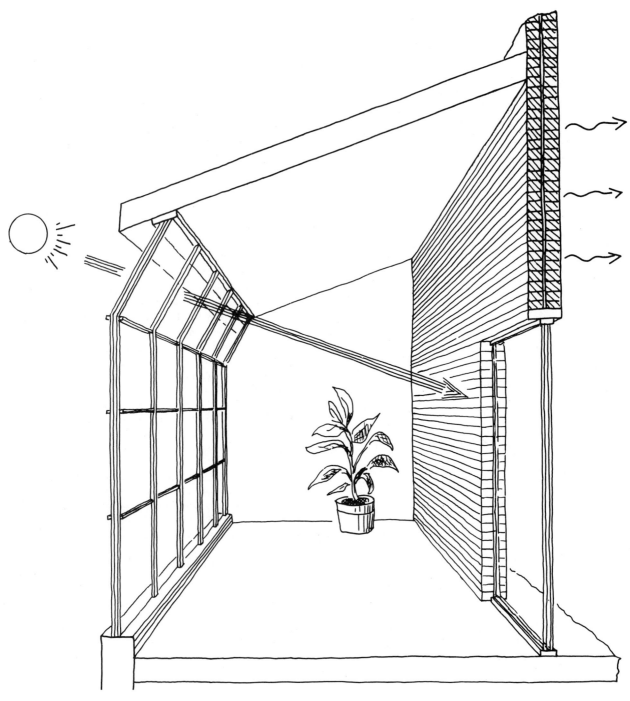

also contribute to comfort at lower daytime temperature settings. In the evening, when restful and relaxing activities take place, warmer air temperatures or local radiant heating may be required for comfort. Although a person at sleep generates the least amount of heat and requires high comfort temperatures when dressed in ordinary indoor wear, the additional body insulation provided by blankets and covers makes appropriate a reduction in nighttime thermostat settings.

Individual needs vary with both personal and environmental elements discussed earlier, but the following range of temperatures can nonetheless serve as an example of

3-4. When greenhouse thermal mass consists of a solid masonry wall between it and the adjoining building, heat can be transferred by conduction through the wall.

thermostat setbacks in a home:

68°–70°F (20°–21.1°C) in the evening, or whenever relaxing activities take place.
63°–65°F (17°–18.3°C) for daytime occupancy with moderate activity.
55°–65°F (12.8°–18.3°C) for unoccupied periods and nighttime settings.

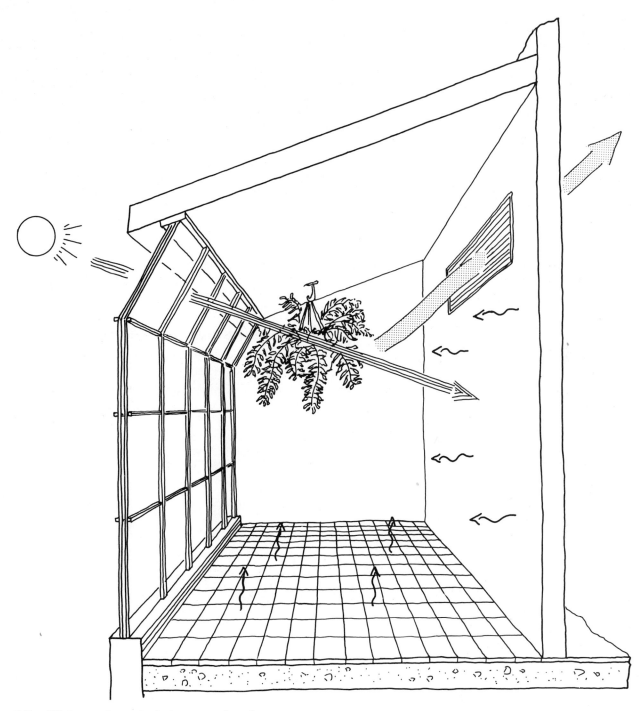

3-5. *When greenhouse heat storage consists of water containers or masonry floor slab, heat can be transferred to adjoining rooms by natural or forced air convection.*

Temperature setbacks in a home can result in considerable savings in energy costs. The Edmond, Oklahoma Project, a two-year study of homes by Honeywell in 1980, tested two daily temperature setbacks of 5–14°F (2.8–7.8°C). All of the homes in the study had a net energy savings ranging from 17 to 25 percent of the total heating cost without setbacks. According to this study, the greater the duration and amount of the setback the greater the savings.

Although day and night temperatures can be set manually, savings are often reduced by occasional forgetfulness. An automatic dual setback clock thermostat assures temperature decreases in a home with regular work-sleep schedules.

Some claim that the savings from significant temperature setbacks are offset by the cost of reheating a space at required periods during the day. The results of the test cases studied by Honeywell indicate that savings accomplished by temperature setbacks far exceed the cost of reheating.

Space Orientation Due to Activity and Internal Heat Gains

In order to maintain thermal balance, an active individual requires lower temperatures and adequate ventilation. The thermal balance of an interior space, however, depends on the sum total of all the thermal influences upon it. With the exception of mechanical heating and cooling, the thermal influences upon a space consist of the following negative and positive elements.

Heat Loss

a. Conductive heat loss through walls, floors, and the roof.
b. Heat loss by radiation from outside "skin" of the building.
c. Conductive loss by wind upon exterior surfaces.
d. Heat loss by infiltration of cold air.
e. Cold air entering through open doors.

Heat Gain

a. Solar radiation upon the exterior surface of a building.
b. Solar radiation entering into space through transparent opening.
c. Conductive heat gain when outside air is warmer than inside air.
d. Warm air entering through openings.
e. Internal heat gain from lighting, equipment, open flame, and appliances.
f. Heat gain from people.
g. Heat gain from steam in cooking and bathing.

The design goal of interior spatial distribution is to achieve a good balance between these thermal influences.

Orientation can be broken down into four different categories, as outlined in the solar chart, figure 7-1, chapter 7.

1. SW SOUTH SE: Best for winter heat gain. Good for living spaces and areas requiring direct solar radiation in winter. Entering sunlight can be diffused or direct.

2. EAST: Significant heat gain and solar radiation in summer mornings. Good exposure for kitchens where internal heat gain is greatest in late afternoon, the assumed meal-preparation period. Adjustable shading useful for summer.

3. WEST: Heat gain and solar radiation significant in summer afternoons. Exposure needs efficient shading. Wintertime heat gain is minimal.

4. NW NORTH NE: Generally sunless and windy wintertime exposure. Exposure needs wind shelter or windbreak. Can be useful orientation for areas with excessive year-round internal heat gain.

Spatial Orientation and Design Factors

In addition to external and internal thermal influences, other design factors need consideration in planning interior area orientation. Social and psychological needs of indi-

3-6. *Living spaces on south wall benefit from winter sunlight and solar heat gain, while utility and buffer spaces absorb the effects of the less desirable cold north exposure.*

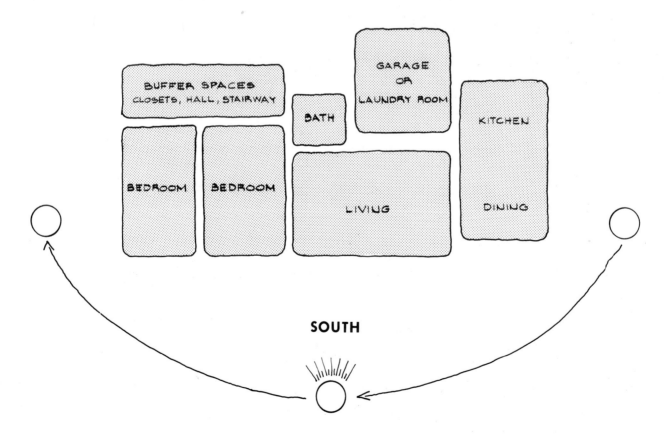

viduals, along with functional and structural properties of the building, are all determinants of final design decisions in the arrangement and subdivision of interior spaces.

Figure 3-6 shows the optimum orientation of interior spaces within a home, living spaces and rooms with continuous daytime occupancy having top priority. General south exposure provides direct sun during the winter for warmth and light. In the warm seasons, when the sun is high in the sky, overhangs and shading devices can shield these exposures from direct sunlight. Support spaces need less consideration in heat and light; areas with significant internal heat gain such as kitchens, however, need adequate natural ventilation and a minimum of direct sun during the summer season. Closets, garages, laundry rooms, and other buffer spaces can serve as extra insulation from the negative thermal influence of north walls.

Optimum orientation of interior spaces is not always possible. Design considerations often conflict with each other, necessitating compromises in layout and orientation. Physical access between certain interior spaces or between interior and exterior areas is often required. Visual access between a living area and a favorable view is sometimes desirable despite the adverse thermal influences of that exposure. Since the interaction of all these considerations can be somewhat complex, there is no single solution to interior spatial layouts. The designer of the interior is the one who ultimately determines the suitable orientation for each interior space, and solves conflicts of interest by appropriate design techniques.

Design Solutions to Adverse Orientations

Below are some design alternatives that can minimize unwanted climatic influences on interiors with unfavorable exposures.

INDOOR SPACES
Condition: View is N–NW, the direction of cold winter winds.
Proposed Solution: Small window areas with triple glazing. Mostly sealed windows to prevent infiltration. Effective nighttime insulating cover over glass.

Condition: Entrance is from general north.
Proposed Solution: Insulated door with effective weather-stripping. Vestibule entrance with 90° turn (see figure 3-7).

Condition: Entrance is from west.
Proposed Solution: Provision for summertime shading of entrance. Light color for exterior face of door. Vestibule and insulated door for wintertime thermal shelter.

Condition: View faces west.
Proposed Solution: Effective insulating shading devices. Light-reflective glass. Exterior shading through trees and vegetation when possible.

Condition: Fixed unfavorable orientation.
Proposed Solution: Light scoop-type windows to catch a more desired orientation. See chapter 11 for case studies and design solutions.

3-7. *Unfavorable entrance orientation can be redesigned with the addition of a vestibule and rotated doorway.*

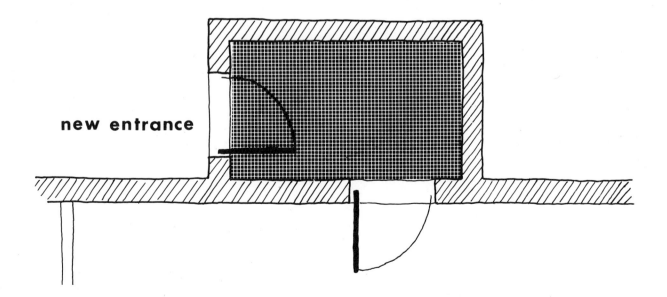

N

new entrance

OUTDOOR SPACES

Condition: Gardens, terraces, or balconies on the south side of a building.

Proposed Solution: High and full deciduous trees when outdoor space is on or close to grade level. Lattice, vine, ivy, or overhead fabric or louver shading.

Condition: Outdoor spaces face west.

Proposed Solution: Low, full trees for shading; vertical adjustible louvers or lattice with vines or ivy.

Like all living beings, humans are at their best when surrounded by a congenial environment. In the following chapters, utilization of available natural energies in the design of an interior shows how such an environment can be created.

Chapter 4

INVESTIGATING THERMAL BEHAVIOR OF INTERIOR MATERIALS

THE MATERIALS USED IN THE CONSTRUCTION AND interior of a shelter traditionally reflect their availability in an area and their suitability for a specific climate. Although this still holds true to a certain extent today, more types of materials are now available for a commercial space or home than ever before. For this reason, most interiors contain a large variety of materials. Some of these serve a purely aesthetic purpose, while others perform a specific function. In the behavior of a living space as shelter, however, the importance of interior materials is often underestimated. In reality, the materials selected for an interior space can make a dramatic difference in its function as shelter.

Each individual space has a different set of thermal influences upon it. Appropriate materials used within can work to emphasize what is desired and minimize what is not, in both summer and winter. To accomplish an optimum environmental condition for any given space, it is necessary to analyze the thermal characteristics of materials intended for the space.

Thermal Function of Materials Within

Interior materials generally perform two types of thermal functions. Some materials within behave thermally as part of the shelter, providing additional insulation from the extreme effects of outdoor climate. Other materials in a space relate only to individuals, creating changes in human thermal sensations. Among the materials that serve as a barrier between indoors and outdoors are curtains, shades, venetian blinds, and shutters; carpets, tiles, or other floor covering

over floors on grade or above uninsulated basements or crawl spaces; interior treatment of exterior walls in the form of paneling, fabrics, or rugs and tapestries used as wall hangings; furniture or cabinets built into exterior walls. Among materials that affect only human thermal sensations are beds, chairs, couches, and other seating where contact is frequent; desks, tabletops, and other furniture where contact is less frequent; and floors over heated rooms, especially when contact with bare feet may be frequent, such as bathrooms and bedrooms.

The most important thermal characteristic of any material is its resistance (R) to the passage of heat. The higher the resistance value of a material, the lower the rate of heat flow through a given thickness of that material. Conversely, since the conductance of a material is the reciprocal of its resistance, or $C = 1/R$, the higher its conductance, the greater the rate of heat passing through it. The R-value of an interior material, therefore, determines its ability to insulate either the house, by slowing down heat loss to the outside, or an individual, by decreasing the rate of heat flow away from the body upon contact.

The conductance of a material, regardless of its thickness, is the amount of heat in Btu/hour (kcal/hr.) passing through one square foot of that material for each 1°F (1°C) temperature difference between its sides (see figure 4-1). For a comparison of the thermal value of various materials, however, a unit value of conductance, or a material's conductivity (k), is appropriate. The conductivity of a material is the rate of heat flow in Btu/hr. sq. ft. °F (kcal/m² h °C) through a one-inch (1 m) thickness of a material. The unit

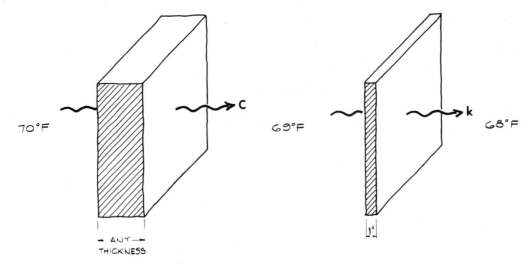

HEAT FLOW

(R) resistance, or resistivity (r), of an inch-thick material is then 1/k.

Figure 4-2 shows the k and r values of many common interior materials. These values are useful in evaluating the materials' thermal effectiveness and aid in their final selection for an interior space.

Whereas some of the materials listed in figure 4-2 are commonly used in thicknesses greater than an inch, the thickness of others, such as fabrics, may be only a fraction of an inch. The overall insulating value R, therefore, increases or decreases with these variations in material thickness. Because fabrics for an interior differ in density and weave, insulating values are often given by the manufacturer. In some instances, two or more materials are combined to achieve a desired thermal effect.

A quick comparison of material conductances can give an indication of the type of thermal sensation a material is likely to produce upon contact with an individual. With regard to heat loss from a house, however, a more accurate thermal effect of a particular interior treatment can be calculated.

In order to compute the heat flow through a material, it is necessary to know the material's resistance value, the temperature difference between its sides, the total area of the material, and the resistance value of the air film trapped on both sides of a material's surface.

Textures and Trapped Air

All gases, including air, are poor conductors of heat. Therefore, any time air is trapped within a material, the overall insulating value of the material increases significantly. Materials used in building insulation and fabrics woven for thermal wear are all based on this principle. Goose down, for instance, is a highly effective thermal barrier because of the trapped air pockets it creates. When wet or compressed, however, these materials lose most of their insulating value.

Air can also work as an insulating layer upon surfaces.

4-1. *Conductivity (k) is a unit heat flow through a one-inch thickness of material. Conductance (C) is the heat flow through a material of any thickness.*

Air molecules become trapped along surfaces within a room. This thin sheet of still air upon a surface acts as insulation and has a resistance value on both the inside and outside surfaces of a building. The amount of air that becomes trapped upon a surface depends on the texture of that surface. Rough textures tend to trap greater quantities of still air than do smooth finishes.

Due to the thermal forces of natural gravity convection, the resistance values of still air layers vary with the position of surfaces within the room. The resistance (R) value of indoor surfaces can be assumed to be the following, where R = sq. ft. $\times$ hr $\times$ °F/Btu (or m² $\times$ h $\times$ °C/kcal):

wall: R = .68 (.139)
ceiling: R = .61 (.125)
floor: R = .92 (.189)

Although still air layers also form on the exterior surfaces of a building, wind velocities generally reduce their significance. With winds under 15 mph (24 km/hr.), the outside air layer is assumed to have an approximate resistance R = .17 for all directions. The resistances of both inside and outside air films can be added to the total resistance ratings of walls, floors, and ceilings in the computation of heat loss from a building shell.

Air Space as Insulation

In addition to being trapped within a material and upon its surface, air can serve as insulation of an interior any time it is enclosed between two successive layers making up the building's shell (see figure 4-6).

The factor that makes an air space like this a good insulator is the minimal air convection that takes place within it. In an open air space, as between a window and

METALS	CONDUCTIVITY		RESISTIVITY	
	(k) (Btu/hr. sq.ft.°F/inch)	(kcal/m²h°C/m)	(r)	1/kcal
Silver	2,897	359	.0003	(.0027)
Copper	2,670	331	.0004	(.003)
Aluminum	1,463	181	.0007	(.0055)
Brass	638	79	.002	(.013)
Steel	310	38	.003	(.026)
Chromium steel	150	(18.6)	.006	(.054)
MASONRY				
Marble (white)	22.6	(2.8)	.04	(.36)
Marble (black)	19.88	(2.5)	.05	(.4)
Slate	13.6	(1.7)	.07	(.59)
Terrazzo	12.5	(1.55)	.08	(.65)
Concrete	12.5	(1.55)	.08	(.65)
Clay (fire hardened)	6.06	(.75)	.16	(1.33)
Common brick	5.0	(.62)	.20	(1.6)
Plaster	5.0	(.62)	.20	(1.6)
Paster board	1.13	(.14)	.88	(7.1)
WOOD				
Fir, pine & similar softwoods	1.10	(.136)	.91	(7.4)
Maple, oak & similar hardwoods	.80	(.10)	1.25	(10.0)
Plywood	.80	(.10)	1.25	(10.0)
Fiberboard wood plank	.35	(.04)	2.86	(25.0)
FABRICS				
Leather (cowhide)	1.2	(.15)	.83	(6.7)
Linen	.61	(.08)	1.64	(12.5)
Felt (dark gray)	.43	(.05)	2.33	(20.0)
Cotton	.39	(.048)	2.56	(20.8)
Silk	.35	(.04)	2.86	(25.0)
Feathers with air	.17	(.02)	5.88	(50.0)
Vegetable fiber with air	.19	(.024)	5.26	(41.7)
Vegetable fiber without air	4.1	(.51)	.71	(1.96)
Flannel	.10	(.0124)	10.00	(80.6)
PLASTICS				
Polystyrene	.2±	(.025)	5.00	(40.0)
Urea formaldehyde	.24	(.03)	4.2	(33.3)
Expanded polyurethane	.18	(.02)	5.55	(50.0)
MISCELLANEOUS				
Ice	16.5	(2.0)	.06	(.5)
Water	3.7	(.46)	.27	(2.2)
Glass	5.0	(.62)	.20	(1.6)
Dry sand	2.7	(.33)	.37	(3.03)
Rubber	1.6	(.20)	.625	(5.0)
Cardboard	1.45	(.18)	.69	(5.6)
Dry soil	.95	(.12)	1.05	(8.3)
Paper	.87	(.11)	1.15	(9.09)
Cork	.37	(.05)	2.7	(20.0)

The values listed all apply for a 1″ (1 m) thickness of each material.

4-2. *Conductivity and resistivity values of interior materials.*

a loose curtain (see figure 4-3), air convection currents circulate heat from the room through the air space, making it ineffective as a thermal barrier. In a closed, or dead, air space, on the other hand, airflow is stopped and the air space acts as an additional layer of insulation.

Each separate air space has an R-value that can be added to the total resistance rating of the building's shell.

Highly insulating window shades that form a honeycomb of separate air spaces achieve their thermal efficiency due to this principle. Similarly, double and triple glazing increases the thermal resistance of single glazing significantly, mainly because of the extra air space or spaces formed.

Whereas the resistance values of more than one dead air space are additive, increasing the thickness of a single air space beyond one inch does not further raise its insulating value. On the contrary, as an air space is increased over

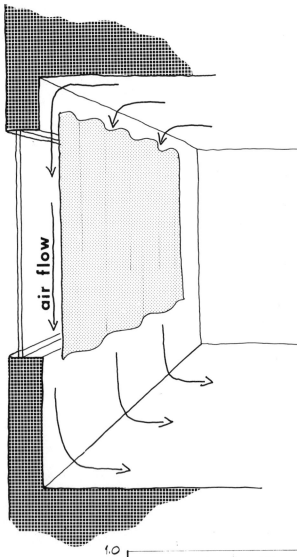

4-3. *Insulating value of air space between insulating curtain and window is negated by a flow of warmed room air through it.*

4 inches (10.16 cm), air currents within the space transfer heat from the warmer surface to the cooler one, reducing its overall thermal effectiveness. Figure 4-4 shows how the thermal resistance of an air space within a wall varies with its thickness.

The list in figure 4-5 indicates the insulating value R of one-inch (2.54 cm) dead-air spaces. Again, due to air convection within the room, the position of the air space within the room determines its effectiveness. The thermal resistance of an air space increases significantly when a material with a high thermal reflectance, such as aluminum foil, is placed on the cool side of an air space (see figure 4-6).

Conductive Heat Flow Through Materials

The heat escaping from the interior of a building by conduction travels through the successive layers of the building shell until it reaches the outside face. Because each square foot of exterior surface area has a unit heat loss, the greater the area of the shell enclosing a space, the more heat is lost through it. To evaluate the effectiveness of alternative interior surface treatments, a heat-flow analysis can be made. For example, the heat transfer through a window before and after the addition of a particular thermal device can reflect projected savings in fuel costs.

The first step in such an analysis is to find the existing resistance value of the window alone. A typical double-glazed window has a total R rating of 1.82 hr. sq. ft. °F/Btu (.37 m^2 h °C/kcal). This rating is arrived at by totalling up all elements through the window having an R-value, since

4-4. *Thermal resistance values for various space thicknesses within a vertical space.*

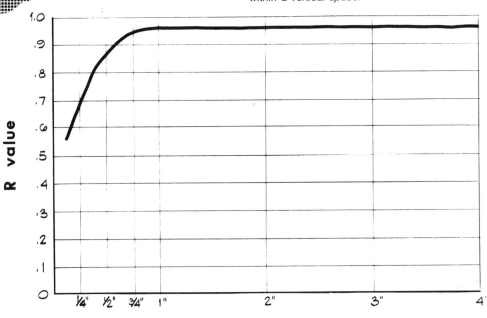

air space within a wall

Position of Air Space	R-value		R with Reflective Coat	
	sq. ft. hr. °F / Btu	$\left(\dfrac{m^2 h °C}{kcal}\right)$	sq. ft. hr. °F / Btu	$\left(\dfrac{m^2 h °C}{kcal}\right)$
wall	.92	(.1886)	2.64	(.54)
roof	.80	(.164)	1.84	(.377)
floor	1.10	(.226)	5.00	(1.025)

4-5.   *Thermal resistance of dead air spaces one inch in width.*

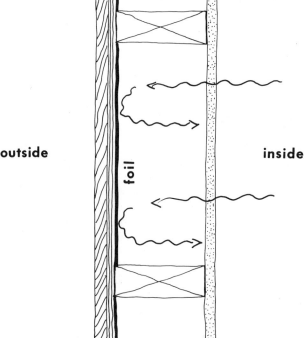

outside   foil   **inside**

4-6.   *Escaping heat is reflected back to the interior by foil.*

the thermal resistances of all materials in the path of heat flow are additive:

     .17 (.035)—exterior air film
     .92 (.189)—air space between panes
     .68 (.139)—interior air film
     .05 (.010)—two panes of glass
    1.82 (.373)—R total (R = m² h °C/kcal)

It is evident from these figures that the thermal resistance of a double-glazed window is mainly the result of the insulating quality of air, not glass.

Once the total resistance is known, the total heat flow, U, is simply the reciprocal of the R total, or $U = 1/R_t$. In this case, the total heat flow through the glass is 1/1.82 = .55 Btu/hr. sq. ft. °F (1/.37 = 2.7 kcal/m² h °C). In other words, each square-foot section of the window allows .55 Btu (2.7 kcal) to pass through each hour for each 1°F (1°C) temperature difference between indoor and outdoor air.

If this window is fitted with thermal shades having an R rating of 3.5 (.72), the total resistance (neglecting the window frames) changes:

    1.82   (.37) —double-glazed window, as before
    3.50   (.72) —thermal shade
     .92   (.189)—newly formed air space
    6.24 (1.28) —R total (R = m² h °C/kcal)

The total heat flow through the window assembly after the addition of the shade is 1/R or 1/6.24 = .16 Btu/hr. sq. ft °F (1/1.28 = .78 kcal/m² h °C). This window treatment, therefore, slows the rate of heat loss from .55 (2.7) to .16 (.78) Btu/hr. sq. ft (kcal/m² h °C), which is a 71 percent improvement.

In order to find the total heat flow in Btu/hr. through the entire window at any given time, U must be multiplied by the window area and by the temperature difference between inside and outside air. With a window area of 50 sq. ft. (4.65 m²), an outdoor temperature of 25°F (−3.9°C), and indoor temperature of 65°F (18.3°C), the total heat loss is .16(50)(40°) = 320 Btu/hr. (.78(4.65)(22.2) = 80.5 kcal/hr.).

By filling in the corresponding R-values, areas, and temperature differentials, conductive heat loss through any combination of materials can be computed.

In the total heat loss from a house, however, other, more complex factors come into play. Radiant heat loss from the exterior surface of a house, convective losses due to wind chill, and losses due to air infiltration and opened doors are more difficult to trace. Nevertheless, simple conductive heat transfer figures are valuable in determining the thermal and cost effectiveness of various interior design treatments.

Two Kinds of Material Contact Determine Rate of Heat Flow

Contact 1: A Material's Behavior as Part of the Shelter

Conductive heat transfer takes place any time two materials are in contact with each other. The more complete the contact, the faster the rate of heat flow from the warmer to the cooler material. To achieve good heat transfer, therefore, materials with high conductance that are designed to make complete contact work best. For instance, the good contact achieved between the flat surface of an electric range and a pot is the chief reason for high heat transfer efficiency.

When heat transfer must be discouraged, as in the shell of a building, the contact area between materials making up that shell should be minimized. Heat travels through a homogeneous material at a rate determined by its thermal

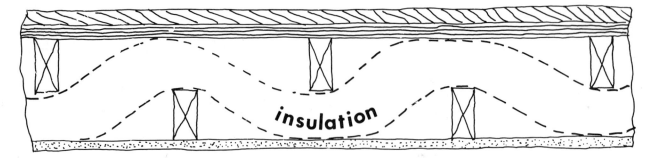

4-7. *Staggered wall studs create a more effective thermal barrier.*

characteristics. Any single material that is in contact with the inside and outside surface of a building's shell aids the flow of heat through it. When a thermal break or a change of materials occurs, contact between inside and outside is inevitably less complete. For example, staggered wall studs (see figure 4-7) create a thermal break within a wall and reduce contact between the interior and exterior surfaces.

When insulating efforts are made through interior design treatments, minimum surface contact can provide similar thermal advantages. The main determinants of the effectiveness of an interior design treatment are the thermal resistance of the material selected, the method of installation for minimum contact, and tight edge seals to discourage room airflow.

Contact 2: The Material as It Relates to Individuals

The second aspect of contact has to do more directly with individual thermal sensations. A great portion of the time an individual spends indoors involves bodily contact with some interior material. Both the initial and the long-term thermal reaction to these contacts becomes significant in a wintertime interior and has an impact on comfort and energy conservation efforts. The magnitude of the thermal sensation received by an individual upon contact varies with the temperature of the material, the conductance of the material, the type of contact made, and the insulating quality of clothes worn.

It is evident from discussions in chapter 1 that individual thermal needs differ in winter and summer interiors. In addition to this, the actual environmental conditions within a home also vary with the different seasons. The increasing cost of energy makes it unfeasible to maintain constant year-round temperature and humidity levels within a home. Instead, indoor temperatures are often allowed to drop close to 65°F (18.3°C) in the winter and may rise to 80°F (26.6°C) or higher in the summer. Therefore, the term *average room temperature* has a different meaning at various times of the year. Because of this seasonal variation, a material may feel colder to the touch in the winter, placing more emphasis on individual contact with objects in the interior and making the creation of a "warm" interior environment through the use of insulating and highly textured materials an important design priority.

The following provides an overview of some common interior materials in their function both as part of the shelter and in human contact.

Metals

Structural strength and easy maintenance are the main advantages of metals for use in interiors. Metals can be found as part of the shelter in exterior doors, door and window frames, and shading devices. Because of their high thermal conductivity, however, they act as a wick in drawing heat from a space. Manufacturers of metal doors and frames have increased the overall efficiency of metal units by placing a thermal break or insulating material within the core of their products (see figure 4-8). Because thermal breaks are not built into all available metal units, product specifications should be checked before a purchase is made.

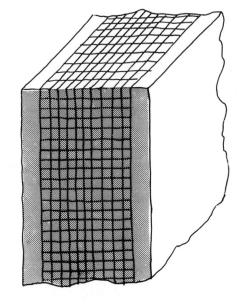

thermal break

4-8. *Insulating core within metal unit reduces thermal conductivity.*

4-9.   *Seat cushions on metal chairs minimize sensations of*
cold.

The high conductivity and generally smooth surface finish of metals make them a poor choice for seating and other surfaces of frequent human contact. Metals feel cold to the touch in both winter and summer interiors and should therefore be combined with fabric or cushions to reduce their adverse thermal effects.

Masonry

Although masonry materials are poor insulators, in many instances masonry floors or walls are desirable. Masonry is used for its fireproof quality around fireplaces and wood-burning stoves. In kitchens, bathrooms, and entrance halls it is preferred for its washability and durability. Passive solar interiors utilize the heat-storage capability of masonry materials. Whereas masonry alone has poor thermal resistance, insulating it on its exterior surface reduces the overall heat loss without interfering with its function within the space.

Even when a masonry material is well insulated on its exterior surface, it produces a cooling sensation upon contact with the body. A smooth, glazed surface finish further accentuates this "cool" feeling. In many instances, masonry has functions that do not involve human contact. When masonry is used as a finished floor in living areas, kitchens, or bathrooms, or as built-in seating, however, contact with individuals may become a consideration. Movable and removable thermal barriers such as throw covers, cushions, and rugs create "warm spots" on masonry surfaces. These "warm spots" can also be built into a masonry surface by alternating materials such as wood, cork tiles, or carpeting. With these methods, the advantages of masonry are utilized while its thermal side effects are minimized.

Wood

Wood is used extensively as a construction material as well as in interiors for finished flooring, walls, and window shutters. Of the major construction materials, wood has the highest insulating value. One inch (2.54 cm) of hardwood is 417 times more insulating than one inch of steel, and 15½ times more insulating than one inch of concrete. In other words, it would take 417 inches of steel or 15½ inches of concrete to provide the same R-value as one inch of hardwood. For this reason, the heat flow through a typical uninsulated wood-frame structure is usually lower than the heat loss through uninsulated masonry.

Even though wood is relatively insulating as a building material, the smooth surface-finish of wood used as furniture makes it somewhat cooler to the touch than most interior fabrics. Although the thermal discomfort produced by bare wood is not as great as with metals and masonry, pads or cushions can improve "contact comfort," especially in a wintertime interior.

Plastics

Plastics in many forms serve as part of the shelter. Because of its nature, plastic can be expanded or foamed, making it highly insulating. Plastic insulation within wall cavities and on building exteriors is very effective in reducing heat loss from a space. Because most plastics are combustible, their exposed use in an interior is restricted by

fire codes. When plastic is used to insulate a surface from within, it must be protected by fire-rated finishing materials on its interior face. Foam-core insulating panels are now available for windows, but should be encased in fireproof materials when used as interior shutters.

The most common types of plastics used in building insulation and insulating panels are the following:

Urethane, a cellular plastic foam that entraps fluorocarbon vapor, making it very low in heat conductance. Urethane is combustible and must be protected from fire by surface materials.

Expanded polystyrene, a lightweight plastic, available in standard-size boards. It is easily cut and resists moisture penetration. Polystyrene is combustible and must be protected by fire-rated materials.

Urea formaldehyde, a low-density foam that has been used to insulate existing cavity walls. Although urea formaldehyde is treated to be noncombustible, it is known to give off toxic vapors as it cures and highly toxic fumes when it does burn. Because of the health hazards associated with this type of insulation, its use was banned by the Consumer Product Safety Commission in February 1982.

Plastics for an interior come in such a large variety of textures and densities that "contact comfort" can vary considerably. In general, the family of plastics can be divided into two basic categories.

Rigid or hard plastics such as acrylic, when used as seating, can feel cool and uncomfortable in a winter interior, and create a sticking problem during the summer. Pads or cushions are often built into plastic seating to alleviate this problem.

Foamed or soft plastics such as polyurethane foam are insulating, and feel warm upon contact, especially when brushed fabrics are stretched over them.

Fabrics

Fabrics in an interior often contribute significantly to the thermal effectiveness of the function of that space as shelter. Carpets and pads, curtains and drapery, wall hangings and fabric wall coverings, can be selected for added insulation of a surface. Studies indicate that carpet and carpet underlayment can reduce the heat loss through an uninsulated concrete slab floor by as much as 72 percent. For window and wall insulation, heavy thermal fabrics are most effective; however, even sheer fabrics, when tightly woven and properly sealed along the edges, can discourage room airflow along a cold surface. This effect is possible only when sheer fabrics intended for cold wall surfaces are stretched on a wooden frame and mounted with a minimum of contact between it and the cold wall. In addition to reducing the actual heat loss from a space, fabric treatments can increase the temperature of surfaces surrounding an individual, minimizing the adverse radiant effects of cold surfaces.

Fabrics, leather, and vinyl used in seating and bedding are usually stretched over insulating padding or cushions. Therefore, heat loss from the body to the surrounding air is not directly related to fabric conductances. In fact, the thermal sensation received by an individual upon contact with these materials is almost totally dependent on the

4-10.   The dense wool fibers of this Oriental carpet make it insulating and "warm," both as part of the shelter and in terms of how it feels against the body.

4-11.   Wool rug hung behind seating reduces adverse effect of adjacent cold wall. (Photo: Thomas Wieschenberg)

surface texture of the fabric. Smooth leather, vinyl, or fabrics feel cool in a wintertime interior, which can discourage their use. Conversely, brushed fabrics such as suede, flannel, velour, or shaggy textures are known to feel "warm," and are thus inviting to occupy.

Permanent and Flexible Materials

Because interior materials affect both energy considerations and personal comfort, their selection is an important step in the preliminary stage of interior design. The two separate functions of these materials necessitate analysis of the influence of outdoor weather on the interior environment as well as a study of the needs and comfort of the occupants within. All selected materials can then be subdivided according to their use within the space as either a permanent or flexible part of the interior.

Built-in furniture as well as installed flooring, window, and wall covering may be considered permanent, while movable window treatments, area rugs, wall hangings, cushions, and fabrics used for bedding and seating may be categorized as flexible, or versatile.

Flexible materials can often be designed to be moved or removed with ease during seasons when they are thermally inappropriate. Just as movable partitions create private space only when required, materials designed for versatility can be used for a specific thermal purpose during a given season (see chapters 8 and 9 for flexible heat-storage materials and flexible insulation).

Material Selection

Because the materials we select for our living spaces have a great influence on our comfort and well-being, we should consider the thermal properties of these materials along with their functional and aesthetic qualities. In this way we can create an interior environment that is pleasing not only to the eye but also to the touch.

4-12. Heavy rug hung on exterior wall behind bed increases human comfort. (Photo: Thomas Wieschenberg)

4-13. Although the natural texture of leather reduces contact area, it feels cool to the touch.

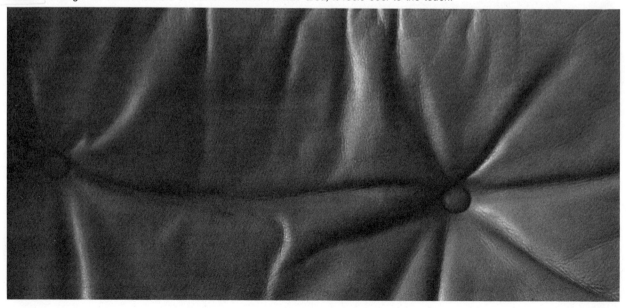

Chapter 5

MAKING THE MOST OF SUNLIGHT AND ARTIFICIAL LIGHT WITH DESIGN AND COLOR

OVER 20 PERCENT OF ALL THE ELECTRICITY GENerated in the United States is used for lighting. While this figure represents approximately 6 percent of total energy consumption in the U.S. directly, lighting is indirectly responsible for some additional expenditure of energy as well.

Approximately 60 percent of the total electricity consumption in commercial spaces is from lighting. Because of the significant wattage required to light these spaces, extra energy is needed to cool them. This additional cooling load is directly related to the waste heat given off by lighting systems (see chapter 1) and becomes an indirect form of energy consumption related to lighting. These additional cooling costs are not offset by savings in wintertime heating, since the warmth acquired from lighting fixtures can be supplied more efficiently by heating systems.

Lighting usage in residences is not as significant as in commercial and public spaces. Nevertheless, efficient use of lighting in homes can provide desired illumination levels with reduced electric costs.

Increasing Consumption in Energy for Lighting

Recommended illumination levels for public spaces and commercial structures have been on the rise for decades. Since the 1950s, lighting-level recommendations for areas of comparable use doubled and in some cases tripled, often leading to overillumination of various spaces. These increased lighting recommendations are now being challenged by environmental designers attempting to create a more energy-efficient interior.

Uniform lighting systems are another cause of excessive lighting, especially in commercial spaces. To provide layout flexibility or for purely aesthetic purposes, lighting, equally spaced regardless of task areas, has added to overillumination and higher costs. Lighting levels required for circulation or waiting areas, for instance, are only one-third of those needed for desk work. If inefficient systems were redesigned for individual task lighting, up to 50 percent savings could be achieved.

Design-Related Inefficiencies

In private homes, inefficient use of lighting, not overillumination, is the main cause of excessive wattage consumption. Lighting efficiency is related to the type of illumination desired and the amount of light interreflected between room surfaces versus the amount of light absorbed as heat by the fixture, surfaces, and objects within the room.

A number of design elements determine the effectiveness of a light source, be it natural daylight entering through windows and skylights or artificial lighting produced by electric fixtures. The efficient utilization of the light within a space is important in both cases. In the case of artificial lighting, design techniques can achieve maximum lighting per watt of energy consumed. In maximum utilization of daylighting, less glass area is needed to provide sufficient light during the day. This technique has special significance in spaces with adverse exposures, such as west, which can create excessive heat during summer periods, or north-northwest, which has the highest rate of wintertime heat loss.

Design Approaches for Maximum Lighting: Natural Daylight and Artificial Illumination

Maximum-lighting design techniques work on the principle of maximum utilization of minimal light. A number of design considerations have an impact on efficient lighting within a space, the light source itself being the primary consideration. With natural lighting, shape, size, and orientation of window openings determine the amount of daytime light available for a space. With artificial lighting, bulb efficiency, fixture design, and its placement within the space are important factors. Artificial lighting is most efficient when it is selected to provide the type and level of illumination required by a particular space.

The second design element influencing effective light distribution is the color scheme of surfaces in a space. Although surface reflectances are major determinants of overall spatial brightness, fabric colors and furniture finishes can be additional factors.

Finally, indoor lighting is influenced by the architectural design and orientation of a structure and the man-made and natural elements surrounding it. Although exterior surroundings are often permanent, planned landscape may increase or decrease the amount of light entering a space, as may light-reflecting window glazing, another light-regulating tool.

Placement of Artificial Light Sources Within a Space

Lighting serves functions besides general, necessary illumination in an interior space. In some instances, lighting is used for dramatic effect upon works of art or to create shadows on sculptural and architectural elements. Although these uses may have some aesthetic validity in the realm of interior design, they have limited functional value.

There are two basic requirements to consider in designing for maximum light efficiency. First, well-distributed light, without glare, is often desired in a living space. And second, task, or selective, lighting is preferred when localized tasks or activities are to be performed. In each case, the placement of the light source within a room affects the efficient use of available wattage.

Well-Distributed Lighting: General Brightness

The light from a source is emitted in all directions. If a single object is present in a spatial void, only the rays emitted toward the object are reflected; the remainder of the light is dissipated within the void (see figure 5-1). When, however, the source is enclosed in a defined space, the light rays will be absorbed or reflected by the surrounding surfaces (see figure 5-2). As light is interreflected between the surfaces, an overall brightness in the space is created. As a general rule, therefore, a fully exposed or multidirectional lighting fixture, lowered by at least 12 inches (30.5 cm) from the ceiling level and centrally located, is most efficient in

5-1.   In a spatial void, all light rays are dissipated except the rays emitted toward an object. A portion of the light is absorbed and the rest reflected by the object, which becomes a secondary source of light.

creating a general brightness within a room. The degree of brightness can be regulated by adjusting the wattage within the fixture itself.

The intensity of light diminishes in proportion to the square of its distance from the source. Therefore, when a fixture is localized within a space, in a corner, for instance, the areas more remote from the source of light will be poorly illuminated. With this type of arrangement, two or three additional sources may be necessary to bring the overall illumination to the desired level.

Well-distributed lighting is often desirable in a room that is used exclusively as a living space. As individuals move to different areas of the room, the lighting from a centrally located source remains relatively constant.

It is important to note that general brightness is closely related to wall brightness. Vertical surfaces are primary in human visual perception. In instances where central lighting is combined with dark, light-absorbing walls, the appearance of brightness greatly diminishes.

In large or open planned spaces, such as lofts, only certain sections of the room may be used as living space. Entrance hall, circulation, book shelving, or dining area may be integrated into this type of interior space. In these cases, lighting concentrated in the immediate area of occupancy is useful in illuminating desired sections of the space. Lighting selected for general brightness of a given portion of a room should have characteristics similar to fixtures selected for an entire room. In both cases, multidirectional light and wall brightness are the major elements.

Localized lighting such as spotlights or track lighting

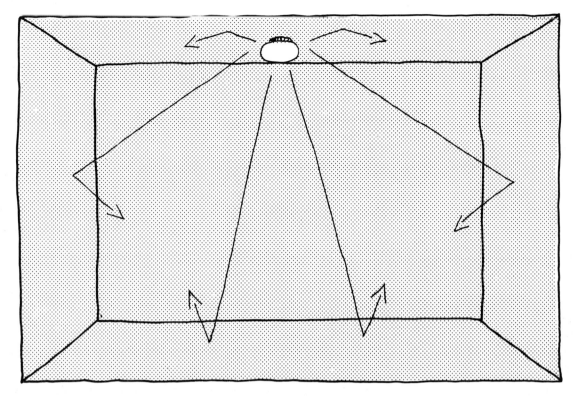

interreflected light

5-2.   *In an enclosed space, all light rays are in part reflected or absorbed by the surrounding surfaces.*

concentrate a high-intensity light in a relatively small area. For this reason, concentrated lighting is a poor choice when general illumination is desired, and necessitates increased wattage consumption.

Selective: Task Lighting

Although a typical bulb emits light in all directions, bulbs and fixtures can be designed to provide a beam of light in a specific direction (see figure 5-3). As light is given off by the bulb, the reflector bounces the light rays in the direction of the lamp opening. In this way, much of the light is directed selectively.

Selective, or task, lighting is desirable when localized visual task work such as writing, reading, sewing, or typing is performed. Selective lighting is available in desk and floor lamps, as well as wall and ceiling fixtures.

Individual task lighting is most efficient when placed close to the work surface. When ceiling fixtures are used, a downlight pattern is most effective in illuminating a horizontal work surface (see figure 5-4). In a dining room, for example, a downlight-type fixture above the eating surface creates the desired illumination for eating without making the entire space excessively bright.

Most rooms in a residence, especially dual-function spaces, should have both general and task lighting fixtures available for use as individual activity may require.

Placement of Natural Light Sources Within a Space

Although the arrangement of artificial light sources within a room is relatively unrestricted, location of natural light sources may be restricted by architectural layout and structural elements.

Any window opening has two separate relationships in illuminating a space. The first has to do with primary and secondary sources of light upon the exterior of the glazing surface. Direct sunlight is the sole primary source of natural light. The amount of direct solar radiation entering a space is dependent on the window exposure, as well as the season and time of day. The most significant secondary light source is diffuse sky radiation. Sky brightness can vary, depending on atmospheric conditions, but it is nonetheless a relatively consistent source of daylight. Another significant secondary source of natural light is light reflected from ground surfaces. Ground reflectance is especially significant in low-rise structures. Nearby structures or natural surroundings can be another source of indirect natural light, especially important on sunless exposures.

The second relationship of a window opening in illuminating a space involves the path and dispersion of the available light rays after they have passed through the glass. In general, a short, wide window provides a wide elliptical light distribution in a space. A tall, narrow opening

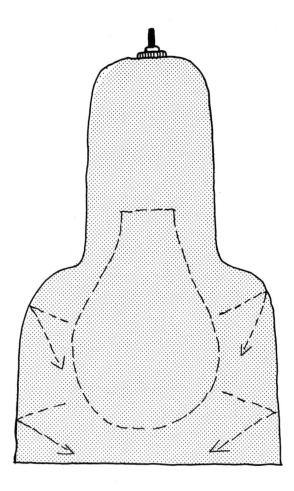

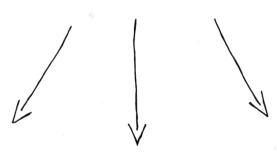

5-3.   In task lighting, light rays can be reflected by the fixture to produce light in a single direction.

diffused light into an interior space. Bubble skylights admit light but reflect much of the overhead solar radiation. When glare is a problem, a light-diffusing surface below the skylight can produce a more evenly distributed light. Vertical south-facing openings such as clerestory windows and light scoops, admit daylight high in the space with the additional advantage of collecting wintertime heat.

Because of day and night and seasonal variations, sky-lights may need adjustable shading or insulating covers for increased efficiency; a greater selection of shades and insulating covers is now becoming available (see chapter 8).

Fixture Design

Bulb efficiency is a prime consideration when maximum utilization of artificial light is a priority. The light output of a bulb is measured in units called *lumens*. The quantity of light produced by one lumen is equivalent to that given off by 12½ candles. The efficiency of any lamp is therefore measured in the amount of light produced per unit of energy, or lumens/watt. The efficiency ranges of the two most common types of lamps used in a home are 31 to 84 lumens/watt for fluorescent light and 4 to 25 lumens/watt for incandescent light. Individual efficiency of each type of bulb depends on design quality as well as on the wattage of the lamp.

In an incandescent bulb, the diameter of the tungsten filament increases as lamp wattage increases. Because heavier filaments can be heated to higher temperatures, an increase in efficiency results. This means that two 60-watt bulbs producing 740 lumens each can be replaced by one 100-watt bulb producing 1480 lumens for equal illumination, with an energy saving of 20 watts. Energy saving can be achieved any time several low-wattage bulbs are replaced by one bulb providing equal illumination with fewer watts. However, in spaces with little need for brightness, low-wattage bulbs should not be upgraded. Lumen output, hours of life, and wattage listed on lightbulb packages can be compared in selecting the most efficient bulb for a specific need.

Fluorescent tubes provide equal lumens at about one-third the energy used by incandescent bulbs. In addition, fluorescent bulbs last about seven times longer. Whereas the initial cost of a fluorescent bulb is high, its long life brings the cost per hour of use down to about half that of an incandescent bulb. Because fluorescent bulbs give off less heat per unit of light than incandescents, they may be appropriate for interiors with excess internal heat gains.

Even with all its benefits, fluorescent lighting may not always be desirable in an interior. The quality of light available from a fluorescent bulb is usually an even, shadowless type, giving off a bluish or greenish light. In addition, the potent unnatural wavelengths given off by unsheltered fluorescent lights have been blamed for certain genetic health problems. For this reason, fluorescents used in living spaces are best when shielded or used as an indirect light source.

provides a deeper penetration of light with less distribution on either side of the window. In north temperate climates, a sense of general brightness in a space can be achieved when room depth is limited to a distance of two to two and a half times the height from the floor to the top of the window opening. Skylights or clerestory windows are excellent providers of light for deep spaces. Each square foot of skylight opening admits about as much light as produced by a 40-watt lightbulb. Skylights, however, present problems of heat loss in the winter and excessive heat gain in the summer. Recently developed insulating skylights minimize adverse thermal effects while utilizing lighting benefits. One of these, the Skyshaft, was invented by architect Richard Crowther. This directional skylight is composed of several layers of insulating air, with reflective surfaces to channel

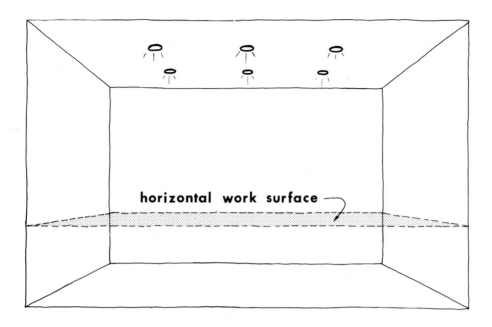

horizontal work surface

5-4. In work areas with ceiling fixtures, a downlight pattern produces maximum illumination on a horizontal work surface.

5-5. Tall, narrow openings allow deep penetration of light with little distribution. Shallow, wide openings allow a wider elliptical distribution of light.

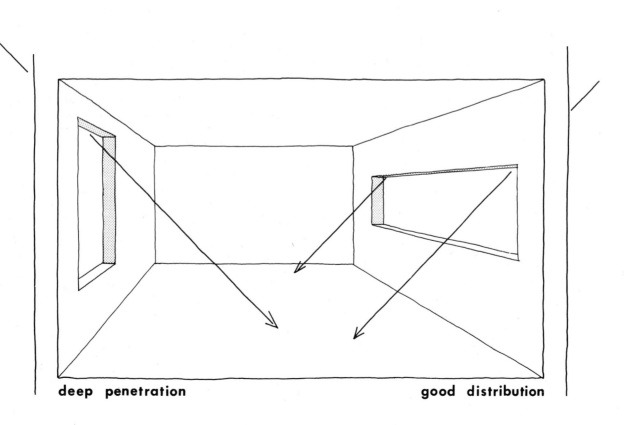

deep penetration   good distribution

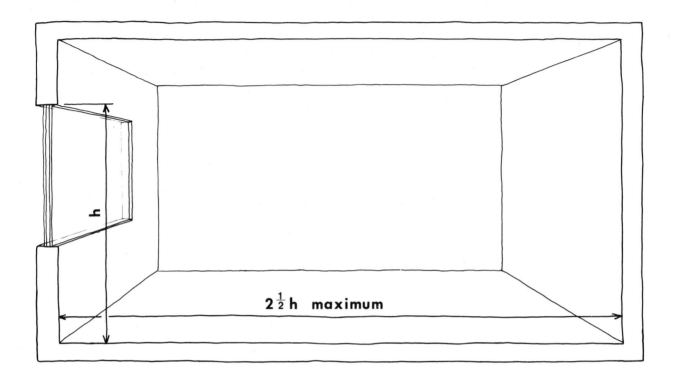

5-6.   For proper daylighting, room depth should be kept to approximately 2½ times the distance from the floor to the top of the window opening.

A more expensive fluorescent-type bulb that gives off light closer to that of natural daylight is available for interiors in which a higher quality of lighting is desired.

5-7.   Layers of insulating air and reflective surfaces to direct diffused light inside are features of Crowther's Skyshaft.

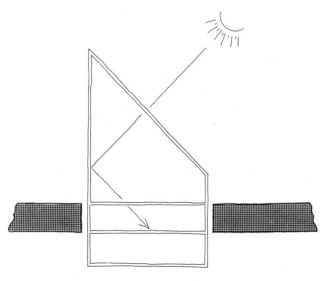

Effect of Fixture Shape and Reflectance

Any type of fixture or light shield involves some loss of efficiency which is magnified when dark or excessively shielding devices are used to cut down harshness. Recessed lighting may have similar effects. When some degree of shielding is desired, a high-transmission, light-diffusing material reduces glare with a minimum loss of efficiency.

The most important characteristic of a lighting shield is its transmission of light. The type of material, its color, and its thickness are all determining factors of light transmission (see figure 5-9).

Light sources are often encased in reflector devices that are used for direct or diffuse lighting. The overall efficiency of these fixtures depends on the shape and the reflectance of the interior surface of the device.

Lampshade and Shielding Materials

Lampshades and shielding materials come in a variety of shapes, colors, and transparencies. Opaque and dark-colored shades allow little or no light to pass through, creating essentially a combination of uplight and downlight. Lampshades with good light-transmission qualities, however, create a more distributed general brightness in a space. The area of illumination depends primarily on the shape of the lampshade and the size of the openings.

In summary, design considerations in selecting efficient lighting include:

1. Good-quality, high-efficiency bulbs; use of one high-wattage in place of several lower-wattage bulbs, where possible.
2. Shields or deflectors that produce the desired effect

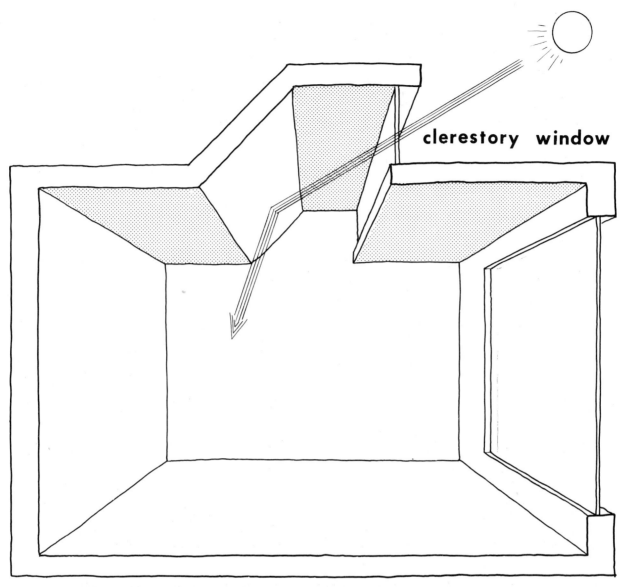

clerestory window

5-8.   *Unlike skylights, clerestory windows are vertical as well as above eye level.*

with the highest possible light transmission.
3. Reflectors, when used, with high-reflectance inside surfaces rather than fixtures with dark colors on the interior surface of the reflector.
4. Light, translucent lampshades in preference to shades that are dark and shield excessively.
5. Selection of the type of fixture meant to produce the desired illumination: concentrated or selective lamps for task lighting and multidirectional ones for general brightness.

Color Schemes of Surfaces Within a Space

Light utilization and distribution in a space is directly related to the colors of surfaces within. Although appropriate location and high quality are important elements of light sources, overall efficiency declines when combined with light-absorbing color schemes. It is therefore essential to select interior surface colors with consideration for spatial lighting plans.

The surface that is most influential as a secondary light source within a space is the one toward which a primary light source is directed. This principle holds true for both artificial and natural lighting. With an uplight system, for instance, the ceiling becomes the major secondary light source, providing evenly distributed diffuse illumination. In a space having horizontal skylights as the sole source of daylight, the floor and other horizontal surfaces such as tabletops act as major indirect light sources. In the latter case, reflectance values of floor and work surfaces determine the amount of light interreflected among the other major surfaces within the room. Since each interior has a different set of light sources, individual spatial analysis is essential in color-scheme decision making.

Maximum daylighting techniques are not always an im-

MATERIAL	TRANSMISSION
Clear glass or plastic	80%–94%
Colored glass (red)	8%–17%
(blue)	3%–5%
(green)	10%–17%
Acid etched glass	
(toward the source)	80%–90%
(away from the source)	65%–80%
Opal white glass	12%–40%
White plastic	30%–65%

5-9. *Materials most often used in shielding lighting.*

MATERIAL	REFLECTANCE
Direct Light Reflection	
Silver	90%–92%
Chromium	63%–66%
Polished aluminum	60%–70%
Stainless steel	50%–60%
Diffused Light Reflection	
White paint	70%–90%
White porcelain enamel	60%–83%

5-10. *Materials primarily used as luminaire reflectors for direct and diffused light reflection.*

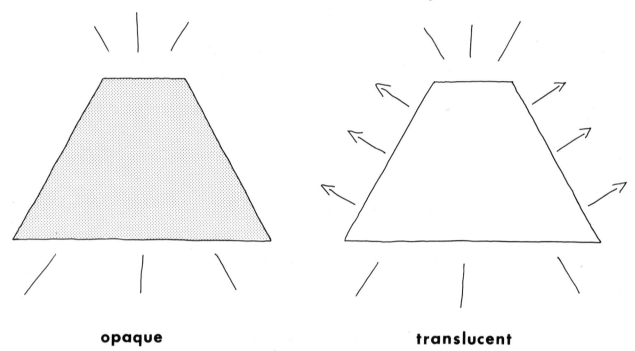

opaque

translucent

5-11. *Opaque shades restrict light distribution; translucent shades create a multidirectional lighting effect.*

portant design priority. Spaces with such favorable exposures as south, southwest, or southeast that have large areas of glass intended for solar heat gain receive more than adequate natural daylight. In these instances, glare and excessive brightness may, in fact, be the main design considerations. Many times, however, interiors lack adequate daylight. This can occur in spaces with limited possibilities for window openings, in spaces within the inner core of a building, or in rooms where daylight entering through windows is diminished due to natural or man-made obstructions. In spaces where only limited or inadequate natural light is available, maximum daylighting design techniques become a major consideration. In a space designed for maximum utilization of daylight, carefully selected surface finishes, fabrics, and furniture with good light-reflecting qualities can take advantage of whatever light is available and can reduce the need for daytime artificial illumination.

Although maximizing daylight is not a consideration in spaces with abundant sunshine, efficient utilization of artificial lighting is equally important in all interiors.

Maximum utilization of available light is not synonymous with a well-lit, bright interior space. It is simply a design technique whereby the desired lighting level and type of illumination for a space is determined, and then supplied with the minimum wattage possible. Maximum lighting utilization, therefore, produces desired illumination at significant cost savings.

The most appropriate surface finish in lighting design is a diffuse one such as flat paint, as it reflects light in a dispersed fashion. Shiny or polished room surfaces such as mirrors, with direct light-reflecting properties, produce glare and have little value in dispersing light within a space.

Figure 5-13 indicates the reflectances of various types of light-diffusing surface finishes. The values represent the percentage of incident light reflected by each surface. Because natural materials such as marble vary in surface texture and coloring their reflectances are hard to predict.

As colors and lighting plan in a space are coordinated, choices in patterns and textures can be limited to those fabrics, carpets, or shades of paint that have reflectances

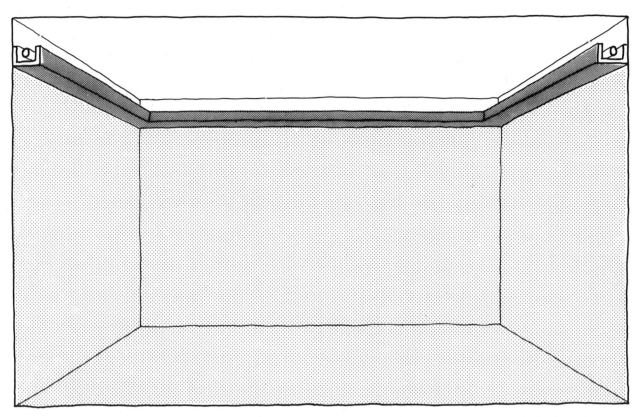

5-12. *Uplights use the ceiling as the chief source of secondary light.*

MASONRY & STRUCTURAL	REFLECTANCE
White plaster	90%–92%
White terra cotta	65%–80%
White porcelain enamel	60%–83%
Sandstone	20%–40%
Marble	30%–70%
Gray cement	20%–30%
Brick (red)	10%–20%
Brick (light buff)	40%–45%
Brick (dark buff)	35%–40%
Paint (new white)	75%–90%
Paint (old white)	50%–70%
White semigloss	70%

COLORS (GENERAL)	
Ivory white	70%–80%
Ivory	60%–70%
Pearl gray	70%–75%
Buff	40%–70%
Light gray	45%–70%
Tan	30%–50%
Dark gray	20%–25%
Azure blue	50%–60%
Pink	50%–70%
Sky blue	35%–40%
Brown	20%–40%
Green	25%–50%
Olive	20%–30%
Red	20%–40%
Black	2%

5-13. *Surface finishes and their corresponding reflectances.*

within the desired range. Because every surface in a room serves a different function, selection of colors and reflectances may be limited by practical and maintenance considerations.

Horizontal Work Surfaces and Floors

The floor and other major horizontal surfaces are not usually considered useful for light dispersion within a space. In certain instances, however, floor and horizontal surface reflectances play a significant role in lighting a space.

Efficiency of lighting systems is generally measured by a unit called the Coefficient of Utilization (C.U.), which specifically measures the ability of a lighting system to illuminate a horizontal work plane, approximately 30 inches (76.2 cm) from the floor level. The Coefficient of Utilization is expressed as a decimal fraction, and signifies the actual percentage of those lumens generated by a light source that are directly useful in producing light upon a work surface. A lighting system having a C.U. of .55, for instance, indicates that 55 percent of the available lumens illuminates a horizontal work plane.

In spaces where ceiling fixtures are used as the main source of light upon work surfaces, the C.U. is helpful in efficient system selection. Work surface illumination is most effective with a downlight pattern of fixtures. Since this type of system concentrates much of the light on horizontal surfaces, it is less useful in creating an overall spatial brightness. The level of spatial brightness with this type of system depends largely on reflectance values of the floor and the work surfaces themselves. When these values are high, spatial brightness is maximized through the interreflection of light within the space.

For practical reasons, floor reflectance values are most often lower than those of other room surfaces. Raising the floor reflectance from an average of 20 percent to 40 percent or more will have a beneficial effect on lighting efficiency, especially in spaces where primary light is directed toward the floor surface (see figure 5-14).

Walls

Wall surfaces are very important in creating a sense of brightness within a space. The reflectance of wall finishes is therefore a determining factor of the efficiency of various types of lighting systems. When brightness control is a priority, lower-wattage fixtures can be used to produce the desired effect. Brightness control through dark surface colors is a poor choice, since in creating low brightness by absorbing lumens lower efficiency results.

Not all walls in a space must necessarily have light surface finishes. Dark walls are sometimes desirable for contrast or spatial effect. In these cases, care must be taken to avoid illuminating the space with methods that directly involve the dark wall as a secondary source of light.

In passive solar interiors, heat-storage surfaces are low in reflectance to allow good heat absorption. In these spaces, non-mass surfaces should be light in color to provide good light distribution.

Curtains, shutters, and wall hangings often make up a large percentage of vertical surfaces in a space. Extensive wall coverings and fabrics used in this manner become significant as "wall surfaces" for lighting purposes and should be treated with equal consideration for their light-reflecting qualities.

The Ceiling

The ceiling is the surface most influential in light dispersion within a space. Uplights use this surface as a chief source of secondary lighting. An uplight with an opaque reflector makes the ceiling the sole source of light. An uplight fixture with a translucent reflector, however, uses both ceiling and light source to illuminate the space.

Natural light from direct solar radiation and sky brightness enters a space at a downward angle. In low buildings, however, a significant portion of natural light entering a space originates from ground surface reflectance. Reflected light from ground surfaces enters a space at an upward angle, making the ceiling reflectance important in daylighting efficiency.

MATERIAL	REFLECTANCE
Dark oak	10%–15%
Light oak	25%–35%
White painted	50%–70%
Red brick	10%–20%
Light brick	40%–45%
Concrete	55%

5-14.   Reflectances of the most common flooring materials.

As a general rule, interior surface reflectances should be high enough to take maximum advantage of light sources. A good range for wall and ceiling reflectances is 60 to 90 percent, while floor finishes can be 40 percent or higher. An increase of wall, ceiling, and floor reflectances from 50-10-10 to 80-60-50, for instance, increases the lighting level within a space by approximately 35 percent. This has great significance in spaces where specific lighting levels are required. In two rooms, each 18 by 22 feet (5.5 by 6.7 m) with identical illumination requirements, the room having low surface reflectances needs 1060 watts while the room with high surface reflectances needs only 800 watts to maintain the necessary lighting level.

Although lighting studies are most often conducted for office and commercial spaces where potential savings are greatest, test results have significance on a small scale as well. Efficient use of lighting in private residences can reduce the number of fixtures and the wattage necessary to provide desired lighting levels.

Furniture Selection

In a space with limited natural lighting, furniture selection becomes an important part of maximum lighting design. Shelving, cabinets, dining table, and sofas take up relatively large areas and have the potential to reflect or absorb incident light. Although furniture reflectances are not as important as surface reflectances, in a limited-lighting situation furniture interreflectance can become the deciding factor between sufficient and inadequate daylighting. Fabrics, carpets, painted finishes, and wood types or stains in the light-to-moderate reflectance range are appropriate for these instances (see figure 5-16).

WOOD	REFLECTANCE
Pine	40%
Light birch	35%–50%
Light oak	25%–35%
Dark oak	10%–15%
Mahogany	6%–12%
Walnut	5%–10%

5-16.   Reflectances of wood types used in furniture.

Architectural Design for Natural Daylighting

The architectural design of a building is the most important element affecting natural daylighting. Building orientation and orientation of individual spaces determines the nature of available daylighting. The hours of daylight in a region are determined by latitude and time of year; and the time of day, in any orientation, can dramatically change the quality of available light. In winter, at noon, sky brightness on south orientations is two and a half times that on the east or west and over four times that of north exposures. In autumn and spring, sky brightness on south exposures at noon is still nearly twice as great as of east and west,

5-15.   A room with limited natural light utilizes light Canadian
elm furniture and white walls for maximum utilization of natural
daylight.

and three times as great as on north. During the summer months, east has the greatest brightness in the morning hours, and west during the afternoon.

Space planning and layout are a major influence in using natural daylight. When small, enclosed spaces are placed on a building's perimeter, daylight is closed off from the inner spaces of the building. In many instances, spatial function is compatible with *open planning,* or free flow of spaces. Open planning allows daylight to be shared by more spaces within the building. In addition, beneficially oriented window openings, shared by many, can minimize the need for windows on adverse exposures.

Landscape

In addition to orientation, the natural landscape and structures surrounding a building have an important role in natural daylighting. In dense urban areas, lower stories often have limited access to natural lighting because of shadows cast by surrounding structures. These low spaces become dependent on light reflected from the ground and adjacent buildings.

In low buildings, light reflected from the ground surface provides up to 50 percent of the total daylighting on a sunny day and 10 to 25 percent in overcast conditions. The type of ground cover immediately surrounding a building is therefore influential in the amount of light reflected into a space located close to these surfaces (see figure 5-17).

Use of Insulating or Light-Reflecting Glass

Often, efforts to reduce heat loss or heat gain through windows conflicts with natural daylighting considerations. Tinted, light-reflecting, and insulating glass all produce losses in daylight transmission. Figure 5-18 compares the transmittance value of various types of ¼-inch (.635 cm) glazing materials.

Light-reflecting glass may be appropriate for buildings in mild climates or ones with excessive year-round internal heat gains. In these buildings, however, energy expenses due to increased artificial illumination during the day resulting from loss of daylighting should be weighed against savings in air cooling costs. It is sometimes more efficient to use adjustable solar shading to allow daylight penetration, except during hours of direct sunlight (see chapter 8).

Light and Heat

Because artificial lighting can be sized in terms of wattage as required by spatial function, the amount of heat given off by fixtures can be calculated. This internal heat gain is

GROUND COVER	REFLECTANCE
Grass	6%
Vegetation	25%
Earth	7%
Snow (new)	75%
Snow (old)	60%
Concrete	55%
Brick (buff)	45%
Brick (red)	30%
Gravel	13%
Asphalt	7%
Painted (new white)	75%
Painted (old white)	55%

5-17. *Reflectances of typical ground covers.*

SINGLE GLASS		TRANSMITTANCE
Clear glass	¼"	87%
Blue green	¼"	75%
Gray	¼"	44%
Bronze	¼"	52%
THERMOPANE INSULATING GLASS		
Clear	¼"	77%
Blue green	¼"	66%
Gray	¼"	35%
Bronze	¼"	38%
VARI-TRAN REFLECTIVE GLASS		
Silver	¼"	8%–20%
Golden	¼"	8%–20%

5-18. *Transmittance of various ¼-inch glazing materials.*

constant, and can be utilized or exhausted as indoor conditions demand. Natural daylight, on the other hand, depends on orientation, weather conditions, seasons, and the hour of day, making it somewhat unpredictable. In addition, some orientations may involve long periods of direct sunlight. In these instances, the heat gained through windows can become significant and needs consideration as a separate design element. Evaluating spatial lighting and heating needs can lead to a number of design choices: heat and light can be used immediately and directly; light can be allowed to penetrate while heat is stored for later use; a portion of the light can be allowed to enter while storing much of the heat for later use; or both heat and light can be partially or totally rejected when not required by the space. Chapters 6 and 7 explore such ways of regulating the heat and light entering a space.

Chapter 6
SOLAR HEAT ABSORPTION AND STORAGE

AS SUNLIGHT ENTERS A SPACE AND STRIKES OBjects and surfaces, some of the solar radiation is absorbed as heat by each object or surface; the remainder is reflected as light. The value of a color, its lightness or darkness, is the main determinant of the proportion of light reflected to light absorbed. Light colors reflect a large percentage of solar energy, whereas darker colors reflect very little light and absorb much of the solar radiation as heat. Surfaces or objects intended to store heat from the sun should therefore have a surface color with good heat-absorbing capability.

Flat black achieves the highest solar absorption, but black is not always aesthetically desirable, especially in interiors in which most major surfaces are designed for solar heat storage. When many room surfaces are of heat storage quality, varying the value of their colors regulates the amount of heat collected by each surface. Making walls moderate to light in color and floors darker results in a tendency for heat to accumulate low within the space. This is advantageous, since the floor is the surface to which occupants are usually closest.

When colors other than black are desired, dark colors with good heat-absorbing qualities can work well. A number of dark-value colors can achieve heat storage efficiencies very close to that which can be achieved by black. As long as the desired color has a solar absorptance value of .70 or more, the loss of solar heat collection efficiency should be no greater than 10 percent (see figure 6-1).

Although color value has the largest effect on solar heat absorptance, hue can also influence heat absorption. Studies conducted by Faye C. Jones at the University of Arizona

Agricultural Experiment Station indicate that for painted surfaces of equivalent lightness, hues in the middle wavelength such as green and yellow are best absorbers of solar radiation. Those in the long wavelength range such as red and orange are next best, while purple and blue in the short wavelength range are the poorest absorbers.

Thermal Mass

An object the sun shines upon is warmed by the sun's rays. Most objects so warmed give off heat to the surrounding space almost instantaneously. Materials that can absorb and keep absorbing heat for a long period of time before giving it off to the surrounding environment are termed *thermal mass* materials. In a space designed for maximum wintertime solar heat gain, the amount of heat received by the space on a sunny day exceeds its daytime heating requirements. For this reason, thermal mass materials are incorporated in these spaces to hold daytime heat until the evening, when it is needed.

The relationship between the living space, the south-facing glass, and the thermal mass determines how solar heat is received by an interior. When sun is allowed to penetrate a living space, warming the space and the mass, the passive solar design is referred to as a *direct gain system*.

When unlimited direct sun penetrating a space is not desired, the thermal mass is placed between the solar glass and the living space. This system is called an *indirect heat gain system,* since the living space receives its solar heat

MATERIAL	ABSORPTANCE
Flat black paint	.95
Dark gray paint	.91
Dark brown paint	.88
Dark green lacquer	.88
Medium brown paint	.84
Medium rust paint	.78
Red bricks	.70
Wood (pine)	.60
Uncolored concrete	.65
Medium orange paint	.58
Medium yellow paint	.57
Aluminum paint	.55
Medium blue paint	.51
Copper	.35
White semigloss paint	.30

6-1. *Solar absorptance values of heat-storage materials and common colors.*

mostly through thermal radiation and conduction from the mass itself, and not the sun.

6-2. *In a direct solar heat gain system, sunlight is allowed to penetrate into all parts of the living space.*

Thermal mass materials have some common properties that make them appropriate for solar heat storage. First, they can store relatively large amounts of heat per pound (per kg), depending on their specific heat; and second, they can distribute heat efficiently throughout the material, depending on their conductivity. Efficient heat absorption by any type of mass is largely controlled by its surface color.

Specific Heat

The specific heat of a substance determines how much heat in Btu's (kcal) one pound (1 kg) of that substance can hold each time its temperature is increased by 1°F (1°C). A material's specific heat is important in measuring the amount, in weight, of thermal mass necessary in a space. When a minimum of weight is essential, a material with high specific heat, capable of holding more Btu's per pound for an equal temperature increase, is desirable. The specific heats of some building materials are listed in figure 6-4.

Conductivity

Although having a high specific heat is a good quality for a thermal mass material, it is not, by itself, enough to make it an efficient heat storage material. Because the heat distribution within the mass is dependent on its con-

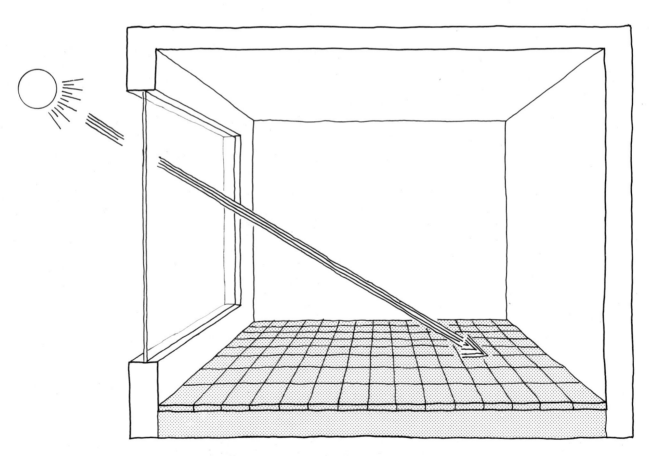

DIRECT SOLAR HEAT GAIN

MATERIAL	Btu's stored/lb./°F temp. rise kcal stored/kg/°C temp. rise
Water	1.0
Softwood	.45
Wood, oak	.57
Corkboard	.50
Brick	.20
Sand	.191
Wool (fabric)	.32
Concrete	.156
Adobe	.24
Steel	.12
Thermol 81-The Energy Rod	.34 (solid)
(phase-change heat storage)	.53 (liquid)

6-4.   *Specific heats of common building substances.*

ductivity, materials with a low k value are poor in transferring heat from their surface throughout the entire mass. When the material conductivity is very high, as in metals, heat is transferred too quickly throughout the mass and is given off too soon. Materials with a moderate k value such as

6-3.   *In an indirect solar heat gain system, sunlight is absorbed by the mass and passes into the living space later in the day in the form of heat.*

concrete, water, or brick soak up heat more slowly, and later in the day give off heat at a slower rate, creating a good thermal balance day and night.

Thermal Time-Lag

Material conductivity and thickness are the two elements determining the length of time it takes heat to travel through a material. This time span is called its *thermal time-lag*.

Thermal time-lag is especially important in indirect gain interiors, where mass materials are between the glass and the living space. When the heat storage mass has excessive time lag, its inside face remains relatively cool. When the time lag is too short, on the other hand, heat is transferred through the mass and is given off more rapidly during the day when the stored heat is not yet needed by the space (see figure 6-5).

In an indirect gain system, therefore, the optimum thickness of a thermal storage wall varies with its conductivity. The higher a material's conductivity, the thicker the wall must be to function well as thermal mass.

According to the list of material conductances in figure 6-6, adobe walls can have the smallest thickness, while brick with magnesium additive, having a high conductance, should have the greatest thickness. In general, thermal heat storage walls vary from 8 to 18 inches (20 to 45 cm)

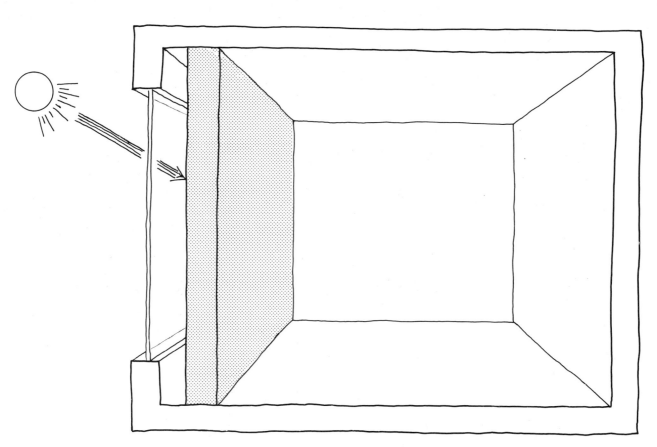

INDIRECT SOLAR HEAT GAIN

MATERIAL	APPROXIMATE TIME LAG
Wood ½″ (1.27 cm)	10 min.
1″ (2.54 cm)	25 min.
Concrete 6″ (15.2 cm)	3 hr. 50 min.
8″ (20.3 cm)	5 hr. 05 min.
12″ (30.5 cm)	7 hr. 50 min.
Brick 4″ (10.2 cm)	2 hr. 20 min.
8″ (20.3 cm)	5 hr. 20 min.
12″ (30.5 cm)	8 hr. 20 min.
Insulation 2″ (5 km)	0 hr. 40 min.
8″ concrete wall with 4″ insulation	6 hr. 55 min.
Wood frame wall with 4″ insulation	2 hr. 45 min.

6-5.   Time lag characteristics of various building materials.

MATERIAL	THERMAL CONDUCTIVITY Btu/hr. sq.ft. °F/inch (kcal/m² h °C/m)
Adobe	.30 (.0372)
Brick (common)	.42 (.052)
Concrete (dense)	1.00 (.124)
Brick (magnesium additive)	2.20 (.273)
Water	3.70 (.459)

6-6.   Thermal conductivity of common building materials.

6-7.   Although water has a high conductivity, heat distribution depends on the convection of warmed water within the container.

in thickness. Water walls are an exception to this rule, since the role of water's conductivity is not great in measuring its thermal time-lag. Heat distribution in a water mass occurs by the gravity convection of warmed water within the container.

Experiments show that, in general, spaces with a large quantity of thermal mass have less indoor temperature fluctuations between day and night than spaces having little mass.

Materials Used for Thermal Mass

Materials that meet the requirements of good thermal mass can be listed in three separate categories: masonry, water, and phase-change substances.

Masonry

The main advantage to using masonry materials for solar heat storage is that they can serve as part of a building's structural system as well as heat storage. When designed to act as thermal mass, exposed masonry floors, walls, and ceilings within a space absorb daytime heat. When a building's structural system consists of non-mass materials, masonry can be added in the form of rock or sand bins, ceramic tiles, or built-in furniture, located in the direct line of the sun to absorb and store thermal energy. The list in figure 6-8 contains the density in pounds per cubic foot of various masonry materials and the amount of heat in Btu's stored by one cubic foot of the material for each degree Fahrenheit temperature rise.

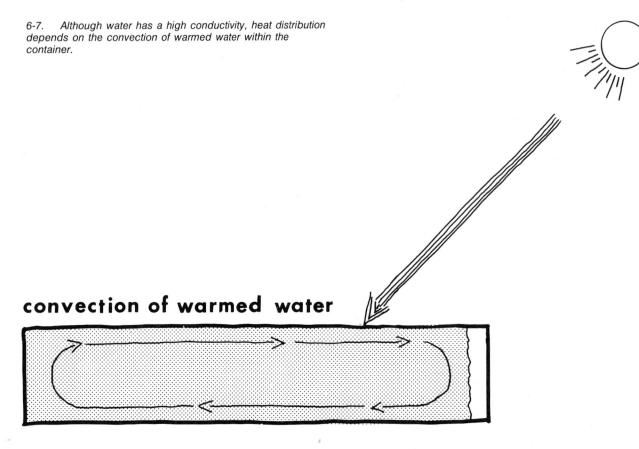

convection of warmed water

MATERIAL	DENSITY lb./cu. ft. (kg/cu. m)	APPROXIMATE HEAT STORED* Btu/lb. (kcal/kg)
Adobe	106 (1,698)	25.0 (14.0)
Brick	123 (1,970)	24.6 (13.7)
Concrete	144 (2,306)	30.0 (16.7)
Sand bin (packed)	94.6 (1,515)	18.0 (10.0)
Sand bin (30% voids)	66 (1,057)	12.6 (7.0)
Rock wall	100 (1,601)	20.0 (11.0)
Rock bin	70 (1,121)	14.0 (7.8)

* per cu. ft. for each 1°F rise in temperature

6-8. Density of masonry materials and amount of heat stored within.

UNIT TYPE OR SIZE			CONTENT in gallons (liters)	HEAT STORED*
	Diameter	Length		
Kalwall tube	12″ (30 cm)	4′ (1.2 m)	24 (91)	200 (90.4)
	18″ (46 cm)	5′ (1.5 m)	66 (250)	550 (248.7)
One Design 53 (black/clear)			53 (201)	442 (199.7)
PVC Pipe	12″ (30.5 cm)	8′ (2.4 m)	47 (178)	392 (177)
Steel drum	Small	Round	30 (114)	250 (113)
Steel drum	Large	Round	55 (208)	459 (207)

* per unit Btu for each 1°F rise in temperature (kcal for each 1°C rise in temperature)

6-9. Water storage containers available for use in passive solar interiors.

Water

The primary advantage of water thermal storage systems is that they can hold approximately five times more Btu's per pound than masonry. When water is added to a space, however, structural support and loss of usable space may become factors. Water storage containers of various sizes and shapes are now marketed for use in passive solar interiors. Listed in figure 6-9 are some water containers, their volume per unit, and the approximate heat stored by each unit for a 1°F temperature rise.

Phase-Change Materials

Phase-change materials are eutectic salt-based substances capable of storing more heat per pound than conventional heat storage materials. Phase-change salts are designed to melt at a relatively low temperature [Thermol 81 rods, for example, melt at 81°F (27.2°C), storing a latent heat of 82 Btu/pound (45.6 kcal/kg)]. As the sun warms them during the day, they melt and absorb a large amount of heat. At night, as they cool and solidify, they release the stored heat into the space. These materials have a high heat capacity not because of their specific heat, but because of the latent heat they absorb when they change their state from solid to liquid. A relatively new development,

phase-change materials are now marketed in containers of various sizes and shapes, as shown in figure 6-10.

Sizing the Mass

In a well-functioning passive solar space, the south-facing glass and the thermal mass must be sized or proportioned to provide a good indoor thermal balance between day and night. Excessive glazing toward the south with little or no thermal mass leads to daytime overheating of an interior. When glazing is limited and mass is excessive, the space cannot fully benefit from solar heat.

The amount of thermal mass material needed by a space is dependent on the size of the glazing facing south, the type of mass, and its capacity to hold heat. The surface color, volume, thickness, and distribution of the mass are additional factors in efficient functioning of a passive solar heating system. The final consideration is the percentage of mass surface receiving direct sunlight. When it is small, the result is inefficient heat absorption by the mass.

Because of differences in the nature of heat gain between direct and indirect heat gain systems, optimum thicknesses and mass distribution differ. In direct gain systems, the

UNIT AND SIZE	PHASE-CHANGE TEMPERATURE	WEIGHT lb. (kg)	APPROXIMATE HEAT STORED
Thermol 81—The Energy Rod 3½″ × 6′ (8.9 cm × 1.8 m) tube	81°F (27.2°C)	32 (14.5)	2,600 Btu (655 kcal)
Thermalrod—27 3½″ × 6′ (8.9 cm × 1.8 m) rod	81°F (27.2°C)	32 (14.5)	2,600 Btu (655 kcal)
Texxor Heat Cells 4″ dia × 7″ (10.2 cm × 17.8 cm) can	81°F (27.2°C)	4.54	345 Btu (87 kcal)
Solar-Pod 48″ × 16″ × 2″ (122 cm × 40.6 cm × 5 cm)	81°F (27.2°C)	29	2,400 Btu (605 kcal)
Sol-Ar-Tile™ 2′ × 2′ × 2″ (61 cm × 61 cm × 5 cm) or 1′ × 2′ × 2″ (30.5 cm × 61 cm × 5 cm)	73°F (22.8°C)		220 Btu/sq. ft. (597 kcal/m²)
Enerphase Panels 14″ × 22″ × 2¼″ (35.6 cm × 55.9 cm × 5.7 cm)	81°F (27.2°C)	20	1,600 Btu (403 kcal)

6-10. Brands of units available storing phase-change materials.

best results can be achieved with well-distributed thermal mass that has some exposure to direct sunlight. For instance, a south-facing room with 4- to 6-inch-thick (10 to 15 cm) concrete floor and walls has more efficient heat absorption and storage than a room with only one massive (16- to 18-inch-thick/40 to 45 cm) wall. Although the total volume of concrete in both spaces may be the same, its distribution throughout the space causes differences in the thermal behavior of the interior. With well-distributed thermal mass, day and night temperature swings are kept to a minimum.

Because an indirect gain system most often has a thermal storage mass equal in area to the south-facing glass, these systems are sized according to a region's climate and the area of floor space to be heated.

As a general rule, a space in a cold climate (winter temperature of 15°F, or − 18.4°C) requires a thermal storage wall and glazing area approximately equal to the floor area of the space being heated. In milder climates or in well-insulated homes, the ratio of mass and glazing area to floor area can be reduced to as little as 25 percent. Because the indoor climate and the energy requirements of various spaces differ, design professionals can calculate the glass and mass area best suited for a particular space.

Although optimum thicknesses of masonry materials can be determined by their conductances (see figure 4-2), water is generally sized by volume, since heat within a water-storage container is more evenly distributed by convection. As a rule of thumb, a dark-colored water wall exposed to the south sun should have at least 8 gallons of water for each square foot (325 liters/m²) of south-facing glass. As the volume of water is increased to a maximum of 22 gallons per square foot (896 liters/m²) temperature fluctuations within the space are minimized. A water wall not exposed to direct sunlight, however, needs several times the volume mentioned above to maintain efficient heat absorption.

Because phase-change materials store significantly more heat than masonry or water storage systems, they can be valuable for use in interiors with limited space or structural capacity. Rods, trays, or tiles containing phase-change salts can be used for thermal storage in either direct or indirect systems. Although indoor temperature fluctuations have not yet been recorded in any published study for this type of thermal storage system, it can be assumed that overall thickness or method of stacking determines time lag characteristics. To maximize the regulation of heat flow from this type of mass, movable insulation or thermal covers placed over the mass after sunset can help to contain the heat within the mass until it is needed.

Glazing Area

The amount of mass needed by a direct gain system is usually given in terms of the south-facing glass area. The size of glazing necessary to supply adequate solar heat for a space depends on the space's size in square feet of floor area and the climate of its location. Although it is not feasible to design a passive solar system to supply 100 percent of a space's heating requirements, such a system can provide for 32 to 98 percent of its heating needs, depending on the insulation of the space and the outdoor climate. As a general rule, the amount of south-facing glass/floor area of living space necessary for a well-insulated space with distributed mass varies from 20 to 35 percent in cold climates to about 10 to 15 percent in milder climates. Because the energy requirements of interior spaces vary, individual consideration is necessary to determine the optimum amount of solar heat appropriate for each space.

Poorly insulated spaces have greater heating needs and require larger solar glass areas. Because the overall heat gain through solar windows is greatly diminished by nighttime heat loss through these large glazed surfaces, night insulating covers can be used to increase the total usable heat provided by these systems.

Quality of a Passive Space

The quantity of thermal mass and the area of solar glazing may be the basic ingredients for indoor thermal balance, but the quality of the space as an interior environment is equally important. Decisions regarding the type of mass to use and how to incorporate it into an area can affect the everyday lives of individuals occupying that space.

Considerations should include glare, discomfort, and fading of fabrics due to prolonged exposure to direct sunlight entering the area, the cold sensation created for an individual upon contact with masonry surfaces below skin temperature, the space and structure necessary to support water systems, the conflict caused by dark or black surfaces designed for maximum heat absorption with maximum daylighting design, and the tedious ritual necessary with manually operated night shutters and thermal covers.

The functional, personal, and thermal requirements of individuals in an interior may involve some compromises to achieve a high-quality design solution.

Chapter 7

EXPOSURE OF THE LIVING SPACE: CLIMATIC ANALYSIS OF AN INTERIOR

AN INTERIOR SPACE HAS A CLIMATE OF ITS OWN. Although this "indoor climate" is directly related to weather conditions outside, two houses, side by side, can have completely different indoor climates.

Much of what determines indoor climate has to do with the architectural and interior design of a structure and the manner in which it responds to the external environment. Thermal effects of people, lighting, and other heat-generating equipment are also important factors. Although HVAC (Heating, Ventilating, and Air Conditioning) systems overcome most of the adverse influences upon the interior, it is becoming increasingly costly to compensate for inefficiencies in building design. In fact, even highly sophisticated mechanical systems cannot totally negate the effects of the outside environment upon the comfort of those within. Extreme outdoor temperatures and cold winter winds are the major cause of infiltrating air and interior surface temperature changes that produce uncomfortable living conditions. Solar radiation is another significant external force affecting the interior space. When allowed to penetrate in the summer, sunlight accounts for a major portion of an interior's cooling costs, while in winter its presence becomes a warm contribution, considerably cutting into heating costs.

Control of solar radiation entering a structure is one of the keys to energy-efficient building design. By maximizing solar penetration during the cold seasons and minimizing it throughout the summer season, the interior climate can be moderated and the cost of environmental conditioning reduced.

Sun

The sun is the source of all forms of energy on earth and is the fundamental origin of global weather patterns. The earth's position relative to the sun causes the seasonal and daily temperature variations and induces continental wind currents. Yet solar radiation also produces a very individual thermal relationship between the source and the object. The sunlight that shines on the sunbather or the sun that radiates into the living area, warming and brightening that space, is individualized sun. Solar radiation entering the living space for a given number of hours each day becomes an inherent part of its interior design, and is just as important to it as its other design features.

Solar Analysis

Since solar radiation is an important design element as well as an abundant energy source, detailed solar analysis is a desirable part of every design development. Some basic information required for this type of analysis includes azimuth and altitude angles of the sun at various latitudes and heat value of the sun expressed in terms of Btu's.

In planning new projects, solar analysis helps in site selection and structure orientation. In the renovation of existing architecture and interiors, solar data helps determine the exposure of various interior spaces and their solar relationship.

Generally, in the northern hemisphere, direct south ori-

JANUARY 21

Time AM	Azimuth	Altitude	N	NE	E	SE	S	SW	W	NW	Horiz.	Time PM
8	55.3	8.1	5	17	111	133	75	6	5	5	14	4
9	44	16.8	12	13	154	224	160	82	12	12	55	3
10	30.9	23.8	16	16	124	241	213	51	16	16	96	2
11	16	28.4	19	19	61	222	244	118	19	19	124	1
12	0	30	20	20	21	179	254	179	21	20	133	12
Daily Totals			124	137	523	1,256	1,638	1,256	523	137	711	
			N	NW	W	SW	S	SE	E	NE	Horiz.	

FEBRUARY 21

Time AM	Azimuth	Altitude	N	NE	E	SE	S	SW	W	NW	Horiz.	Time PM
7	80.2	11.4	2	23	51	47	14	2	2	2	4	5
8	62.2	15.4	10	50	183	199	94	10	10	10	43	4
9	50.2	25.0	16	22	186	245	157	17	16	16	98	3
10	35.9	32.8	21	21	143	246	203	38	21	21	143	2
11	18.9	38.1	23	23	71	219	231	103	23	23	171	1
12	0	40.0	24	24	25	170	241	170	25	24	180	12
Daily Totals			168	235	731	1,296	1,639	1,296	731	235	1,098	
			N	NW	W	SW	S	SE	E	NE	Horiz.	

MARCH 21

Time AM	Azimuth	Altitude	N	NE	E	SE	S	SW	W	NW	Horiz.	Time PM
7	80.2	11.4	9	93	163	135	22	8	8	8	26	5
8	69.6	22.5	16	91	218	211	74	16	16	16	85	4
9	57.3	32.8	21	47	203	236	128	22	21	21	143	3
10	41.9	41.6	25	27	153	229	171	29	25	25	186	2
11	22.6	47.7	28	28	78	198	197	77	28	28	213	1
12	0	50.0	29	29	31	145	206	145	31	29	223	12
Daily Totals			227	413	944	1,306	1,390	1,306	944	413	1,529	
			N	NW	W	SW	S	SE	E	NE	Horiz.	

APRIL 21

Time AM	Azimuth	Altitude	N	NE	E	SE	S	SW	W	NW	Horiz.	Time PM
6	98.9	7.4	11	72	88	52	5	5	5	5	11	6
7	89.5	18.9	16	140	201	143	16	14	14	14	61	5
8	79.3	30.3	22	128	224	188	41	21	21	21	123	4
9	67.2	41.3	27	80	202	203	83	27	27	27	177	3
10	51.4	51.2	31	37	152	193	121	32	31	31	217	2
11	29.2	58.7	33	34	81	160	146	52	33	33	243	1
12	0	61.6	34	34	36	108	154	108	36	34	252	12
Daily Totals			314	656	1,115	1,198	978	1,198	1,115	656	1,916	
			N	NW	W	SW	S	SE	E	NE	Horiz.	

7-1.   Solar position and approximate heat available on a vertical surface throughout the year at 40° north latitude. Daily totals are the total Btu's available for each orientation, obtained by adding down the AM column and up the PM column for the same exposure. The 12 noon reading is added only once.

MAY 21

Time AM	Azimuth	Altitude	N	NE	E	SE	S	SW	W	NW	Horiz.	Time PM
5	114.7	1.9	0	1	1	0	0	0	0	0	0	7
6	105.6	12.7	36	128	141	71	10	10	10	10	31	6
7	96.6	24.0	28	165	209	131	20	19	19	19	87	5
8	87.2	35.4	27	149	220	164	29	25	25	25	146	4
9	76.0	46.8	31	105	197	175	53	30	30	30	195	3
10	60.9	57.5	34	54	148	163	83	35	34	34	234	2
11	37.1	66.2	36	38	81	130	105	42	36	36	257	1
12	0	70.0	37	37	40	82	113	82	40	37	265	12
Daily Totals			421	831	1,191	1,077	713	1,077	1,191	831	2,165	
			N	NW	W	SW	S	SE	E	NE	Horiz.	

JUNE 21

Time AM	Azimuth	Altitude	N	NE	E	SE	S	SW	W	NW	Horiz.	Time PM
5	117.3	4.2	10	21	20	6	1	1	1	1	3	7
6	108.4	14.8	48	143	151	70	13	13	13	13	40	6
7	99.7	26.0	37	172	207	122	22	21	21	21	97	5
8	90.7	37.4	30	156	216	152	29	27	27	27	153	4
9	80.2	48.8	33	114	192	161	45	32	32	32	201	3
10	65.8	59.8	35	63	145	148	69	36	35	35	238	2
11	41.9	69.2	38	40	81	116	88	41	38	38	260	1
12	0	73.5	38	38	41	72	95	72	41	38	267	12
Daily Totals			500	914	1,220	1,018	629	1,018	1,220	914	2,251	
			N	NW	W	SW	S	SE	E	NE	Horiz.	

JULY 21

Time AM	Azimuth	Altitude	N	NE	E	SE	S	SW	W	NW	Horiz.	Time PM
5	115.2	2.3	1	2	2	1	0	0	0	0	0	7
6	106.1	13.1	37	125	137	68	11	11	11	11	32	6
7	97.2	24.3	30	163	204	127	21	20	20	20	88	5
8	87.8	35.8	28	148	216	160	30	26	26	26	145	4
9	76.7	47.2	32	106	193	170	52	31	31	31	194	3
10	61.7	57.9	35	56	146	159	81	36	35	35	231	2
11	37.0	66.7	37	40	81	127	102	43	37	37	254	1
12	0	70.6	38	38	41	80	109	80	41	38	262	12
Daily Totals			438	838	1,180	1,059	703	1,059	1,180	838	2,150	
			N	NW	W	SW	S	SE	E	NE	Horiz.	

AUGUST 21

Time AM	Azimuth	Altitude	N	NE	E	SE	S	SW	W	NW	Horiz.	Time PM
6	99.5	7.9	12	68	82	48	6	5	5	5	12	6
7	90.0	19.3	17	135	191	135	17	16	16	16	62	5
8	79.9	30.7	24	126	216	180	41	23	23	23	122	4
9	67.9	41.8	28	82	197	196	80	28	28	28	174	3
10	52.1	51.7	32	40	150	187	116	34	32	32	214	2
11	29.7	59.3	35	36	81	156	141	52	35	35	235	1
12	0	62.3	35	35	38	106	149	106	38	35	247	12
Daily Totals			331	661	1,094	1,166	951	1,166	1,094	661	1,885	
			N	NW	W	SW	S	SE	E	NE	Horiz.	

SEPTEMBER 21

Time AM	Azimuth	Altitude	N	NE	E	SE	S	SW	W	NW	Horiz.	Time PM
7	80.2	11.4	9	84	146	121	21	9	9	9	25	5
8	69.6	22.5	17	87	205	199	71	17	17	17	82	4
9	57.3	32.8	22	47	194	226	124	23	22	22	138	3
10	41.9	41.6	27	28	148	221	165	30	27	27	180	2
11	22.6	47.7	29	29	78	192	191	77	29	29	206	1
12	0	50.0	30	30	32	142	200	142	32	30	215	12
Daily Totals			238	409	907	1,257	1,344	1,257	907	409	1,477	
			N	NW	W	SW	S	SE	E	NE	Horiz.	

OCTOBER 21

Time AM	Azimuth	Altitude	N	NE	E	SE	S	SW	W	NW	Horiz.	Time PM
7	72.3	4.5	2	20	45	42	12	2	2	2	4	5
8	61.9	15.0	11	49	173	188	89	11	11	11	43	4
9	49.8	24.5	17	23	180	235	151	18	17	17	97	3
10	35.6	32.4	21	22	139	238	196	38	21	21	140	2
11	18.7	37.6	24	24	71	212	224	101	24	24	168	1
12	0	39.5	25	25	27	165	234	165	27	25	177	12
Daily Totals			175	238	710	1,250	1,578	1,250	710	238	1,081	
			N	NW	W	SW	S	SE	E	NE	Horiz.	

NOVEMBER 21

Time AM	Azimuth	Altitude	N	NE	E	SE	S	SW	W	NW	Horiz.	Time PM
8	55.4	8.2	5	18	108	129	72	6	5	5	14	4
9	44.1	17.0	12	13	151	219	156	13	12	12	55	3
10	31.0	24.0	14	14	113	232	210	55	14	14	77	2
11	16.1	28.6	19	19	61	218	240	116	19	19	123	1
12	0	30.5	20	20	21	176	250	176	21	20	132	12
Daily Totals			120	134	504	1,164	1,606	1,164	504	134	670	
			N	NW	W	SW	S	SE	E	NE	Horiz.	

DECEMBER 21

Time AM	Azimuth	Altitude	N	NE	E	SE	S	SW	W	NW	Horiz.	Time PM
8	53	5.5	3	8	67	84	50	3	3	3	6	4
9	42	14	10	11	135	205	151	13	10	10	39	3
10	29	21	14	14	113	232	210	55	14	14	77	2
11	15	25	17	17	56	217	242	120	17	17	104	1
12	0	27	18	18	19	178	253	178	19	18	113	12
Daily Totals			106	112	434	1,107	1,559	1,107	434	112	565	
			N	NW	W	SW	S	SE	E	NE	Horiz.	

entation provides the maximum radiant heat during the winter season. Any structure, new or existing, that has a clear access to the south obtains in wintertime a net heat gain through all windows facing that direction, whereas windows facing the east, west, or north experience a net heat loss. In terms of passive solar principles in the design of an interior space, increasing south-facing window openings results in an increased heat-collecting potential. Even when the building orientation is as much as 25° off true south, as in the case of the Manhattan street grid, 90 percent of the available solar heat can be collected.

The vertical angle at which south-facing collecting surfaces trap the maximum amount of solar energy in any given area is approximately 15°–20° plus the north latitude of that region. For the New York vicinity, for instance, which is located at approximately 40° north latitude, this means a tilt of 55°–60° with the horizontal. Utilizing this principle assures maximum heat collection and is especially critical when costly active solar systems with flat-plate collectors

are employed for home heating. Although vertical south-facing glass admits much of the available solar radiation, the designer of passive solar spaces can take advantage of the optimum angle by using it in the design of greenhouse and skylight glazing.

In some instances, the potential for solar heating a space may exist but is not fully utilized. This is true when there is unobstructed access to the south, but few or no window openings facing that direction. In such cases, installing new windows or enlarging existing ones creates a solar heating opportunity. When the size of the window opening is limited by structural or architectural elements, inserting a solar bay window increases the area of the glazing and in turn the solar intake.

Solar Bay Window

The amount of heat gained through a window on a clear day depends on its size and orientation, as well as the

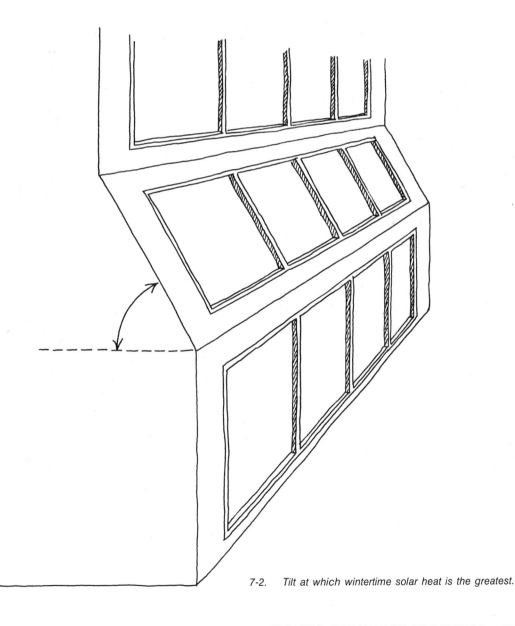

7-2.   Tilt at which wintertime solar heat is the greatest.

7-3.   Solar bay windows can better realize the potential for solar heating.

season and time of day. Each square foot of glass gains a certain number of Btu's each hour (see figure 7-1). Bay window design makes it possible to increase the glass area inserted into a window opening without increasing the size of the opening itself. However, while a conventional bay window inserted into a south-facing window opening increases the overall glazing area, it reduces the square

footage of glass facing directly south and therefore does little to increase the wintertime heat gain of the window.

Solar bay window design makes it possible to increase both glazing area and wintertime heat gain by tilting the top portion of the window. As the tilt angle approaches the optimum, 15°–20° plus the latitude of the region, heat gain efficiency is maximized.

MONTH	VERTICAL SURFACE	60° TILT	% INCREASE
October	1,770 (4,802)	2,140 (5,806)	21%
November	1,760 (4,775)	1,950 (5,290)	11%
December	1,700 (4,612)	1,860 (5,046)	9%
January	1,810 (4,911)	2,000 (5,426)	10%
February	1,860 (5,046)	2,240 (6,077)	20%
March	1,660 (4,503)	2,270 (6,159)	37%

7-5.   *Average clear-day heat gain on glazing surfaces at 40° north latitude in Btu/square feet (kcal/m²).*

Figure 7-5 compares the average daily heat gain on a square foot of vertical glazing to that achieved by a 60° tilt at 40° north latitude for the duration of the heating season. The average increase in heat gain through the tilted glazing varies from 9 percent in December to 37 percent in March.

Although the tilt is a definite advantage in the winter, it represents a greater heat gain problem in the summer than does a vertical surface, since the gain on a south-facing vertical surface actually decreases during the summer, but the heat gain through a tilted surface often increases. Because of this, a tilt should be used only when effective shading of its surface is possible. Natural shading with large trees or vines is best, although exterior window insulation and shading devices can be nearly as effective (see chapter 8).

In order to be efficient, the east and west wings of a solar bay window should be opaque and well insulated to prevent excessive wintertime heat loss and summer heat gain. As with all windows intended for solar heat gain, provision for night insulation greatly increases heat-collecting efficiency.

Glazing Transmittance

In addition to the size and style of a window, the type of glazing also affects the overall heat gain through it. Solar transmission through glazing materials can vary significantly, depending on the type, content, and thickness of the glazing. In many instances, an effort to decrease heat loss through a window with additional glazing layers cuts down on the amount of sunlight able to pass through it.

As sunlight strikes a glazing surface, solar energy can be lost by reflection from the outside surface of the glazing and by thermal radiation and convection from the warmed glass. Further reduction of solar transmittance occurs with weathering of plastic glazing materials or accumulation of dirt on the glazing surface.

Several special-composition glazing materials are available on the market to answer the need for high-transmittance glass in solar designs (see figure 7-6). Among these is a 3M Company product called SunGain, a thin plastic film that lets in more solar heat than glass does. Another product, Solakleer, developed by General Glass International, is a glass with reduced iron content having a higher solar transmittance than conventional clear glass.

Solar Gain Windows

For effective solar heating, an interior located in a cold

GLAZING MATERIAL	SOLAR TRANSMITTANCE
3M's SunGain	93%–96%
ASG's Sundex (tempered flat ⅛" glass)	91.6%
International's Solakleer	90%
⅛" clear glass	80%
¼" clear glass	75%
½" clear glass (heavy duty)	61%
GE's Lexan (double wall plastic)	80%
Kalwall's Sunwall (two panels with air space)	77%
Thermopane Insulating Glass	
⅛" clear	69%
¼" clear	59%

7-6.   *Some commercially available glazing materials especially created for maximum solar heat gain.*

climate with average winter temperatures of 20° to 30°F (−6.6° to −1.1°C) requires double glazing and a solar window area of approximately 20 to 35 percent of the total floor area of the space. In regions with milder climates, single glazing is suitable and the glass area can be reduced to 15 percent or less of the total floor area.

The quality and design of solar windows as well as their method of installation influence their overall efficiency as a heat-collecting element. Double-glazed windows with a wood frame construction, for instance, are 20 percent more insulating than metal units. The thermal performance of metal-framed windows improves when a thermal break is built into the frame. Window units should fit well and be properly caulked to prevent air infiltration around the window opening. Weatherstripping around the operable portions of the window assures a tight seal when closed.

The specific type of window unit most appropriate for a space depends on the priorities of the owner and the function the space itself will serve. Since passive solar heating usually involves a vast glazing surface, most of the glass should be fixed and sealed to avoid infiltration of air, but some panels at the top and bottom should nevertheless be operable to allow for summertime ventilation.

Solar Model

A preliminary model of the interior space, showing the existing or proposed window openings, is useful in representing its solar relationship. By placing the model on a base with the south direction indicated, the designer can simulate some critical solar conditions.

To simulate any solar position, use a full-size copy of the sundial for the desired north latitude shown on pages 70–72. After making a basic model of the space to be tested showing all window openings, mount the sundial on the base of the model so that the south arrow is parallel to the "south" marked on the base. Then place a one-inch (2.54 cm) peg or pin vertically in the place indicated on the sundial. Take the model outside on a sunny day and rotate and tilt it until the shadow of the top of the peg touches the intersection of the time and date lines being simulated. Observe how the solar relationship of the interior of the model changes with the various times of day and seasons. Also note how changes in window shapes or sizes affect the path of the entering sunlight.

After completing the solar analysis, the designer can evaluate the solar heating possibilities of the space. When it is clear that solar heating is not possible, further study can lead to alternate design approaches as discussed in later chapters. When a solar heating opportunity does exist, it remains to choose the method that best serves the thermal and functional requirements of the space.

Since the thermal requirements of a space depend largely on its indoor climate, some interiors may need instant solar heat while others benefit only from solar heat that is delayed until later in the day. In some instances, the very space receiving solar radiation may not need any of its heat at all. The intention, then, is to formulate solar alternatives as an integral part of the interior design scheme. In this way, heat from the sun can be utilized as it is needed by each individual space.

Instantaneous Heat Gain

When a space needs solar heat instantly, thermal mass is not provided and the interior materials that absorb the entering thermal energy release it simultaneously. A need for instantaneous heat gain may exist under any of the following conditions: a home with poor insulating qualities resulting in a high rate of heat loss; people such as young children or the elderly requiring warm air temperatures; smoking, kitchen odors, or other conditions that necessitate a high ventilation rate; a space where the proportion of south-facing glazing to floor area is small.

Direct Gain

The most obvious way to accomplish instantaneous solar heat gain is to allow sunlight to penetrate unobstructed into a space. In this direct form of heat gain, the sun plays a major role as a design element, affecting not only the space but also the people occupying that space. For this reason both the design scheme as well as the occupants of a space must be compatible with the sun. It is necessary to stress this issue, since the key to the effectiveness of a direct gain system is the ability of the occupants to live in a room filled with sun.

In the design of the interior of a space intended for direct gain, one of the priorities is to eliminate glare without sacrificing effective distribution of natural light. As we know, when sunlight strikes an object, a certain portion of the light is absorbed as heat while the rest is reflected, and the proportion of reflected to absorbed light varies according to the color and finish of the object (see figure 6-1). A low-reflectance color scheme and matte finishes in areas of the room receiving long periods of sunlight can moderate excessive brightness. A second important quality of materials selected for direct gain systems is their durability and resistance to fading. Moreover, because prolonged exposure to the sun may make surfaces uncomfortably warm, they should be textured to make them comfortable to the touch. Lastly, light-diffusing ceiling finishes and light accent colors will balance the overall color scheme and distribute natural daylight within the space.

Even when the problem of general glare is solved, localized glare may occur. Glare makes activities such as reading, writing, drawing, or typing difficult. Locating task areas out of the direct path of the sun solves this problem.

One final but important consideration in direct gain systems is the thermal effect of sunlight upon the individual. In a recent case study, the comfort of several people in an office was investigated. With a uniform indoor air temperature of 70°F (21.1°C), most of the people in the office felt comfortable. Two people sitting in an area exposed to long periods of direct sun, however, felt uncomfortably warm. In this case, the radiant heat of the sun was adversely affecting these two individuals, even though the space itself was not overheating. A person in the direct line of the sun, therefore, feels warmer than other people occupying that space and requires cooler air temperatures to be comfortable. Clearly, direct gain systems work well only when the human and design elements are coordinated to form a harmonious interior environment.

Indirect Gain

When the problems associated with direct gain systems become major, partial or total shading of the interior may be necessary.

After sunlight enters a room through a transparent opening, most of its energy is turned into heat and trapped. When the required shading is accomplished with light-colored shading devices, however, as much as 90 percent of the solar radiation may be reflected back outside before it can be absorbed by objects within the room. Shading a room in this manner results in very little heat trapped inside and a significant loss of beneficial solar heat. Using darker, more light-absorbing shading devices prevents the waste of solar heat. Such a "solar window" acts very much like a flat-plate solar collector where the dark shading device functions as the absorber, getting hot and transferring its heat directly into the room. Conductive heat transfer from the warm surface of the absorber, as well as convective transfer by air circulating along the face of the warmed

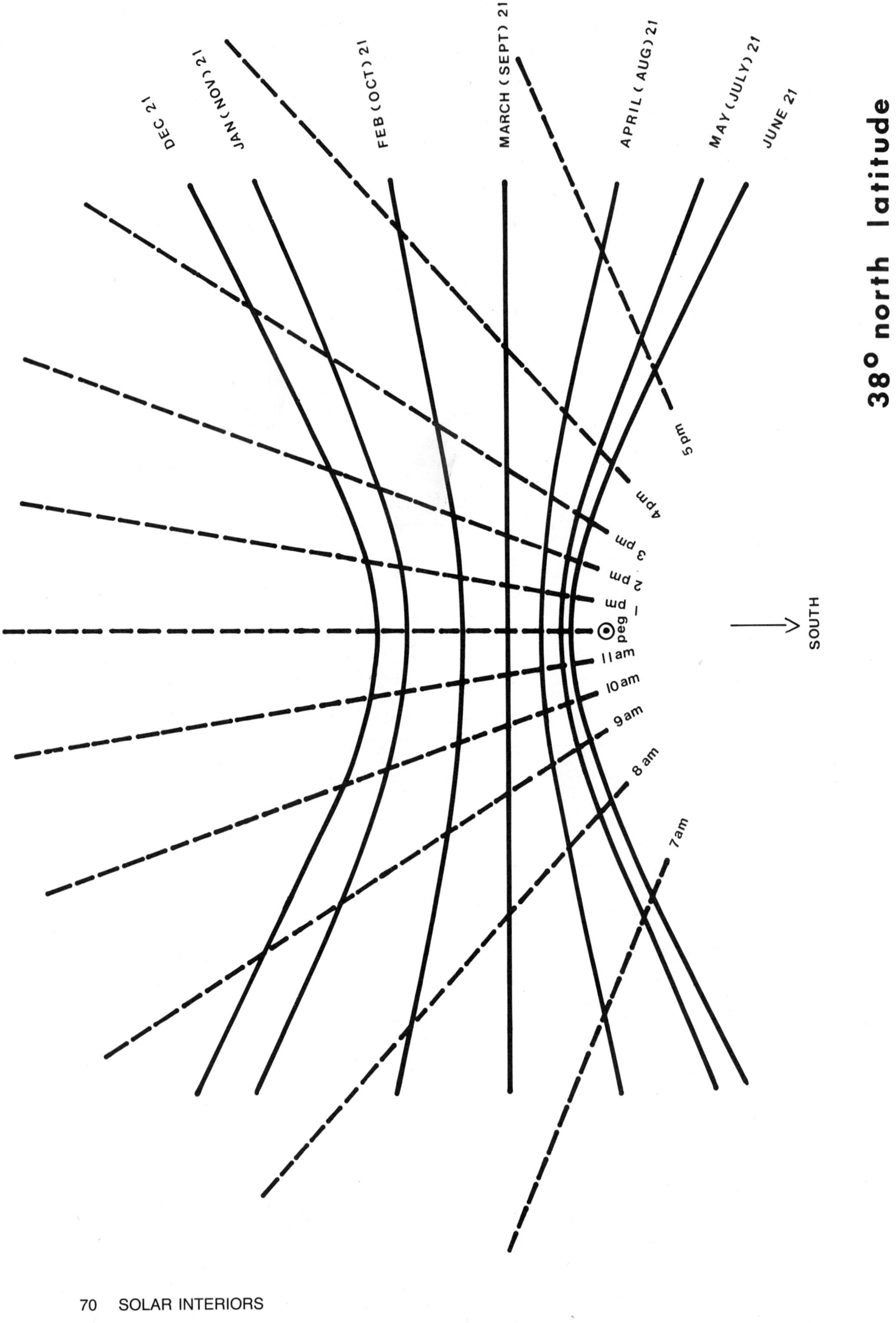

38° north latitude

DEC 21
JAN (NOV) 21
FEB (OCT) 21
MARCH (SEPT) 21
APRIL (AUG) 21
MAY (JULY) 21
JUNE 21

noon
1 pm
2 pm
3 pm
4 pm
5 pm

11 am
10 am
9 am
8 am
7 am

SOUTH

7-7. *Sundial at 38° north latitude*

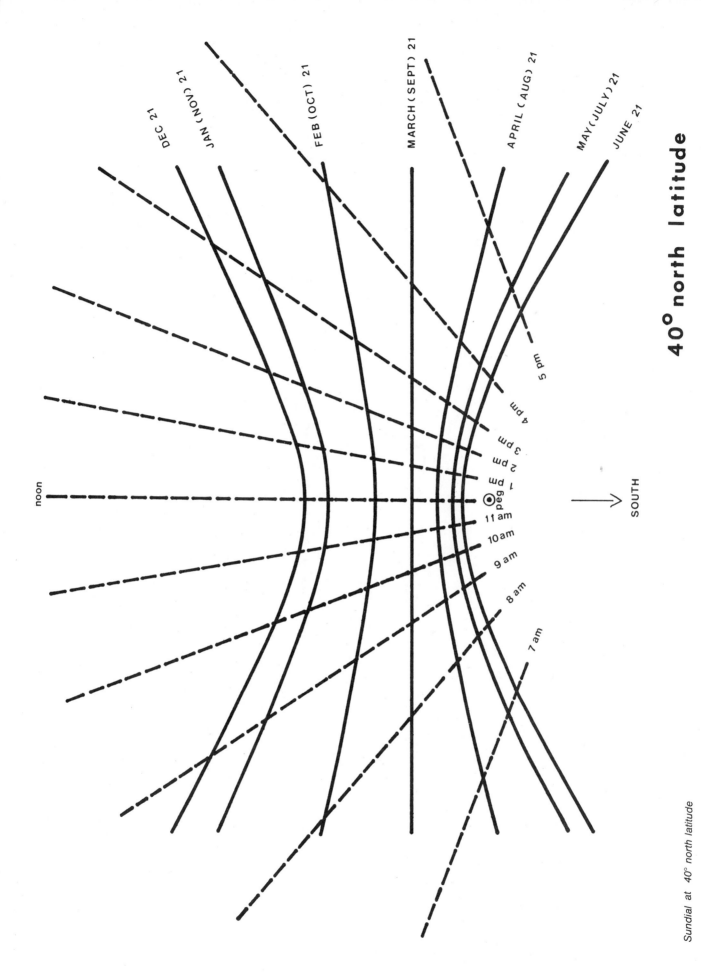

DEC 21
JAN (NOV) 21
FEB (OCT) 21
MARCH (SEPT) 21
APRIL (AUG) 21
MAY (JULY) 21
JUNE 21

40° north latitude

5 pm
4 pm
3 pm
2 pm
1 pm
peg
11 am
10 am
9 am
8 am
7 am

noon

SOUTH

Sundial at 40° north latitude

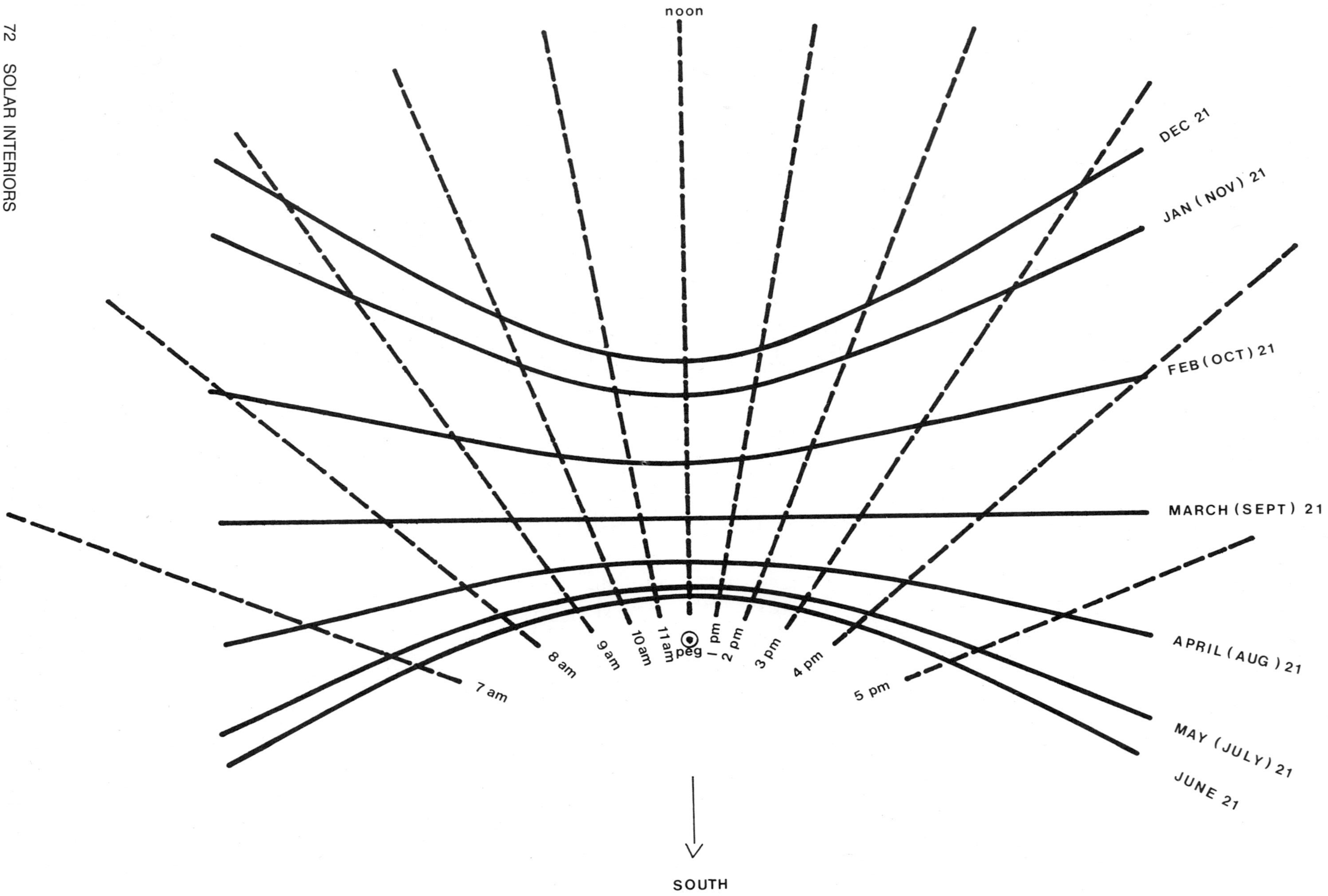

Sundial at 42° north latitude

42° north latitude

DEC 21
JAN (NOV) 21
FEB (OCT) 21
MARCH (SEPT) 21
APRIL (AUG) 21
MAY (JULY) 21
JUNE 21

noon
1 pm
2 pm
3 pm
4 pm
5 pm
11 am
peg
10 am
9 am
8 am
7 am

SOUTH

7-8.   By tilting and. rotating the model , any time or
season of the year, as indicated by the peg's shadow, can be
simulated. The solar penetration into the space at these times
can then be noted with a glance: page 73 shows 11 AM on
May or July 21; page 74 shows 12 noon on June 21; page 75
shows 11 AM on February or October 21; page 76 shows 10
AM on January or November 21. (Photos: Robert Panchyk)

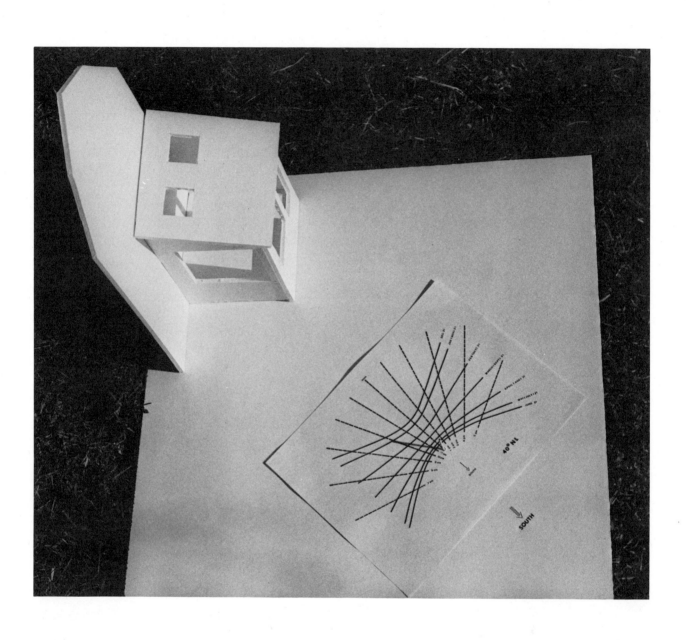

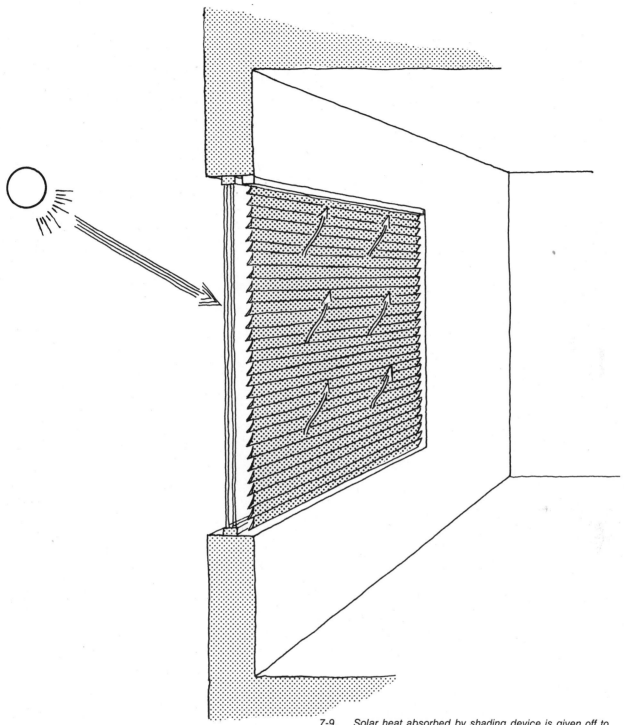

7-9.   Solar heat absorbed by shading device is given off to the room by conduction and convection.

shading device, allows most of the heat collected to enter the living space.

The effectiveness of this system depends largely on the ability of heat to pass through the shading device. For this reason, insulating shades or quilted curtains are not appropriate. Vertical or horizontal dark-metal venetian blinds or thin dark shades work best (see figure 7-9). The shading coefficient chart in figure 7-10 lists the heat-absorbing qual- ities of various types and colors of shading devices. The devices with the highest percentages have the best heat absorption properties; the ones with the lower percentages reflect much of the sunlight and are excellent for summertime use. Since shading devices used as solar absorbers are ineffective for summertime shading, or insulation, it is best to use supplementary devices such as light-reflecting exterior shutters for these purposes.

TYPE OF SHADING DEVICE	% OF SOLAR HEAT GAINED
Interior Blinds and Shades	
Dark-colored roller shade, fully drawn	80%
Light-colored roller shade, fully drawn	40%
Dark-gray curtain, fully drawn	60%
Light-gray curtain, fully drawn	50%
Off-white curtain, fully drawn	40%
Dark-colored blinds, adjusted for full shading	75%
Light-colored blinds, adjusted for full shading	55%
Metallic aluminum blinds, adjusted for full shading	45%
Black matte-finish blinds	70%
Insulated shade (sealed edges)	10%
Interior pop-in panel (sealed edges)	5%
Light-Reflecting Glass	
¼″ gray plate glass	65%
¼″ medium-dark tinted glass	50%
Light-gray metallized reflective coating on glass	35%–60%
Dark-gray metallized reflective coating on glass	20%–35%
Reflecto-Shade solar film	30%
Exterior Shading	
Typical tree, light shading	50%–60%
Dense tree or building	20%–25%
Continuous overhang or awning	25%
Movable horizontal louvers	10%–15%
Off-white outside venetian blinds	15%
Exterior light-colored shade	10%–15%
Fixed vertical fins or louvers	30%
Movable vertical louvers	10%–15%
Outside light-colored venetian blinds	15%
Outside rigid insulating shutters (sealed edges)	0%

7-10.   *Assuming that the solar heat gain through clear glass is 100 percent, this list indicates the percentage of heat gain with the addition of various shading devices to clear, unshaded glass.*

No loss of absorber efficiency results when the inside face color of the heat-collecting device is light in order to enhance artificial lighting. Shades and blinds with a dual color scheme have the added benefit that they can be reversed during the summer months. Bali manufactures such dual color blinds under the name Duotone, with a black matte finish on one surface and a choice of colors on the other. This system of heat collection is aesthetically flexible, permitting the regulation of sunlight entering the living space without sacrificing solar heat gain.

Delayed Heat Gain

In well-insulated spaces, or ones especially designed for passive solar heating, the amount of thermal energy gained through solar windows during the midday hours generally exceeds the hourly heating requirements of the space. This condition leads to daytime overheating of the space and a need for thermal mass to absorb and store some of the entering solar radiation.

Thermal mass is most often an integral part of passive solar designs. Interiors that are retrofitted for solar heat gain also need thermal mass to moderate day and night temperature variations. Adding thermal mass to an existing interior can be a problem and may require structural support. Often thermal mass may be found in the space itself as masonry or concrete in the structural system of a building. In most cases, however, the thermal mass materials are covered with wood, carpeting, or other insulating materials, making their heat storage property mostly ineffective. Resurfacing a thermal mass with masonry finishing materials can make it effective as a heat sink.

Since thermal mass gives off its heat in all directions, insulating the mass from the exterior is essential so that most of its stored heat is reradiated toward the interior space. Sizing thermal mass and methods of adding it to an interior are discussed in chapters 6 and 9.

Direct Gain

As with instantaneous heat gains, delayed heat gains achieved by the addition of thermal mass can be direct or indirect. In a delayed direct-gain system overheating is prevented by thermal mass materials that absorb a significant amount of solar energy. Problems similar to those with direct instantaneous heat-gain systems, such as excessive brightness, glare, and fading of fabrics, may occur. With delayed gain systems, however, it is important to make mass materials moderately dark for absorbing heat while keeping the non-mass materials light to diffuse sunlight and create well-distributed brightness within. When thermal mass materials exposed to prolonged direct sun are located in places of frequent human contact, they should be lighter in color to prevent an uncomfortably warm sensation.

Indirect Gain

When there is a need to control the flow of sunlight into the space, indirect delayed gain works best. With thermal mass between the living area and the glazing, direct sun can be blocked from entering the living space. Most often, it is not necessary to block the sun totally, and openings may be left in the mass to permit some solar radiation to enter the living space (see chapter 9). For interiors where this arrangement is impractical, an alternate is the Reflective Insulating Blind (RIB), developed by Oak Ridge National Laboratory, which can admit solar radiation into a space without the usual problems associated with direct gain systems. Its 3½-inch wood slats, covered with foil on the exterior side, reflect the incoming sunlight to the ceiling. When the ceiling consists of heat-storage materials, it can absorb solar heat directly. If not, a light-diffusing ceiling finish will disperse the light throughout the space to be absorbed by thermal mass materials within. The additional advantage of these blinds is their high insulating value. In the closed position, they form a tight seal between the slats and effectively reduce nighttime heat loss. Preliminary tests show that the RIB can save up to 50 percent of a space's energy costs.

Another way to accomplish indirect delayed heat gain

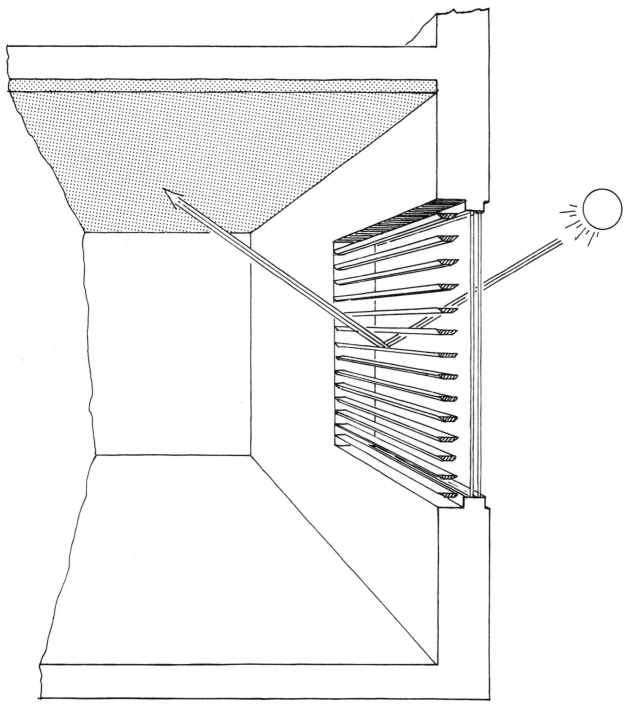

7-11.   The shiny flat surface of the Reflective Insulating Blind
(RIB) reflects incoming sunlight toward the ceiling heat storage tiles.

is to use a small space such as a vestibule or entranceway facing south as a heat collection and storage space. Often, because of poor planning, closets or hallways are oriented toward the south, and these spaces can also be converted to serve as a solar heat reservoir for the adjoining spaces.

The amount of useful heat transferred from small heat-collecting spaces to occupied areas depends on the amount of glazing area toward the south, the type and location of thermal mass materials, and heat lost from the collecting space by conduction or through opening of doors.

The best place to locate thermal mass in this type of heat-collecting space is directly between it and the living area. This can be accomplished by constructing a heat storage wall or placing jugs of water or containers of phase-change materials on shelves that serve as a partition between the two spaces.

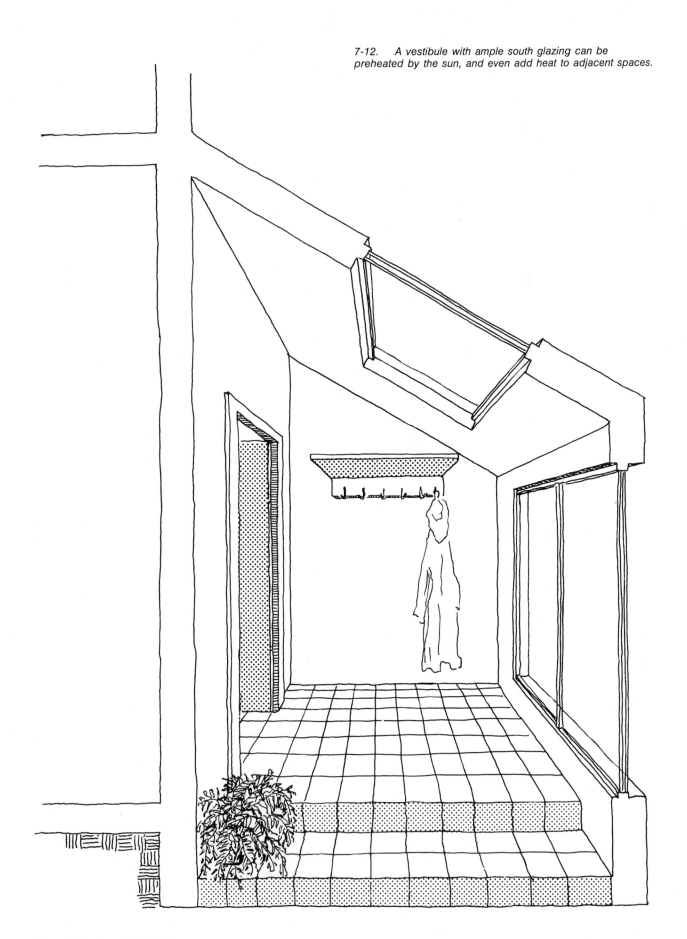

7-12.	A vestibule with ample south glazing can be preheated by the sun, and even add heat to adjacent spaces.

Efficient heat absorption by the thermal mass is especially important in heat-collecting vestibules. Due to the relatively high air exchange rate in vestibules, solar windows without mass are less effective since the warmed air is constantly vented out.

Heat Gain Not Desired

In many cases, because internal heat gain from people, lights, and equipment is considerable, solar heat gain may be totally undesired. It is not unusual to find office spaces that are cooled during the winter because of excessive internal heat gains. In fact, there are instances when one portion of a building is cooled while another is heated. In private homes, internal heat gain is not as significant as in commercial spaces; nonetheless, location of heat-generating equipment such as boilers or wood-burning stoves may make certain areas of the house warm, with little need for extra heat from the sun. In these cases, dark-colored shading devices used as absorbers can collect solar heat, and the warmed air between the absorber and glazing can then be ducted out of the room into other areas where the additional heat can be utilized.

Solar Awareness

Awareness of the pattern of solar radiation entering a space can lead to a higher quality of interior design. Treating sunlight as a design element as well as a heat source combines the practical and aesthetic facets of solar radiation. After careful consideration of all the options, a designer can select the solar utilization method most suitable for the physical qualities of a space and the personal needs of the individuals within.

Chapter 8

WINDOWS: SHADING AND INSULATING DEVICES

BECAUSE DIRECT SOLAR RADIATION EXERTS ONE of the greatest thermal forces on the interior environment, the summertime control of its penetration is an important consideration. Whereas admission of unobstructed sunlight into a space is desired during the heating season, the reverse is required for the cooling season. Choosing effective shading devices (see the shading coefficient chart, figure 7-8) can reduce the cooling requirements of a space significantly by minimizing radiant heat gain. Shading devices with aluminized interior surfaces can also work to cut radiant heat loss from a space in winter by reflecting the escaping radiant heat back into the room.

An additional way to reduce heat transfer through a window is by slowing the conductive flow of heat through it with window insulation. Although many shading devices have some insulating value, they most often are not truly efficient window insulation.

Window insulating devices can be distinguished by two features. First, their relatively high insulating value makes the combined resistance-rating of the window plus the device comparable to that of an insulated wall; and second, their tight fit blocks convection by sealing the top, bottom, and sides around the window frame. In the wintertime, window insulation is removed from the window during the day to allow the warming sunlight to penetrate and replaced at night to minimize heat loss through the glazing. Using window insulation to reduce conductive heat gain during the summer, however, is not so simple. To reduce summertime conductive heat gain, it is necessary to use window insulation in the daytime. In most cases, however, this results in inadequate daylight within the space. Compensating for that with artificial illumination in turn adds undesired heat to the space. Furthermore, because window insulation is well sealed, it prevents outdoor-indoor airflow, and this may be a problem for those interiors that might otherwise benefit from natural ventilation.

The usefulness of shading and insulating devices must therefore be evaluated in terms of the need for shading, daylight, and ventilation, as well as personal priorities of individuals within the space.

Shading Devices

Efficient shading is an important design consideration in warm climates and during the summer season in temperate regions. Some shading devices do no more than cast a shadow upon a window area, while others contribute to the insulation of the window surface.

In mild climates, solar shading and free airflow through windows may take priority over other considerations. In temperate climates, window insulation is an additional factor to consider. When a shading device is selected to perform more than one function, it must be able to respond dynamically to the changing weather conditions. In addition to efficient shading, insulating and light-filtering qualities of a device can be important in the final evaluation of its year-round effectiveness.

Exterior Shading Techniques and Architectural Elements

The shading coefficients of external shading devices indicate that they are the most effective in keeping out sunlight. This is mainly due to the fact that all external devices intercept solar radiation before it enters the space, allowing very little radiant heat to be trapped inside. On south orientations, building overhangs, awnings, or exterior horizontal louvers provide maximum solar shading. Since east and west orientations receive the most significant amount of solar radiation during the summer months, the efficiency of shading devices for windows in these directions is even more critical. Because of the lower angles of the summer sun in the east and west, vertical louvers or a combination of vertical and horizontal elements are effective exterior treatments for these exposures.

Exterior window shades, light in color, are very effective for all orientations. Most exterior shades can be electronically lowered or raised, while some come with photoelectric sensors that lower them automatically. Opaque shading with shades or shutters is most efficient in reducing solar heat gain; however, its high thermal efficiency may be offset by the need for increased artificial lighting. Translucent shading, while not as effective, reduces heat gain without totally eliminating natural daylight.

Fiberglass solar screens are another excellent method of shading, especially when daylight and outside airflow are required. Solar screens, available under various brand names, can prevent up to 65 percent of the solar radiation from entering a space. The screens are relatively easy to install on the outside of window areas and are low in cost.

The natural landscape can function as one of the best shading devices for all orientations. In a well-planned landscape design, deciduous trees or vines provide natural seasonal shading. Trees can frequently shade an entire exterior wall including the window area, producing even greater reductions in cooling needs. Computer data by Fred S. Dubin and Chalmers G. Long, Jr. in *Energy Conservation Standards* on heat gain through exterior walls show that in the New York region an insulated wall receiving significant sun, such as an east- or west-facing wall, gains nearly four and a half times as much heat as a sunless north wall having the same insulating value and surface absorption. Solar analysis using a sundial and model of various trees can help ascertain the height and spread of trees suitable for shading each exposure.

Deciduous vines on vertical or horizontal lattice allow the sun through in the winter and help to shade and cool the adjacent structure during the summer. An additional advantage of shading with natural vegetation is the evaporative cooling it provides by transpiring moisture into the air. The natural cooling of ground vegetation can also reduce heat gain in nearby structures. October midday temperature readings in Davis, California, revealed significant differences in the temperatures above various ground surfaces. The air temperature above grass mowed to a height of 4 inches (10 cm) was 67°F (19.4°C); above 2-inch (5 cm) grass, it was 79°F (26°C); and above a half-inch (1.5 cm) of grass,

87°F (30.6°C)—all while the air over artificial turf was 125°F (51.7°C). Even when pavements or artificial turf are shaded, natural ground cover generally maintains lower temperatures.

Taking advantage of landscaping techniques for solar control can be advantageous for both indoor and outdoor comfort. With proper care and pruning, natural vegetation will have a long life and should provide continued shading.

Light-Reflecting Glass

Light-reflecting glass is often used in the design of buildings with anticipated excessive internal heat gain that will require shading most of the year. In existing buildings that need year-round shading, a light-reflecting solar film can be mounted permanently on clear windows. This practice does have several drawbacks, however. After a number of years, the effects of window washing and heat buildup may cause the film to peel or crack. Since reflective glazing of any sort is permanent, interiors that need only seasonal shading will not benefit from it. For such purposes, a solar film that operates like a window shade is now available under the name Reflecto-Shade. Manufactured by Madico, this plastic film behaves much like reflecting glass, and can reflect 35 to 80 percent of the sunlight while admitting some light for natural daylighting. In addition to solar shading, some light-reflecting films and shades are made to increase the insulating value of the window by reducing radiant heat loss from the interior during the winter. The solar transmittance of light-reflecting glazing and coatings depends on their color and composition. Whereas some allow considerable sunlight to pass through, others permit as little as 7 percent of the solar radiation to enter a space (see figure 8-1).

Type of Glazing	% Solar Transmittance
Vari-Tran	
¼" clear glass with Vari-Tran	
Silver	9%–20%
Golden	8%–21%
1" Thermopane with Vari-Tran	
Silver	7%–16%
Golden	7%–17%
Tinted glass	
¼" Gray	46%
¼" Bronze	49%
¼" Thermopane Gray	35%
Bronze	38%

8-1. *Types of light-reflecting glass and their reflectances.*

Interior Shades, Curtains, and Blinds

Window treatment in a purely design sense denotes the relationship between an overall interior design scheme and the window. In solar interiors, however, the window represents a constantly changing thermal force upon a space.

With careful management, the thermal influences of window areas can work for the benefit of the individuals within and at the same time relate to the design scheme of the interior. An increasing number of alternatives are becoming available to achieve a desired thermal effect in window design.

When shading is a priority, the color and the position or fit of the shading device are important considerations. Since the function of a shading device is to reflect radiant energy, the lighter the exterior surface color of the device, the more effective it becomes. Additionally, when the device is installed close to the window, a more complete reflectance can be achieved. For instance, an ordinary close-fitting window shade, light in color, reflects up to 60 percent of the solar radiation in the summer and adds to the insulating value of the window area in the winter. With a window shade fully drawn, warmed room air circulates along the surface of the shade rather than the surface of the cold glass, reducing heat loss by as much as 30 percent.

Shades are available in a wide variety of styles and textures, from roll-down bamboo to textured fabric. The solar reflectance of these devices can often be obtained from the manufacturer, and will depend largely on the exterior color finish of the device. When a specific fabric pattern or color is desired for aesthetic purposes, double-layer shading having a light-reflecting outside layer can be used.

Drapes reflect sunlight and can also function as wintertime insulation when they block warmed room air from circulating adjacent to window surfaces. Opaque fabrics, light in color, are best in reflecting solar radiation. When light filtering or partial shading is required, sheer curtains may be suitable. The weave and thickness of the curtain fabric determine the amount of light capable of passing through it. Thin translucent weaves often have a light-diffusing effect for a more dispersed daylighting within.

Because the solar influence of most exposures changes throughout the day, flexibility in shading devices is often desired. Curtains are not well suited in this respect, whereas venetian blinds are among the most versatile of shading devices. Although most venetian blinds are not effective insulators, they function well in reflecting solar radiation and they can be adjusted to regulate incoming daylight. White and aluminum finishes are most effective in reflecting sunlight and can save up to 30 percent of air conditioning costs (see figure 7-10).

Horizontal venetian blinds are commonly available in plastic, steel, or aluminum with one- or two-inch slats. Wooden blinds, although more expensive, are regaining popularity after several decades of decline. Wood has better insulating qualities than metal or plastic. In fact, wooden blinds have the potential to qualify as window insulation. When well fitted into the window opening with tightly sealing slats such as RIB (Oak Ridge National Lab's Reflective Insulating Blind), they function as a multipurpose window treatment.

Vertical venetian blinds in plastic, metal, or fabric also offer shading and adjustability but are somewhat less rigid than horizontal blinds, which minimizes their value as a window insulator.

Interior shutters, quite common in Europe, are picking

8-2. Oak Ridge National Lab's Reflective Insulating Blinds can reflect light up toward a ceiling heat storage or back outside during the summer. When closed, the slats form an insulating seal.

up popularity in the United States. In cold climates, solid shutters can function as night insulation and summertime blackout shading when daylighting is not essential. Solid window shutters that have high thermal resistance values are effective window insulators. In areas of mild climates, fixed louver wood shutters work well as shading devices.

In general, opaque shading devices are most effective in reducing heat gain. Because of the need for daylight, however, a conflict arises any time window treatment materials are opaque. In response, manufacturers have introduced special translucent weaves that shade and insulate while allowing diffused light to enter a space. Studies indicate that a translucent shade mounted within a wood frame with a fairly tight fit cuts heat transfer by 44 percent. One such shade, made with a special Swiss-imported fabric, is Sol-R-Veil. The shade is of a woven vinyl material coated with plastic that reduces heat gain while providing natural lighting.

Window Insulation

Window insulators can have thermal resistances ranging

8-3. *Some existing buildings have exterior shutters that are seldom utilized. (Photo: Robert Stidolph)*

from R-1 to R-8 or more. Data on annual heat flow through windows indicate that an R-5 rating is optimum. Since the first layers of insulation always yield the greatest savings, as thickness is increased much beyond the optimum value, additional savings become minimal.

Not all windows require very high thermal efficiency. Window areas that should be considered first are the ones that lose the most heat. Windows that face a sunless, windward exposure, for example, can have significant heat loss by conduction and infiltration and would benefit from insulation. Dubin and Long's computer study in *Energy Conservation Standards* (1978) shows that in the northern latitudes the north exposures are the biggest energy losers. In the New York region, for example, a double-glazed north-facing window loses 23 percent more heat than a south-facing one. In the same region, the heat loss of a single-glazed opening facing north is 32 percent higher than one oriented south.

Window size is another important consideration. Heat loss through small window areas, especially when inset or sheltered from the wind, is usually minimal. Large glass areas such as window walls, sliding glass doors, and solar windows, on the other hand, account for a significant heat loss during winter nights. Night insulation for these glass areas can represent a large energy savings. On solar windows, night-insulating covers raise the net heat-collecting potential of the passive system.

Window insulation is also useful in minimizing summertime heat gain. Although its usefulness may be limited by the need for natural ventilation and daylight, there are instances when summertime use of insulating covers is appropriate.

Window insulating devices are not at all a new development. Wooden insulating shutters built into the exterior or interior framework of old buildings are not uncommon. Unfortunately, out of neglect, many of these devices have ceased to function. Bringing back simple and effective window insulators would have a favorable impact on human comfort and energy costs.

Exterior Window Insulation

Exterior window insulating devices have benefits as well as disadvantages. Condensation is less likely to occur on or within window panes. In some cases, exterior insulating devices also function as a barrier to intruders. However, exterior window devices need structural strength as well as wear and weather resistance. Since the devices are outside, snow, ice, insects, and leaves from trees may interfere with their operation.

Shutters

Exterior insulating shutters are usually constructed with one to two inches of insulating core plus a weatherproof outer surface such as exterior-grade wood or aluminum. Shutters that support their own weight plus snow loads must be more rigid than other types. The extent of a shutter's framework and bracing determines how it will be able to withstand loads.

The method used to attach a shutter to the exterior of

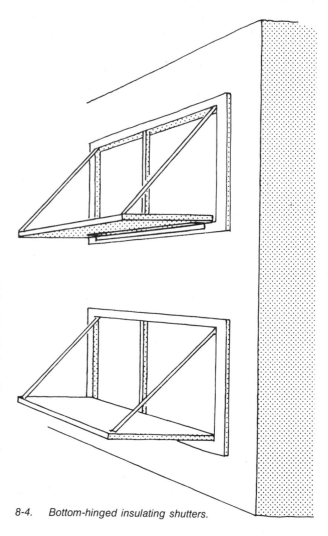

8-4.   *Bottom-hinged insulating shutters.*

the window frame can affect the appearance of a building. Bottom-hinged shutters are generally lowered with chains or cords and may need additional support from below. When used on solar heat-gain windows, the inside face of the shutter can be finished with a mirrorlike surface to reflect additional sunshine toward the glass.

Shutters hinged at the top can be used when there is sufficient architectural overhang to protect them from heavy snow and ice loads. Crank mechanisms or a cord and pulley attached to the building overhang can operate top-hinged shutters.

Perhaps the least obtrusive shutters are the side-hinged ones (see figure 8-3). Small side-hinged shutters can be operated easily from the inside by crank mechanisms. For large glass areas or sliding glass doors, bifolding shutters such as Thermafold Shutters by Shutters, Inc., are appropriate. When opened, the shutters fold flat against the adjacent wall, preventing damage from strong winds and avoiding the shading of solar windows.

Exterior sliding shutters are thermally effective; however, they are often operable only from the outside. New designs

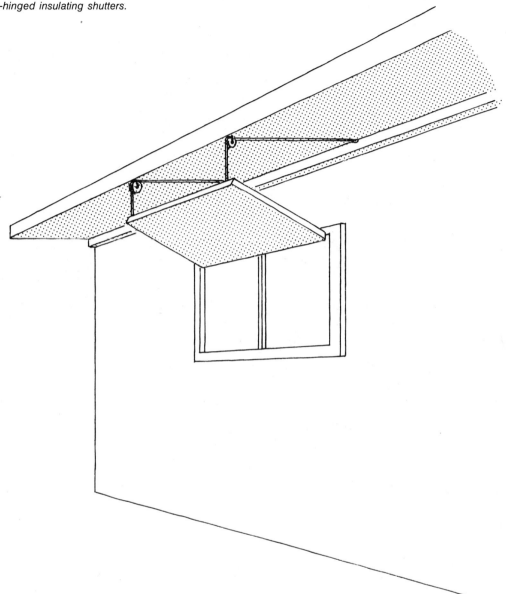

with a series of cords and pulleys permit indoor operation.

Exterior roll-down shutters, commonly called *rolladen,* have been used in Europe for many years. Older models are wood, whereas the newer ones are hollow or foam-filled aluminum or PVC. These devices are excellent for summer shading and are somewhat useful as insulators. Nonetheless, because their construction allows for loosely connected slats, their R-values are relatively low. Tests on the hollow PVC model indicate an R-value of merely 1.6. Solid roll-down devices or those with tightly sealed slats can improve thermal performance. The Roldoor system by One Design, Inc., is a garage-door–type device with a PVC exterior filled with two inches of foam. The thermal yield of Roldoor is over R-10.

The shutter style most appropriate for a window may depend on the size and orientation of the window as well as the visual impact it makes on the exterior of the building.

Additional Glazing as Insulation

Adding glazing layers to existing glass is often the first step in retrofitting window areas. A pane of glass added to single glazing can double the thermal resistance of the window. Triple glazing, or three layers of glass with two air spaces, raises the R-value by an additional 50 percent. The advantage of insulating with multiple glazing is that it is a permanent part of the window and will insulate day and night. Additional glass layers, however, do have an effect on solar and light transmission into a space. Whereas a single pane of ⅛-inch glass allows 86 percent of the light to penetrate, double glazing lets in only 74 percent, and triple glass cuts light penetration to 64 percent. In solar heat-gain windows, therefore, the insulating benefits of multiple glazing should be weighed against its effects on transmission of sunlight .

8-6. *Exterior sliding shutters can work well on large glazed areas at grade level. (Photo: Robert Panchyk)*

In some cases, multiple glazing can cause condensation of moisture on the cold surface of the glass. To avoid this, insulated or double-pane windows are constructed with a tight seal, preventing moisture from entering the space between the two layers of glass. With storm windows, the problem can be solved by leaving vent holes to allow moisture to escape. Any time glazing is added to existing windows, provision should be made to prevent condensation.

There are instances when replacing windows or installing exterior glazing is impractical. Interior glazing is an alternative in these cases. Plastic storm windows, sold as a film in rolls or in rigid sheets, are relatively inexpensive and can be applied to the window from the inside. The plastic film can either be stapled to a wooden frame or be snapped into a specially constructed plastic frame. The plastic frame called Temp-Rite, available from Solar Usage Now, Inc., has a slat to snap in plastic and hold it taut. Solar films of various composition and thickness are available. The life-span and cost of these films vary with their quality. Poly-ethylene film, for instance, is very low in cost but has a

relatively short life-span. A better-quality film of polyester, manufactured by 3M Company, is a little more costly but has an estimated life of fifteen years and a solar transmission of 96 percent. Rigid plastic interior storm windows are available from a number of manufacturers. One product, Defender from Defender Energy Corporation, is made of rigid acrylic, attaching with either a magnetic seal for easy removal or a snap-lock seal. Retrofitting windows with additional glazing is a good beginning in reducing heat loss. Because of the poor insulating quality of glass, however, multiple glazing is inadequate in reducing the adverse thermal influence of window areas.

Interior Window Insulation

Insulating window surfaces from the inside can often be easier and more practical than exterior treatments. Interior insulation, like multiple glazing, however, can create condensation problems. Condensation occurs when moist air from the interior space escapes through and around the insulating panel and condenses on the cold surface of the

8-7.   *Rolladen roll-down shutters. (Courtesy American German Industries)*

window. To minimize this problem, many interior insulating devices have built-in moisture barriers such as vinyl or polyethylene. Devices that are well sealed around the edges are less likely to be permeable to moisture. In temperate climates, the average wintertime indoor relative humidity of 30 percent should not create great condensation problems. In very cold climates, on the other hand, condensation can become a serious problem even at low indoor relative humidity levels. In these cases, exterior window insulation may be more appropriate.

Interior window insulation can simply be a well-designed window treatment or a more elaborate device used specifically to insulate the window.

Shutters

Interior shutters are made with a solid insulating core with fabric or wood exterior. A shutter's thermal efficiency depends on its R-value and fit into the window opening. As with exterior models, interior shutters can be attached a variety of ways, depending on the physical dimensions of the window area and personal priorities.

Pop-in shutter panels, often home made, can be attached with magnetic strips, clips, or simply by friction in the case of lightweight panels. Compression seal weatherstripping around the perimeter of the panel assures tight edge seals. Since pop-in shutters require daily removal and replacement, they may be inconvenient as insulation for most window areas. On those portions of glazing with seasonal adverse exposures, for spaces that have adequate additional windows, pop-in panels may be left in place throughout a season.

Shutters that are attached to the window frame are more convenient and easier to operate than the pop-in types. The type of operation selected may depend on the dimensions of the window opening and the available wall space surrounding it. Top-hinged models must have a ceiling support or a counterweight built into the wall. Sliding shutters, while easier to operate, require wall space on both sides of the window. Bifold shutters may be the best solution for large windows and sliding glass doors. Thermanel insulated shutters by Neilson Company are bifold models with a high R-value available in wood or fabric finish. The Sun Saver shutters, constructed of pine wood, also offer a good R-value. Shutter kits come in three standard sizes and can be ordered from Homesworth Corporation.

Thermal Shades

Design modifications of conventional window shades have brought them into the window-insulating category. The easiest way to improve the thermal efficiency of an ordinary shade is to replace its cloth or vinyl fabric with a foil-faced material that reflects thermal energy. One such fabric especially made for greenhouse shading is Foylon, manufactured by Duracote Corporation. Foylon can be used to replace an existing shade, or it can be attached to the shade at the top on its exterior face. For ease of operation, the Foylon layer should be unattached to the shade at the bottom.

Because each separate air layer has an insulating value,

shades that form several insulating air pockets are now marketed. One such shade, invented by a Connecticut architect, is made up of five separate air layers of aluminized mylar film wound into an ordinary wooden shade roller. As it is pulled down, a honeycomb frame forces the layers apart, and expands the shade to a thickness of about 3½ inches. Its high insulating value stems from the four separate air spaces that it forms, plus the high thermal reflectance of aluminized Mylar. Although factory models are available in mirror or white finishes, the shade can be faced on the inside with any desired fabric.

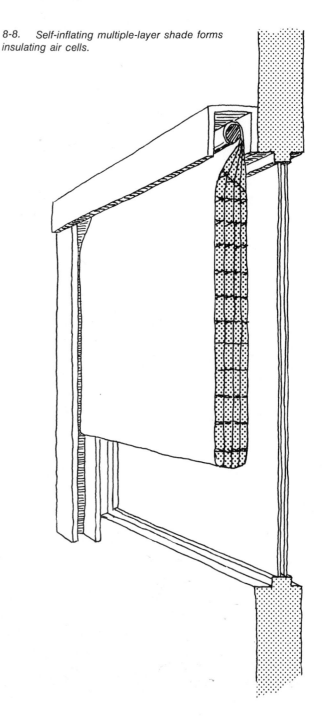

8-8.   Self-inflating multiple-layer shade forms insulating air cells.

8-9. *Sun Saver insulating shutters. (Courtesy Homesworth Corporation)*

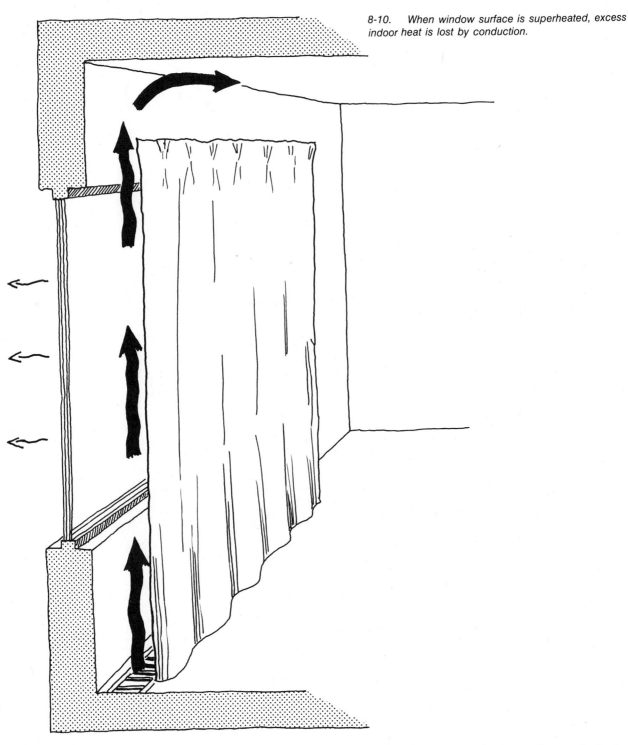

8-10.   When window surface is superheated, excess indoor heat is lost by conduction.

Such multiple-layer shades yield an average R-value of over R-10 and can be purchased from several manufacturers. The Insulating Shade Company, for instance, offers the Insulating Shade-High R Shade, consisting of the above-mentioned five separate air layers. The Insulating Curtain Wall, by the Thermal Technology Corporation, is equally efficient.

Instead of using air pockets, several companies now make shades composed of fiberfill insulation. These shades,

often quilted, are a composite of polyester fibers and reflective plastic materials. One such shade is the Window Quilt, available from Appropriate Technology Corporation, with an insulating value of R-3.5. Sun Quilt, another shade of similar composition by Sun Quilt Corporation, operates on a motorized track.

A rigid shade behaving more like a roll-down shutter is now marketed by Systems for Energy Conservation. Thermo-Shades have interlocking rigid slats that are airtight and

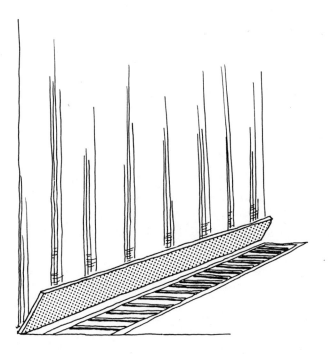

waterproof. The shade moves up and down on side tracks and can be motor driven or operated by hand.

Curtains

Curtains are quite common and have been used as window insulation for years. They can be ineffective insulators, however, unless they are hung and used properly. As with all window insulation, the R-value of the curtain fabric is an important consideration, and will depend on the composition, weave, and thickness of the material. Window Blankets, made especially for window insulation, are quilted drapes of polyester with a cotton lining having an insulating value of R-2. Additional thermal value can be achieved with the use of special drapery liners. One such liner, Wind-N-Sun Shield by Wind-N-Sun Shield, Inc., has a foil coating and reflects thermal energy toward the living space in winter. When reversed in the summer, it reflects solar radiation.

Curtains must be hung to restrict room airflow between the curtain and the glazing for thermal efficiency as well as condensation control. It is especially vital that curtains not block heat from radiators or floor registers. When curtains are draped over a heat source, warm air is forced to flow adjacent to the glazing surface, thus increasing heat loss by conduction (see figure 8-10).

When floor registers are located below windows, a deflector like the one shown in figure 8-11 can assure proper heat circulation within the space. Bulky radiators below window areas call for window-length curtains with a block or deflector sealing the bottom edge. Drapes over window areas without heating elements can be held in place with weights at the bottom of the fabric. For window-length cur-

tains, a pull cord or magnetic strip can be used. A wooden or cloth-type valance prevents air flow at the top.

Other Considerations

Among the practical and safety factors to consider in selecting window insulation is how the device operates. When manually operated devices necessitate tedious daily rituals, their future use may be neglected and their effectiveness reduced. How well they operate in case of emergency is also an important factor. Electronically operable devices over glass doors, for instance, may block a means of egress. Another safety consideration is the flammability of the materials used in an insulating device. Although plastic products, from tablecloths to carpeting, are found in most interiors, plastic, when exposed and used in quantity as interior window insulation may constitute a significant fire hazard, since it is not only combustible but gives off highly toxic fumes when it burns. For this reason, building codes prohibit its exposed use in building construction.

Insulating devices with a fiberglass core are safest. Panels having plastic cores should be enclosed in fire-retardant materials to reduce fire hazard.

Double Window Treatments

Although a few window devices are versatile enough to provide privacy, daylight and ventilation adjustment, and nighttime insulation, most available window treatments are best suited for only one of these functions. Compromise is required, and that often results in sacrifice of efficiency in some of its functions. For example, insulating window covers that also reflect sunlight exclude light and air from the interior; they can be utilized only where there is no need for daylighting or natural ventilation. Similarly, although light-filtering shades can insulate, their thermal resistance is not comparable to that of opaque window insulation.

Double window treatment enables the designer to select those devices that are most efficient in their intended function. With careful design, double window treatment can solve the conflict due to the daily and seasonal changes in the thermal influence of window areas. Since not all window treatments are compatible, however, consideration of the physical properties of the window itself, operation of the devices, and personal aesthetic preference is necessary.

Interior–Exterior Combinations

Interior-exterior window treatment combinations offer a number of benefits. In a practical sense, the two devices, fitted and operating separately, do not interfere with each other; adjustment of one need not affect performance of the other. And in an aesthetic sense, one is not obligated to make sure two separate treatments look good together if one element is on the outside, the other on the inside.

The two options in interior-exterior window treatment combinations are either having the insulating device on the outside with shade control on the inside or having exterior shading with interior insulation. Exterior flexible insulation such as roll-down, hinged, or pop-in shutters leaves the inside of the window area free of heavy drapes or insulating

8-12.   *Pella interglazing shading: Slimshade installed in double-hung sash with double glazing panel. (Courtesy Pella/Rolscreen Company)*

panels. Interior shades, venetian blinds, or sheer curtains can then provide privacy and shading.

Exterior shading with movable horizontal or vertical louvers; adjustable metal or fabric awnings; architectural overhangs; or roll-down shades that are combined with interior quilted or thermal shades; insulating sliding, pop-in, or bifolding shutters; or insulated drapes can also be effective. On sunless orientations, or when natural or man-made surroundings shade window areas throughout the summer, shading devices can be eliminated.

Interior–Interior Combinations

When cost or practical problems eliminate the possibility of exterior window treatment, two compatible interior devices may be selected. Insulating drapes and light-reflecting venetian blinds or translucent shades work well together. Sliding or pop-in shutters can serve as insulation when sheer curtains for privacy and light filtering are desired.

A common problem encountered when attempting dual interior window treatment is inadequate sill depth, making it difficult or impossible to install various devices. A new type of double glass window with a venetian blind built into the air space between the two panes of glass solves this problem. Pella/Rolscreen Company is now marketing doubleglazed windows with miniature blinds between the glazings. Interglazing shading control leaves room for hinged or pop-in insulating elements to be installed within the interior frame of the window.

Considerations in the selection of double window treatment combinations include effectiveness, personal taste, and cost. Because the effectiveness of double window treatment depends on the thermal properties of the devices used, actual solar reflectances and resistance ratings of the products selected should be checked. Very often, the effectiveness of products advertised to be insulating and energy saving turn out to be marginal.

Shading and Insulating Tilted Glazing

Because of the significant summertime heat gain through tilted south-facing glazing surfaces, efficient shading becomes top priority. A number of roll-down exterior shading fabrics are available for shading solar greenhouse and other tilted glazing. Information on the cost and properties of these shading devices is often available from greenhouse manufacturers. The most important property to look for is the shading coefficient. The devices that absorb the least solar heat work best (see figure 7-10).

An even more effective way to reduce summer heat gain in tilted glazing is to place an insulating and light-reflecting cover on its exterior surface. In instances where abundant daylight is provided by remaining vertical glazing the tilt shading-insulating device can remain in place throughout the summer season.

Insulating sloped surfaces from the inside can be difficult. Solar Technology Corporation has developed a system called Sun-Mover especially for sloped glazing. It insulates and its louvered surface is adjustable either manually or through a microcompressor computer. Skylids, from Zomeworks Corporation, are both insulating and solar-control louvers, custom designed for skylights. The louvers move in response to sunlight and provide a high R-value when closed during sunless periods and at night. In the summer, a manual override can keep the shutters closed during hot, sunny days.

Skylights offer significantly more daylight per square foot of glass than does vertical glazing. When facing south, tilted glass admits more wintertime heat than does vertical south-oriented glazing. With the addition of flexible insulation to prevent excessive nighttime heat loss in winter or summertime overheating, the usefulness of skylights can be maximized.

Final Considerations

After consideration is given to adverse and beneficial seasonal solar influences of a window area, as well as the daylighting, ventilation, and privacy requirements of the individuals within, decisions on the type and size of window and its treatment can follow. Whether a building already exists or is newly planned, successful window design and management can produce a significant reduction in the cost of environmental conditioning of the interior space.

Chapter 9

THERMAL MASS IN THE INTERIOR

THE TWO COMPONENTS OF AN INTERIOR DESIGNED or retrofitted to function as a passive solar space are large glass areas facing south and thermal mass to moderate the day and night temperature fluctuations within. The beauty of the passive solar design concept is its simplicity. Yet often the very design compromises the benefits of the passive solar heating opportunity.

Proportioning south-facing glass to floor area and mass size is not enough to produce a comfortable and well-distributed passive system. To function efficiently as a heating system, a space needs an overall design that links the glazing, thermal mass, and spatial plan in a logical and functional manner. The location of thermal mass within the interior and how it relates to individuals as well as all the other surrounding spaces are often crucial. In a direct gain system, for instance, the south-oriented portions of an interior may be comfortable while the north sections remain cool.

In passive solar spaces, thermal mass is a key element and becomes the heat regulator within the space. Thermal mass can have a structural function as well, serving as the floor, ceiling, or walls within a space. It can be spread out within a space or concentrated and centrally located. Often thermal mass has a secondary function other than structural. Mass can have aesthetic appeal, such as a sculpture or a pool of water; it can function as shelving, seating, a fireplace, or a platform for wood-burning devices. Although mass functioning as the walls and floor of a space is most desirable, there is no specific type of mass appropriate for all designs. The type, composition, and location of the thermal mass most suitable for a space depends on layout, solar access, and personal aesthetic preferences.

Floor Mass

Concrete, used as a structural floor or slab on grade, is a common form of thermal heat storage. When a building is designed as a passive solar structure, floor storage can be an intentional part of the design. In retrofitting a space, concrete slab is often found under finished flooring or carpeting. In single-family homes, a concrete basement floor can be utilized for solar heat storage when a south-facing glazing retrofit makes direct solar access possible (see figure 9-1). An existing masonry or concrete slab can often be utilized as mass when a terrace or balcony is retrofitted to function as a solar greenhouse.

A floor used for thermal mass can be left exposed as brick or concrete painted a moderately dark color. In living spaces, exposed concrete is often undesired so it is faced with masonry tiles. Masonry flooring materials are available in a variety of textures, shades, and unit sizes. Room function, personal preferences, and maintenance are factors in the selection of masonry flooring. Although most masonry materials are good conductors of heat, dark matte finishes are most efficient heat absorbers. Rough textures absorb and give off thermal energy most completely, but they are harder to clean than smooth glazed finishes.

In interiors with floor heat storage, the floor serves an important thermal function. For this reason, the design of the space and furniture arrangement must be compatible with the limitations of the heat storage system. Floor heat

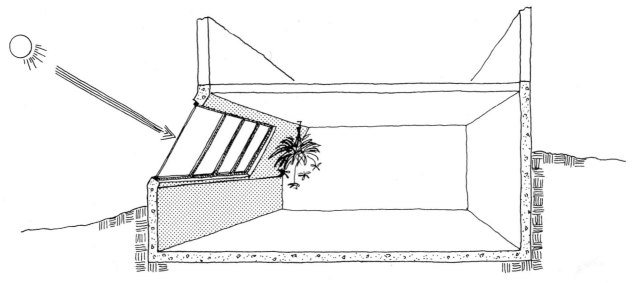

9-1. *Concrete basement floor slab can act as thermal storage mass for incoming solar radiation.*

storage with a direct solar heat-gain system implies that unobstructed sunshine enters the space on all clear winter days. With solar analysis (see figure 7-8) the daily path of the sun entering the space during the winter season can be mapped out. The floor mass can then be located within this path for direct radiant access to absorb a maximum amount of solar heat. Because it is essential that direct sunlight hits the mass surface, carpets or other floor coverings cannot be used. (Small throw rugs, however, are permissible.) Large bulky furniture that blocks the sun or casts a shadow on the floor is also undesirable. Lightweight furniture units covered with fade-resistant fabrics are most appropriate for these areas.

Another factor that determines whether floor heat storage is the right system to choose is the degree to which individual styles and habits involve contact with the floor surface. For instance, if the floor is often used as a play surface by children the physical qualities of thermal mass materials may cause thermal discomfort. When "charged" with sunlight, a thermal floor can be quite warm. On cloudy days and in the morning, however, masonry, because of its high conductance, feels cold to the touch. When these thermal variations are objectionable, a different method of heat storage may be more appropriate.

Heat Distribution from a Floor Mass

Floor heat storage has a favorable impact on individual comfort. With ordinary seating just 16 inches (40 cm) above floor level, the floor is the surface closest to people within a space. In the winter, the coldest air in a room falls to the floor level. Because of this, any air circulation in the room produces a cooling effect at the floor's surface. A floor slab that warms with radiant energy, such as a thermal mass floor, minimizes this adverse thermal condition.

As with all radiant heating systems, a warmed floor gives off mainly radiant heat, minimizing convective air motion within the space. This reduces drafts, dust circulation, and

excessive dryness. In addition, human comfort may be achieved at lower air temperatures due to the increase in the mean radiant temperature within.

The heat given off by a thermal storage slab is usually confined to the room in which it is located. When a floor slab functions as a ceiling for a space below, however, heat is then radiated into both spaces. An effective spatial layout for a floor heat storage system is illustrated in figure 9-2. With most of the interior living spaces receiving direct south sun, heat distribution from the mass is relatively uniform. In cases where physical restrictions make total solar access impossible, there are alternative ways to distribute solar heat. Large glazing surfaces often result in overheating of south spaces; excess heat in these instances can be mechanically ducted to other areas. When south-facing spaces are self-heating with no excess heat, separate thermostatic controls or individual heating units such as wood stoves may be used to balance temperatures within.

Walls as Mass

A thermal mass wall can be a freestanding, non-load-bearing wall or it can be an actual part of the structural system of a building. When retrofitting a space for passive solar heating, it may be feasible to add a masonry wall for thermal storage when a new extension is planned. In some cases, masonry walls are an existing part of the structure. If these walls are to be retrofitted to store thermal energy, they must be solid masonry with no insulation or air space within, and also be insulated on the exterior surface and left exposed on the side that receives direct sun (see figure 9-3). When a masonry wall is an interior wall, as in a Trombe wall system, the glazing and not the wall needs night insulation.

When a wall or walls are used as thermal mass, personal contact or "contact comfort" is not an important consideration but wall texture, color, and ease of cleaning and maintenance are important.

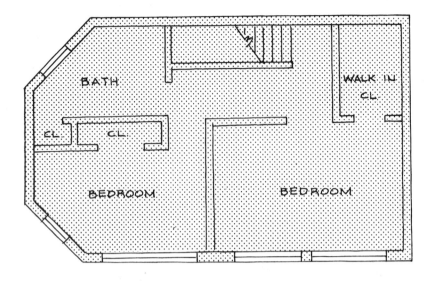

SECOND FLOOR

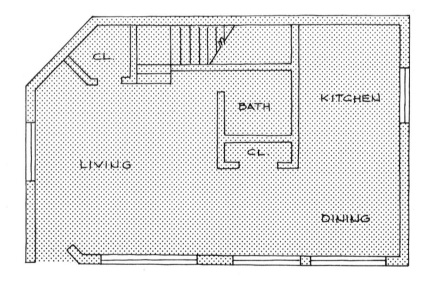

FIRST FLOOR

S

9-2.   *Floor thermal storage system works best when the most frequently used spaces are along the south wall.*

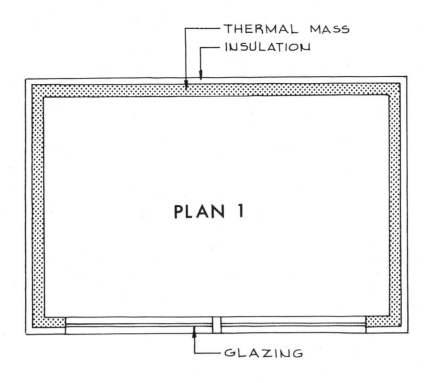

THERMAL MASS
INSULATION

PLAN 1

GLAZING

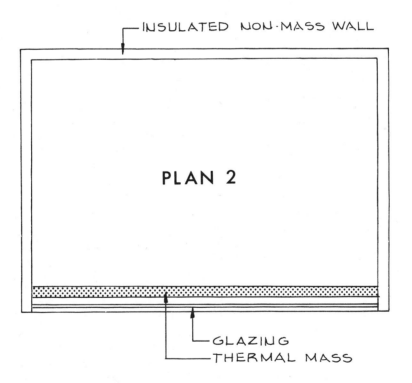

INSULATED NON·MASS WALL

PLAN 2

GLAZING
THERMAL MASS

9-3.   With direct heat gain, Plan 1, the exterior walls,
insulated on the outside, provide thermal mass for the space.
With indirect heat gain, Plan 2, the uninsulated thermal storage
wall is placed behind the south glazing, while the other
exterior walls are well insulated.

When a single wall is used for heat absorption, a dark finish with rough texture works best. Brick, concrete block, or poured concrete walls, left exposed, painted a dark flat color, or finished with masonry tiles are alternatives. When water is the heat storage medium, black fiberglass tubes, stacked barrels of water, and even water containers embedded in a concrete wall can serve as a non-loadbearing thermal storage wall.

The location of the wall with respect to the solar windows determines whether the passive system is a direct gain or indirect gain type (see figures 6-2, 6-3). With an indirect system, the side of the wall facing the space can be any color, since solar radiation is incident upon its other side. Walls used for indirect heat transfer often allow some direct light to enter the space. Masonry walls can be designed with "holes" or windows, water walls with spaces between the tubes or barrels to let in light. In some cases, clear water containers are used to further increase light entering a space. Because of its transparency, however, clear water absorbs less heat than water in dark metal containers or water that is colored dark.

When a direct heat gain system is employed, the need for direct solar access may limit room depth. Because window arrangement and sizes differ, a solar model (see figure 7-8) can be used to show the best location for the heat storage wall. In some instances, a wall can be especially designed to follow the solar path (see figure 9-4).

A space in which most major surfaces have heat storage capability can utilize light-diffusing glazing materials with high solar transmission to disperse light throughout the space. With clear glazing, a moderately light finish on major surfaces acts to disperse sunlight within the space. In all passive systems non-mass materials should never be excessively dark. Since they have no capability to store heat, non-mass materials absorb and give off thermal energy immediately and cause overheating of the interior.

The cost or structural limitations of adding heat storage walls to a space often make this type of retrofitting unfeasible. In these cases, a partition made of phase-change materials, available in long, thin tubes, can be installed instead. Manufacturers should provide installation requirements of phase-change materials intended for passive use. The time-lag characteristics of phase-change materials regulate the rate at which heat is released. When time lag is too short, movable insulating covers may be necessary to regulate heat flow from the tubes.

Heat Distribution from Thermal Walls

In indirect-gain thermal walls, the best heat distribution results when all spaces share the thermal wall (see figure 9-5). When this is not possible, alternate heating in other spaces may be necessary to balance interior thermal conditions. A direct-gain thermal wall, on the other hand, can heat both the direct access space and the adjoining one (see figure 9-6). A thermal wall functioning this way can also be used to provide additional daylight for adjoining spaces. Translucent glazing or glass blocks at the top of the wall allow the benefits of the south exposure to be utilized by these spaces.

Ceiling Mass

A concrete slab, roof ponds, or phase-change substances in the form of ceiling tiles can serve as ceiling heat storage. Since the angle of the sun entering through windows is downward, a thermal mass ceiling, unless heated from above, can receive only reflected light. Window reflectors with their concave shape can direct solar radiation toward the ceiling. Although heat storage may be reduced with this type of indirect system, a ceiling heat storage is convenient, eliminating such problems as shading of the mass with furniture, glare, and fading of fabrics.

Heat Distribution from a Ceiling Mass

Heat distribution from a radiant ceiling has limitations similar to those of radiant floors. Adjoining areas without mass may have to be heated separately for a balanced indoor thermal environment.

Special-Function Mass

Often materials having a special function in a space can be utilized as thermal mass. A masonry fireplace falls into this category. A masonry or concrete stairway under a skylight may also be used to store thermal energy. The heat stored in a stairway radiates its heat at two levels or warms up an entranceway when it is enclosed. Similarly, window seats made of phase-change materials or concrete, planters, fish tanks, or swimming pools are sometimes used as thermal mass. When an unenclosed body of water is used for heat storage, however, it cools off by evaporation, adding moisture to indoor air.

Using thermal mass as a secondary function of materials in a room can work well to supplement other forms of mass, or alone when sufficient in quantity.

Versatile Mass

Versatile or flexible thermal mass is generally movable, and comes in small, manageable units. When water is the heat-storage mass, jugs, bottles, water bags, fiberglass cylinders, and cans are all possible ways to contain it.

The size of the water containers can make a difference in thermal performance. Large containers, such as 55-gallon (209 liter) drums, tend to warm slowly, as the heat gained is constantly distributed within the large body of water by convection. The temperature of water within these containers therefore remains relatively low. Water temperature in narrow containers with significant surface exposure to sunlight, on the other hand, increases more rapidly. The smaller the water container, the greater the temperature increase. The drawback of small containers is that time lag may be reduced so heat is given off too rapidly. To avoid this, stack containers close together to allow conductive heat transfer between the units and to increase the time lag of the mass as a whole.

Phase-change materials, another type of versatile thermal mass, are available in small units within trays, plastic bottles, sacks, rigid tubes, and even translucent window panels. Because phase-change substances are relative newcomers

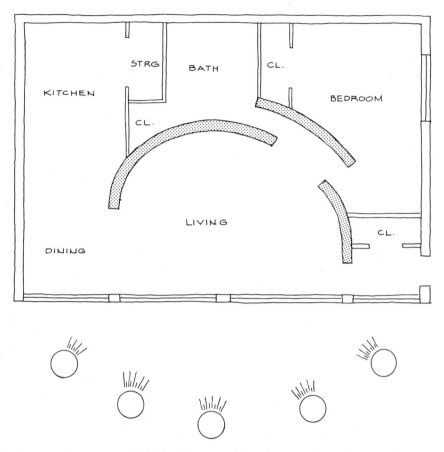

9-4.   The curved walls collect solar heat and distribute it throughout the interior.

9-5.   Because heat collection and re-radiation from an indirect heat-gain thermal storage wall is localized, it is best to locate most major living spaces along that wall.

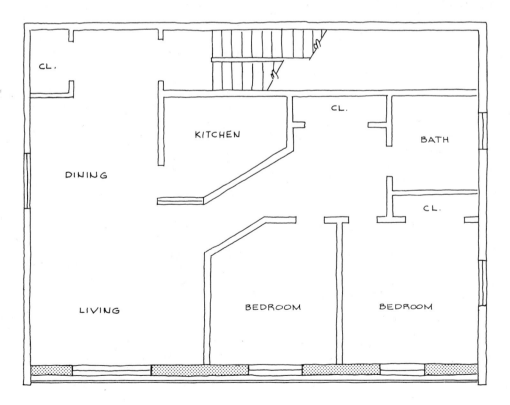

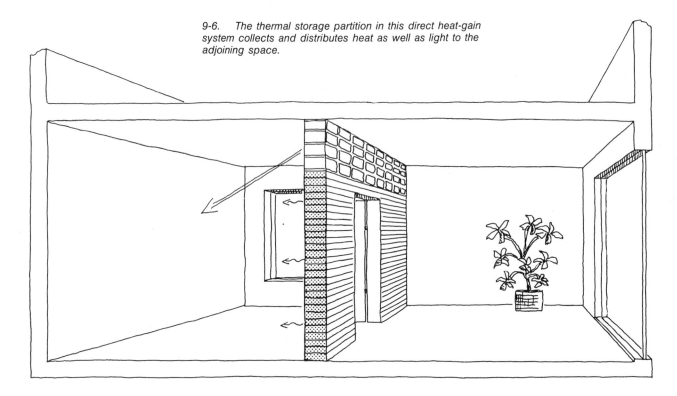

9-6. *The thermal storage partition in this direct heat-gain system collects and distributes heat as well as light to the adjoining space.*

ADJOINING SPACE   DIRECT GAIN SPACE

to the field of solar heat storage, their thermal properties of melting temperature, heat capacity, and time lag, along with their life expectancy, should be checked before a purchase is made.

Phase-change material is expanding the opportunities in passive solar retrofitting. Because its heat storage capacity is much greater than that of traditional thermal mass materials, it is a good alternative in interiors with limited space or structural strength.

Once a versatile heat storage unit is selected, its placement within the space and method of stacking become the task of the designer. Maximum surface exposure to direct sunlight is always the first priority; spatial and visual effects are additional considerations. Sometimes units are stacked and left exposed; in any case, they can make an aesthetic contribution to the design of a given space. Units colored black or other dark shades can create a playful effect. Clear containers filled with water or phase-change materials often produce special daylighting.

When concealed units are desired, cabinets or shelves with movable insulating panels can be adapted or custom designed to enclose heat storage modules. In one solution, wall racks installed at the top of a wall were custom made to support phase-change tubes that received direct sunlight from clerestory windows.

A major concern with all liquid-type heat storage units is leakage. Evaporation may also be a problem. Good-quality containers that are tightly capped will minimize these two occurrences. It is nevertheless generally desirable to

have refillable containers. Yellowing and algae growth in water can usually be prevented by adding chlorine to the water.

Mass and Supplementary Heating: Compatible Systems

In most cases, it is neither feasible nor cost effective to design passive solar heating systems to supply 100 percent of a space's heating needs. Although some passive solar designs for very mild climates can often supply more than 90 percent of the heat required by a space, other passive design features, because of the restrictions of an existing layout or a very cold climate, only contribute a small percentage of the required thermal energy within a space. It is important to remember that unlike active solar systems, the passive solar system is mainly a design concept, and one that need not cost more than any other design. For this reason, any contribution from a design intended to take advantage of the sun for adding wintertime heat to a space is beneficial.

Most passive solar buildings have backup heating systems for cloudy or excessively cold days, the type and size of the supplementary heating system depending largely on the average percentage of heat supplied by the sun. Factors involved in the heating potential of a solar space are percentage of sunny days in a region, and structural, functional, and site limitations to unobstructed south exposure. These elements, therefore, cause variations in the amount of heat an interior receives from the sun. In general, a space partially heated by the sun can fall into one of three categories, high, moderate, or low solar supply, representing the extent to which solar energy is utilized within a space.

High Supply

In underground housing, highly insulated buildings, spaces with a large percentage of shared-party walls, or in sunny, mild climates, a well-designed passive solar space can receive about 90 percent of its heating needs from the sun. Although some people prefer a central heating system, there is usually no need for elaborate auxiliary systems in these cases.

In rural or suburban areas with low-cost or free wood supply, wood-burning devices often provide backup heating. Other popular alternatives are electrical radiant or baseboard systems. Although electricity may be a costly source of heat in some parts of the country, it has several advantages when used as auxiliary heating. Installation of electrical heating is relatively easy; there is no need for a boiler or furnace. More important, individual room temperature control is thus facilitated, and this has great significance in passive solar spaces. Those rooms lacking south exposure that may remain cooler than those with direct sunlight can be heated as needed with such electric space heating.

Moderate Supply

When solar heat is significant but does not supply a major portion of an interior's heating, conventional central heating is often desirable as the supplementary system. This usually consists of hot-water baseboard heating, pipes embedded in a slab for radiant heat, or warm air forced through ducts. Central heating is most efficient when spaces are zoned separately, providing more than one thermostatic control. Individual temperature control may be necessary on each level of open two-story interiors. Rooms used directly as passive solar collectors should also have separate temperature controls since these areas are likely to be warmest. In addition, the radiant heat supplied by thermal mass in these spaces will create individual comfort at lower air temperatures.

Low Supply

In cases where orientation and glazing contribute only slightly to heating a space, a conventional heating system is called for. Major changes in heating this type of space may not be necessary; nonetheless, manual controls such as shut-off values are helpful in preventing overheating of spaces that receive direct sunshine.

Making the Right Choice

After all the options are reviewed, final selection of the type and location of thermal mass and backup heating can be made. As with any design element in an interior, the choice of the thermal mass and supplementary heating system that is most suitable for a space, as well as for the people within it, contributes to a desirable interior environment.

Chapter 10

INSULATING FROM WITHIN

IN RECENT YEARS, GROWING AWARENESS OF ENergy usage in buildings and homes has prompted research as well as production of energy-efficient materials. Perhaps the first response to the need for such materials came from the manufacturers of building insulation. Demand for new composites along with traditional materials to insulate walls, floors, and ceilings is still strong today.

Insulating the exterior surfaces of a space has the dual benefit of reducing heat flow between inside and out and increasing human comfort by raising the mean radiant temperature of the surfaces within. Insulating value, moisture resistance, fire and health safety, and cost are main considerations in selecting building insulation. There are a number of insulating materials on the market. Installation problems in retrofitting existing structures, however, can limit the choices, since there are instances where surfaces to be insulated are inaccessible, or the cost of retrofitting is excessive, or the type of material suitable for installation has questionable fire or health ratings. Nevertheless, insulating cavity walls or installing exterior insulation on a structure is often cost effective if one owns a space. If one rents, on the other hand, adding exterior, or building, insulation is unfeasible. In certain cases, therefore, it may be advantageous to seek out other methods of improving the thermal performance of exterior surfaces.

Insulating from within is a good way to do this. With the exception of surfaces used for solar heat storage, the thermal resistance of any exterior surface can be increased with interior insulating treatments. Innovative interior insulating treatments are now being designed and rediscovered as

an alternative to building insulation. Although not as effective as building insulation, interior treatments have the advantage of accessibility and versatility, and can always be changed or removed in the future.

Initial Insulation

On any uninsulated surface, the initial layers of insulation yield the greatest savings. As a surface becomes more heavily insulated, additional insulating layers produce little further savings.

This can be proven by a simple computation and is significant in attempting insulation from within. A typical uninsulated wood-frame wall with wood siding has a thermal resistance rating of approximately R-4. When one inch (2.5 cm) of insulating wall cover with a thermal value of R-2 is added to the wall, a 33 percent reduction of heat flow through the wall is achieved. On the other hand, when a wall is well insulated to R-19, let's say, a wall covering with an R-2 rating will lower heat loss by only 9.5 percent.

It especially makes sense, therefore, to add interior insulating treatments to uninsulated surfaces. Cold floors, walls, and ceilings can become more energy efficient with these treatments, and occupants will ultimately benefit.

Walls

Traditionally, decisions on wall coverings rarely hinged on their energy efficiency. Most often, choices were based on aesthetic questions of texture and color. Now, insulating value can be included as a factor in the decision. A combination of the R-value of the material itself and the way it is applied to the wall will determine its overall insulating value.

Thin fabric or plastic wall covering applied directly to a wall's surface have little resistance to conductive heat transfer. A surprising result, however, can be achieved with Thermodecor, distributed by Enertec Systems, Inc., a recently developed product that has the ability to reflect thermal radiation and in effect turns ordinary wallpaper into an insulator by reflecting escaping radiant heat back into a space. The covering is made up of a thin layer of pure aluminum coated with a paint that reflects visible light but is translucent to thermal radiation. With this quality, a finish with a desired color or print can reflect about 65 to 75 percent of the radiant heat back into a space.

In tests, when conventional wallpaper was applied to the walls and ceilings of a room, only 13 percent of the thermal radiation was reflected back into the space. When Thermodecor was applied to these same surfaces, 65 percent of the radiant heat was reflected.

Energy savings with a wall covering based on the reflection of radiant heat vary with the type of heating system in the interior. Thermodecor wall covering can save more energy with heating units that give off mostly radiant heat than with systems relying mostly on air convection. To illustrate this, a further test of the effectiveness of Thermodecor was made in rooms heated by a radiator, a forced-air heater, and a radiant floor heater. Thermodecor used in the room with radiant heat yielded the greatest savings of 18 percent. It performed nearly as well with the radiator, requiring 15 percent less energy, and least well when used with forced-air heat, reducing savings to 5 percent.

Because of its ability to manipulate radiant heat, this type of wall covering has great potential for increasing human comfort, since the greatest heat loss from the body in a wintertime interior occurs through thermal radiation to the surrounding surfaces.

Another perhaps more elaborate way to insulate walls from within is by adding coverings that actually reduce the conductive flow of heat through a wall. Cork tiles, wood paneling, quilted or heavier fabrics, even carpeting mounted directly on the wall's surface can slow heat transfer. The effectiveness of these coverings is directly proportional to the R-value of the material used. This type of treatment can be especially successful when one particular wall in a space is uncomfortably cold.

With a thinner fabric, an insulating value can be achieved by stretching it on a frame to form an air space between the fabric and the wall's surface. Once this is properly installed, room air will flow along the surface of the fabric

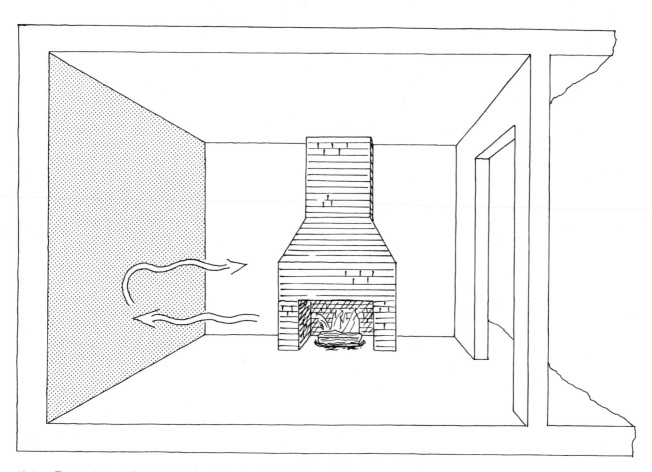

10-1. *Thermodecor reflects escaping radiant heat back into a space.*

instead of the wall's surface, reducing heat loss.

A more effective way to insulate with fabrics involves a polyester insulating pad held by a wall-mounted frame (see figure 10-2). The frame is mounted around the perimeter of the wall and the pad inserted and covered with a decorative fabric. With a half-inch polyester pad the treatment adds an insulating value of R-1.41 to the wall. In the case of a typical uninsulated wood-frame wall with a thermal resistance of R-4, this means a 28 percent reduction of heat flow.

In some instances, such permanent installation of a wall covering is not desired. For these cases, fabrics, hangings, and rugs can reduce the adverse thermal influences of a wall. The effectiveness of these wall hangings usually depends on their thickness and the area they cover. This type of partial wall insulation may not always make a great impact on the energy requirements of a building as a whole, but it can contribute to individual comfort. Decorative wool rugs on cold wall surfaces adjacent to seating and sleeping areas can reduce the direct radiant heat transfer between individuals and the cold surface.

Insulating with Furniture

Strategic placement of furniture is often useful in reducing the adverse effects of a cold wall. Fixed or movable solid units against a cold wall can function as a buffer between the wall and the living space. In planning or redesigning interiors, therefore, cabinets, solid chests, closets, or large modular units may be placed adjacent to a cold exterior wall for the best thermal effect. Seating and other occupied areas are then centrally located or arranged close to interior wall surfaces.

Ceilings

Because of limited available thermal treatments, the ceiling may be the last surface to be considered for insulation from within. Nevertheless, the insulating value and height of a ceiling does make a considerable impact on heat used in an interior. When the ceiling functions as the roof or a floor of an uninsulated attic, it accounts for the largest unit heat loss from the space. An interior ceiling, one that functions as the floor of another space above, does not lose heat directly, but in this case the ceiling height can have an indirect thermal effect on individuals in the space.

High or double-story ceilings often produce a desired spatial effect. In two-story sun spaces, for instance, ceiling height encourages the upward flow of warm air which is then circulated from the top of the space throughout the entire house. Great ceiling heights are generally required in public and commercial spaces, whereas in old residential structures, or lofts retrofitted to function as living spaces, existing high ceilings may be undesired.

The thermal inefficiency of high ceilings can be attributed to the significant amount of additional heat required to heat the extra *air space* created by the excessive ceiling height. Secondly, due to natural gravity convection the top portions of such a "tall room" will often be warmer than the lower parts where the occupants are. This can be an advantage during the summer, providing effective ventilation, but becomes a severe disadvantage during the heating season. To overcome this adverse condition, careful consideration is necessary in designing "tall spaces."

In already-existing high-ceiling interiors, an insulating suspended ceiling can minimize adverse thermal influences. Sometimes flexible design can make a tall ceiling feasible. In a space with clerestory windows high within the room a special insulating panel can seal off the top portion of the space whenever desired (see figure 10-4). In nonheat-gain windows, the high space can be sealed off during the coldest months and then opened for effective ventilation during the summer. When clerestory windows are heat-collecting south-facing surfaces, panels can function as night insulation. In older structures, belvederes and roof dormers can function in much the same way (see figure 10-5). These sections can be closed off by a hatch during the winter to prevent heat loss. Reopened during the summer, they provide an efficient escape route for the warmest air in the structure.

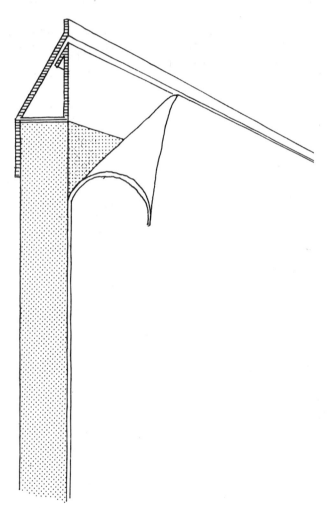

10-2. *Fabri Trak is a specially designed frame for wall coverings. After the frame is mounted on the edges of the wall, the insulating pad is inserted and covered with the desired fabric. An adhesive strip along the frame holds the fabric while it is securely inserted into the frame.*

10-3.   *Kitchen cabinets minimize adverse radiant effect of a
cold exterior wall. (Photo: Robert Stidolph)*

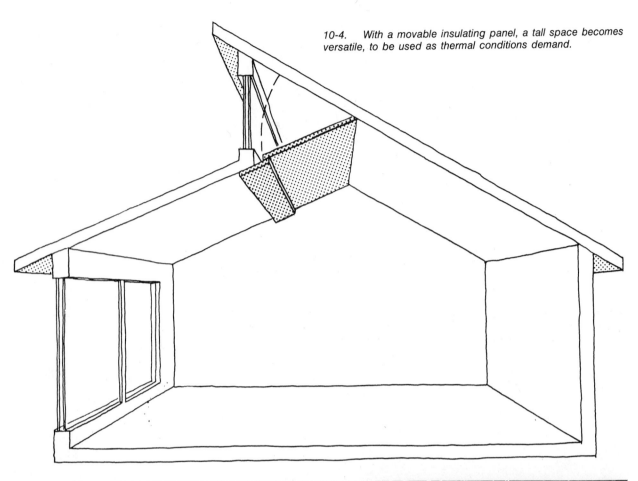

10-4. With a movable insulating panel, a tall space becomes versatile, to be used as thermal conditions demand.

10-5. Existing roof dormer on traditional residence. (Photo: Robert Stidolph)

Floors

The rapid heat flow through an uninsulated floor can be slowed by insulating from within. An insulating covering may be applied to any floor that is not intended for solar heat storage.

The most common materials used for this insulation are carpet and underlayment. A carpet with a foam underlayment has a thermal resistance rating of approximately R-1.23; a carpet and fibrous pad combination yields about R-2.08. Because insulating value of carpets depends on fiber, texture, and thickness, the above values are only approximate. Nevertheless, projected savings can be calculated with these thermal values in mind. On a typical uninsulated wood floor with a thermal resistance of R-3, a carpet and foam underlayment can reduce heat flow by 29 percent. With a fibrous pad, a 41-percent reduction in heat flow is possible. On an uninsulated concrete slab floor with an R-value of approximately .48, the carpet–foam pad combination produces a 72-percent reduction in heat flow, while a carpet and fibrous pad cuts heat transfer by as much as 81 percent.

Slowing Convective Heat Transfer

Air infiltration accounts for a large amount of energy waste in buildings. Although some outside air is continuously required in all interiors, the uncontrolled infiltration of cold outside air encouraged by wind pressure and indoor air currents should be minimized.

The most effective way to reduce uncontrolled outside airflow into a space is by sealing cracks around electrical outlets, window and door frames, and masonry joints. Caulks, weatherstripping, and vapor barriers can be used to tighten a space against air infiltration. Design techniques that effectively seal wall and window surfaces can also cut the volume of outside air entering a space.

Drafts and Indoor Air Circulation

Infiltration of outside air is not the sole cause of drafts within a space; a number of other thermal conditions in a wintertime interior can create indoor air movement. As room air flows along a cold wall, for example, it is cooled by conduction. The cooled air then drops, resulting in the movement of cool air along the floor.

Although both cold air infiltration and drafts due to the effect of cold surfaces indicate a heat loss from the space, all indoor air movement having adverse effects on individuals is not always necessarily the result of heat transfer between inside and outside. Spatial design, as with open vertical heights or the type of heating system or the heat circulation mechanisms can all influence the velocity of airflow in a wintertime interior.

Forced-air heating systems circulate heat by the convective motion of air, which in turn accounts for efficient heat distribution. Radiators, wood-burning stoves, and other high-temperature radiant systems give off considerable radiant heat, but also rely on air convection for heat distribution. Since a radiant heat source has a high surface temperature, the air passing over its surface is heated and rises rapidly,

pulling more cool air along the floor. In open two-story spaces, natural gravity air convection can cause upward air motion resulting in cool air movement at the floor level. Forced-air circulation with ceiling fans or duct systems is often necessary to redistribute heat that accumulates at the top of a double-story sunspace or room. These methods effectively distribute heat, but it should be noted that moving air, especially when moderate in temperature (70°–80°F/ 21.1°–26.7°C), ultimately has a cooling effect on individuals within a space.

The problem that confronts the designer, therefore, is how to shield individuals from the direct adverse thermal influences of air movement in a wintertime interior without obstructing efficient heat distribution.

Designing to Minimize Drafts

Air circulation or air movement can often be manipulated by structural interior design to minimize its cooling influence on individuals.

For instance, because an open door provides a common path for cold outside air to enter a space, techniques that minimize air exchange at entrances are useful. Vestibules and airlock entrances are good solutions. A vestibule can be added on outside an existing doorway or constructed within the space itself when the floor plan permits. Solar heat collecting vestibules, as shown in chapter 7, may be thermally self-sufficient, and in some cases even contribute to the heating of adjacent interior areas.

The vertical airlock or sunken entrance is also very effective in reducing the volume of cold air entering a living space. In a vertical airlock entrance, warm air, lighter than cold, tends to remain above the entrance at the living level, leaving the heavier cold air trapped below (see figure 10-6).

When airlocks cannot be added, shrubs or exterior wing walls can be used to deflect winds from the doorway. Figure 10-7 shows a wing wall perpendicular to the direction of cold winter winds to shelter the entrance from direct exposure. Even the addition of a storm door to an already existing solid door can be useful in deflecting direct winds from the entranceway.

Often, selected areas within a space permit excessive air infiltration and become a significant drain on the interior's energy. This may be true of nonsolar porches or balconies that have been retrofitted to function as part of the living space. These additions, often constructed with uninsulated surfaces and poorly sealed windows, are now energy wasters within the space. It is best to seal cracks, replace old window units, and add insulation to the walls and floors of these spaces; this is, however, often infeasible. Another way to reduce the adverse effects of these areas is with versatile partitions. Such dividers as thermal curtains, sliding glass doors, or movable partitions can be used to isolate these areas during periods of extreme weather conditions; they may be reopened in milder seasons.

In instances where partitions, doorways, or curtains are not desired, occupants can shield themselves from the direct cooling effect of an entrance or an area of excessive infiltration with strategic furniture arrangement. Solid furniture can often deflect incoming drafts from occupied areas. Fig-

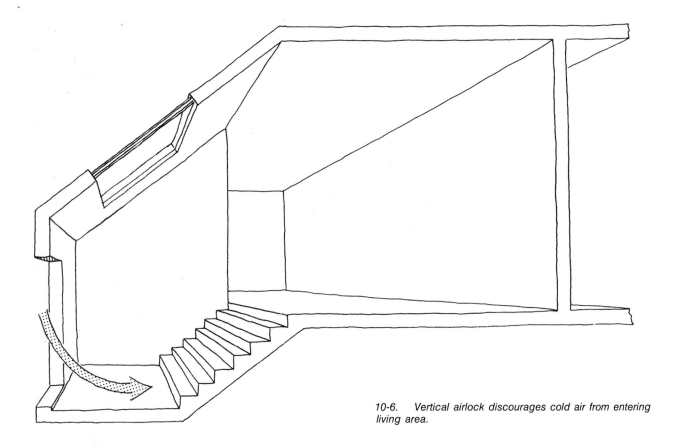

10-6.   *Vertical airlock discourages cold air from entering living area.*

ures 10-8 and 10-9 show ways to use furniture to shelter seating clusters from direct drafts.

Because of natural air convection in a space, the coldest air always drops and flows along the floor. One way to overcome this effect when redesigning a space with ample ceiling height is to create an elevated living surface. When the occupied portions of a space are elevated 16 to 20 inches (40 to 50 cm) above the original floor, the coldest air can be trapped near exterior walls (see figure 10-10). To further discourage cold airflow at occupied level, filtered tubes or ducts beneath the new floor will channel cool airflow below the living surface.

Air motion that is meant to distribute heat within a space should not be obstructed, but interior planning can often reduce its adverse effects on individuals. To avoid the cooling influence of room-temperature air movement on occupants, it is best to locate seating, work, and sleep areas away from the direct path of duct outlets or ceiling fans.

When Airflow Is Desired

Wintertime priorities are to shield occupants from adverse air movement; in summer, however, airflow through a space is to be encouraged. How much air circulates through an interior space depends on such factors as wind speed, air temperature, and the location and size of window openings. The natural and man-made surroundings can sometimes become obstacles to efficient airflow through an interior.

Building orientation and spatial layout determine whether an interior has access to a windward exposure. Even when windows face the windward side of a building, the natural breeze can be reduced by nearby structures or trees.

Town and city planning have a great impact on the general nature of wind flow through an area. In some instances, street grid layout can greatly reduce the natural cooling capacity of a region.

Similarly, the local landscape can either encourage or hinder winds upon a structure. Whereas in the northwestern part of the United States winter winds originate from a general south direction, in the northeast winter winds blow from north to northwest. Evergreens planted to the windward side of a building reduce the adverse effect of cold winter winds, whereas natural ground-level vegetation on the side facing summer breezes allows a free flow of summer breezes. Because natural vegetation absorbs heat, it has a cooling effect on air passing over it. Conversely, concrete and masonry pavements surrounding a structure soak up heat and increase the temperature of air as it flows by.

Airflow Through an Interior—Inlet and Outlet

The force of wind against a building creates positive and negative pressures within. Positive pressure is formed on windward, or inlet walls, while suction or negative pressure is created on the leeward, or outlet, side.

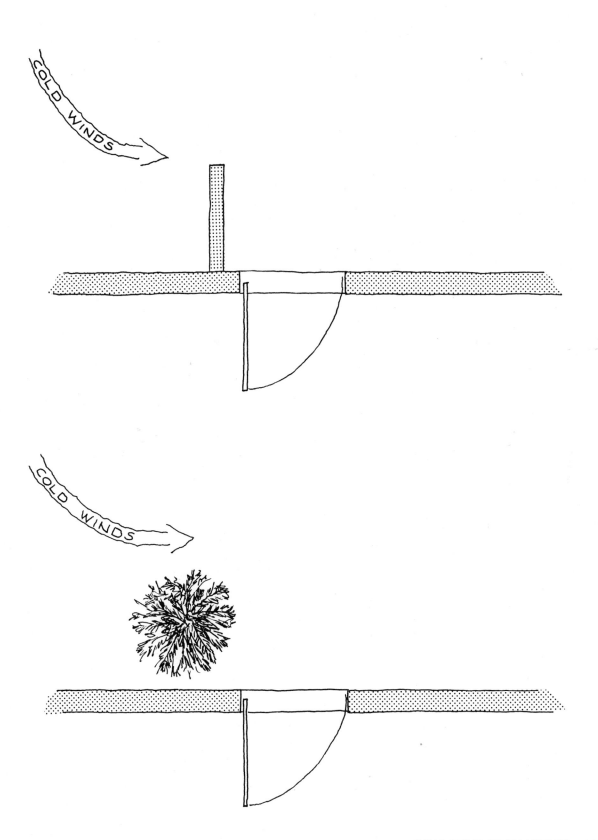

10-7. *Wing walls or evergreen shrubs perpendicular to the direction of cold winds reduce flow of cold air through entry.*

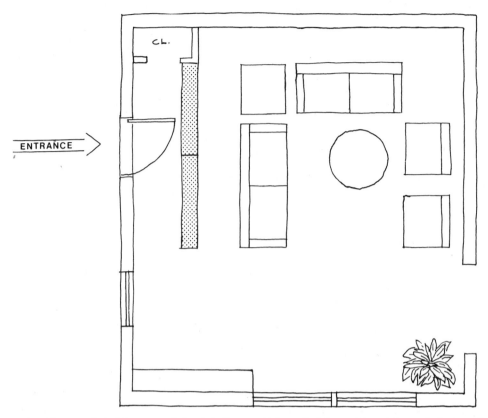

10-8.   Solid wood cabinets and shelving prevent direct draft at seating area.

10-9.   Shelving cabinet deflects drafts from the entrance. Curved solid bar unit further discourages the cold downdrafts at window area from circulating deeper into the living space.

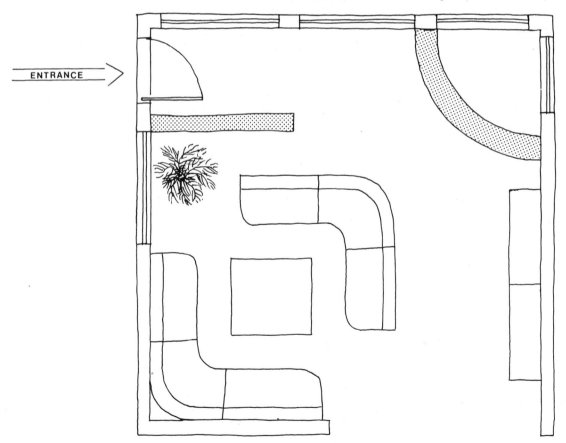

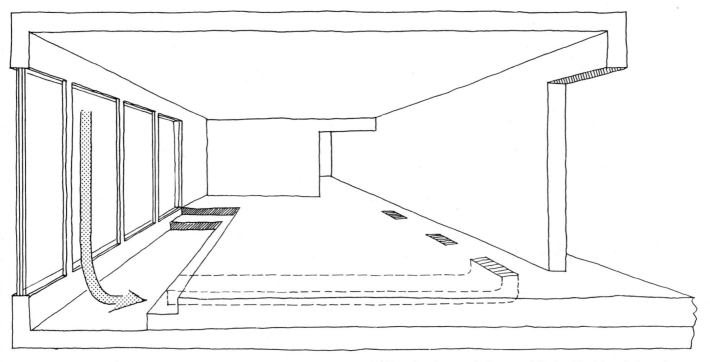

10-10.   With the living level elevated, the coldest air circulates below occupied floor.

10-11.   Landscape design can deflect cold winter winds and encourage summertime airflow into living spaces.

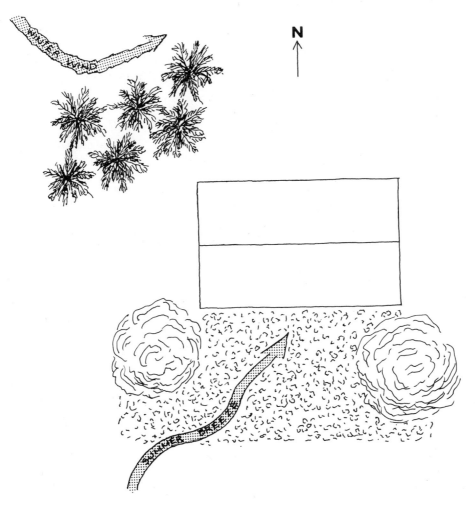

The best way to generate natural airflow through an interior space is with effective cross-ventilation. This is possible by locating window openings on both windward and leeward sides of a space. Maximum airflow occurs when two large openings are opposite each other in this relationship. When the direction of the wind is perpendicular to an inlet opening, maximum airflow across the space takes place, as figure 10-12 shows. Areas on either side of the opening, however, have low air movement. This condition can be corrected by locating window openings obliquely (45°) to the direction of the wind. In this case, as figure 10-13 shows, airflow around the entire space is encouraged. When window openings are on adjacent walls in a space, an inlet receiving direct winds is more suitable for providing good air circulation within the space (see figure 10-14).

Natural ventilation is poor in spaces having only one facade available for window openings, even when the opening faces the direction of the wind. In some cases, window design in a space with single exposure can make considerable improvement in the air velocities within. Window design will have little effect when the openings are located on the leeward side, but it can increase indoor wind velocities dramatically on windward exposures. Two windows on either

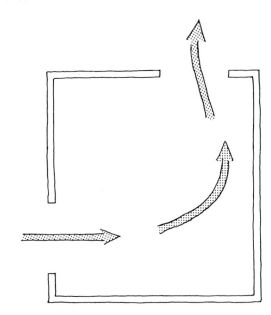

10-14.   When openings are on adjacent walls, a wind direction perpendicular to the window opening promotes good air circulation within.

side of the windward space can double the indoor air velocity achieved by one centrally located window of the same area. Vertical projections along the side of window openings, as shown in figure 10-15, create an artificial inlet–outlet relationship, thereby increasing indoor air velocities by up to ten times the original value.

Effect of Opening Height

The vertical position of openings within is also important in the effective ventilation of a space. For cooling of individuals, it is essential to direct wind flow along levels of occupancy. Since people in a space are closest to floor level, low inlet openings are more effective for convective cooling than higher openings that channel wind flow above the occupants. Pivoted windows or adjustable louvers that can direct wind flow downward are equally effective in providing comfort. In schools and offices where winds at desk level may disturb papers, airflow can be aimed at head level.

The differential of vertical heights of inlet and outlet openings in a space is another determinant of effective natural airflow through a space. The greater the vertical distance between inlet and outlet, the stronger the upward airflow. Interiors with significant vertical spaces such as a stairwell, attic, belvedere, or high ceiling have the potential for good upward airflow. When this type of flow exists, exhaust of hot air from a space is facilitated.

Interior obstructions to airflow at inlet points can reduce indoor air velocities. Curtains or shades, necessary for privacy or prevention of solar heat gain, inevitably cut down on airflow through inlet openings. Abrupt course changes in indoor breeze caused by furniture or interior partitions

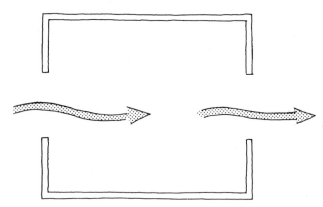

10-12.   When the direction of the wind is perpendicular to openings, airflow is good. Spaces on either side of openings, however, have poor circulation.

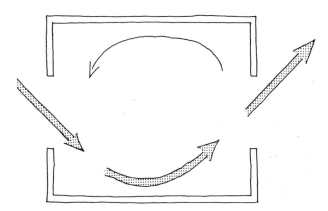

10-13.   When the wind direction is at 45° to opening, air circulation in the room is increased.

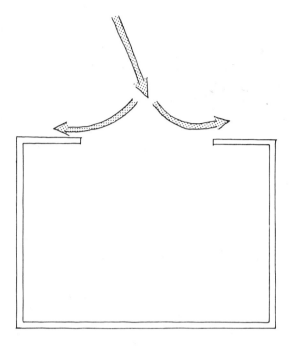

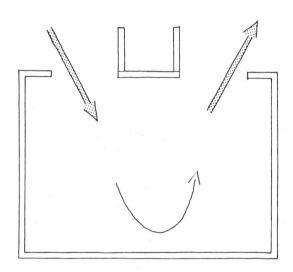

10-15. *When only one side is available for window openings, a single window works poorly even when in a windward orientation. Two separate window openings provide better airflow, while wing walls can further encourage inlet-outlet relationship.*

also reduce air speed significantly. Even screens bring about a considerable reduction in airflow through windows. When outdoor wind velocity is low, a wire mesh screen can cut wind flow through the window opening by about 50 percent. In planning for good airflow through a space, therefore, minimizing interior obstructions to wind flow is an important design consideration.

The planning and design of window openings in an interior space will depend on certain variables. Analysis of climatic and environmental influences, along with specific design choices, can help in choosing where the window openings will go, how large they will be, and what shape they will take. Further design decisions will deal specifically with such considerations as allowing prevailing summer winds to penetrate for natural cooling during warm seasons; examining exterior obstructions to airflow and considering their removal; noting the number of walls in the space with existing or possible window openings; arranging furniture and interior partitions to allow free airflow; coordinating glazing surfaces intended for solar heat gain with operable sections of glass needed for adequate ventilation; selecting windows with tight seal and good insulating qualities; placing air outlets in high vertical spaces to provide efficient exhaust of warm air; adding exterior vertical wind deflectors to improve natural airflow into spaces with a single exposure on the windward side; and/or using such devices as movable horizontal louvers to provide shading and privacy while deflecting incoming air downward for maximum cooling benefit to occupants.

Conflicts

The changing seasons in temperate climates may introduce design conflicts regarding interior thermal priorities. Careful planning and analysis of an interior, however, can often pinpoint a major thermal flaw within the space, which will then be the target of the interior design scheme. Techniques to insulate surfaces and discourage cold air infiltration and circulation within can minimize winter discomfort. Alternatively, selective window design and proper placement of vents can encourage natural summertime ventilation, reducing the need for mechanical cooling.

Chapter 11

SOLAR INTERIORS

NOW THAT WE HAVE EXAMINED THE NATURE OF human thermal reactions and considered what contributes to comfort, and have followed this with an analysis of design factors relating to the interior space, it would seem logical to conclude with how the combination of these elements can best result in the total design of a space.

Entire spaces or buildings can be categorized according to the major thermal influence upon them. Since the orientation or solar exposure often constitutes this major determinant, three general categories will be considered, having to do with direction: *southern exposures,* those spaces with a relatively clear access to the south or 30° east or west of true south, and thus presenting an opportunity for passive solar design, *eastern or western exposures,* those interiors that may have no passive solar opportunity yet receive excessive direct sun during the summer months, and *northern exposures,* for those spaces having a general north orientation, or facing any other direction with an obstructed exposure, creating essentially the same sunless condition as would a northern exposure.

The following case studies involve typical or existing spaces that could be improved with the proposed changes. A variety of spaces, both residential and commercial, in single-family or small buildings as well as in multifamily or high-rise structures, was selected to show design solutions in each exposure category. In many cases more than one option for a particular space is discussed.

Southern Exposures

A large number of existing spaces have ideal conditions for a passive solar retrofit. Although solar conversion is always a benefit, the effectiveness of the passive system depends partially on the design of an existing space. Features like well-insulated surfaces and few window openings on orientations other than south help make the passive system more efficient. It is therefore best to incorporate as many appropriate energy-conserving design techniques as possible to optimize the thermal performance of a retrofitted space.

The extent of the solar conversion and the method selected for each case varies with the scope of a project and the amount of money invested in it, which in turn may hinge on owner's priorities, permanency of the occupancy, and possible secondary functions of the conversion.

Perhaps the most ideal time for a passive solar conversion is when extension or renovation is planned anyway. Incorporating solar design principles during renovation does not always mean an increase in the cost of the project, yet it offers great advantages. In some instances, the main requirements of a passive solar space may be present but not fully utilized. In these cases, a mere redesign of the interior may be all that is necessary for the conversion.

An interior converted to function as a passive solar heat collector inevitably undergoes some changes, not only in the physical nature of the space, but also in its thermal behavior and the effect that has on inhabitants. A space functioning as a passive solar heat collector will, for example, have a wider range of temperatures within a twenty-four-hour period than will a conventional space. Although large temperature swings are not desirable, comfort in a passive space may be greater than in conventional spaces because of the large warmed surfaces involved. Using the sun for heating makes individuals more aware of the movement of sunlight through an area, and emphasizes the importance of opening window insulators in the morning and closing them after the sun goes down.

The following examples present some solar options open to spaces with unobstructed access to the south, and the adjustments that may be necessary within. In each case, the benefits and possible drawbacks of each new system are analyzed.

Case 1: Single-Family Residence

This single-family home located in a residential section of New York City has solid masonry walls and clear southern exposure toward a private garden, which makes a passive solar conversion highly feasible (see figures 11-1, 11-2, 11-3).

Option 1—Trombe Wall Retrofit

A building with solid masonry walls is adaptable for a Trombe wall retrofit. A masonry wall containing insulation cannot function as a heat storage wall, and one with an air space can be used only if the space is filled with concrete. Design professionals can determine the composition and structural stability of existing walls intended for heat storage.

In this case, the wall is suitable to function as a heat storage wall. The major structural aspect of this conversion will be the installation of the glazing. A separate structural framework to support the glazing can be fitted about 6 inches (15 cm) from the existing wall. To avoid excessive heat loss, the unit should consist of double-insulated glass or plastic held by a frame with a thermal break. Perimeter insulation and ground insulation above the frost line are essential. Glazing materials having high solar transmission are available from solar glazing manufacturers, although recycled window units can also be adapted for the glazing to reduce the expense of this conversion. The exterior surface of the wall should have good heat-absorbing qualities. Red brick has a relatively high heat absorption, but a flat black finish achieves the maximum heat gain.

With the glazing fixed in front of the thermal storage wall, heat collection begins, passing through the wall by conduction (see figure 11-4). If warm airflow is desired during the day, top and bottom vents equipped with dampers

11-1.   Case 1: Single-family residence in New York City with solid masonry walls. (Photo: Robert Stidolph)

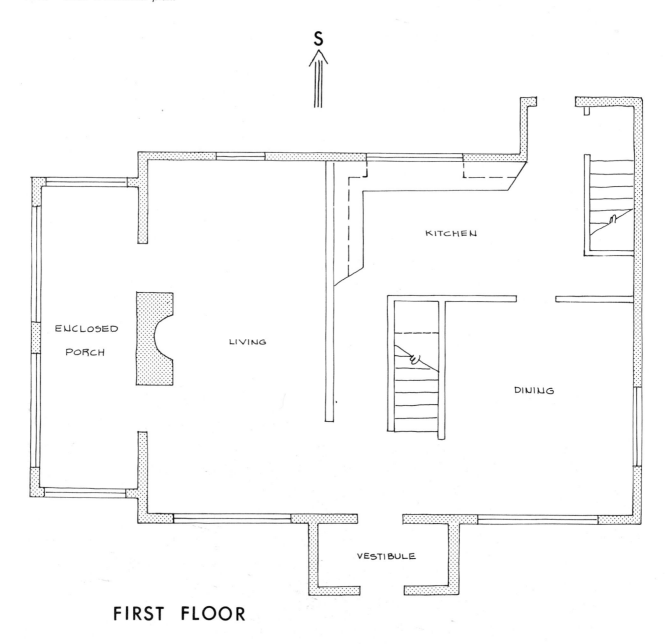

FIRST FLOOR

to prevent back flow can be installed on each floor. Figure 2-1 shows how vents can serve as the path for daytime warm air circulation. The installation of vents can frequently be avoided when adequate windows are located on top and bottom floors to perform this function. As a rule of thumb, top and bottom openings should be equally distributed with a total area of 1 square foot (.09 m²) for every 100 square feet (9 m²) of heat storage wall.

The existing south-facing windows are left in place to allow some direct sunlight to enter the spaces within and provide the option of warm air circulation during the day. Manual operation of windows to provide warm airflow during the day is necessary in this case but may not be practical in all instances. Upper-story windows should be opened at

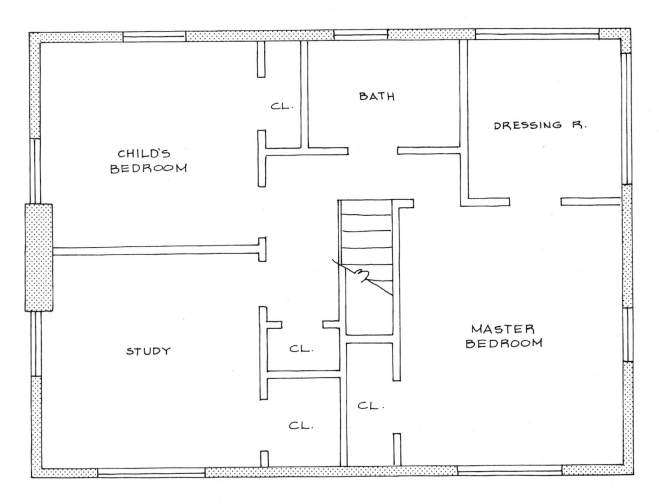

S

CHILD'S
BEDROOM

CL.

BATH

DRESSING R.

STUDY

CL.

MASTER
BEDROOM

CL.

CL.

SECOND FLOOR

the top and the lower-level windows at the bottom for maximum airflow. In the evening and on cloudy days, windows must be securely closed to prevent reverse airflow.

As always, shading of the wall is essential to prevent an adverse summertime condition. In this case, the absence of a large deciduous tree in the flower garden makes natural shading difficult. The existing roof overhang extended with a lightweight movable awning is therefore used to shade the thermal storage wall (figures 11-5, 11-6). Summertime venting of hot air in the air space between the wall and glazing is accomplished with a row of operable windows along the top of the glazing. Ample glazing and skylights at the rear vestibule, equipped with shading devices, provide additional wintertime heat gain.

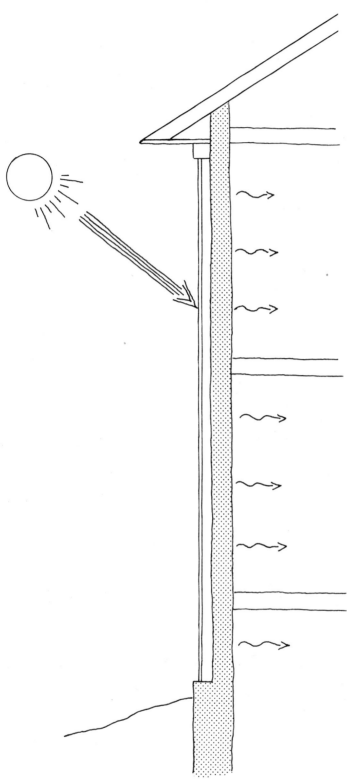

To allow efficient heat flow through the wall, it is best to strip its interior surface of traditional finishing materials such as plaster or paneling that may slow the transfer of heat. When the wall is solid brick, it can be cleaned and refinished on its interior face. Most masonry walls, however, have brick exterior with a concrete block backing, which may be undesirable as an interior finish in these instances. The way a thermal storage wall surface is finished depends on aesthetic preferences. A decorative masonry finish such as quarry tile is appropriate since it does not slow the transfer of heat. In other cases the wall can be painted any desired color, or covered with thin copper wall tiles to reduce cost of refinishing.

The second interior change may involve furniture arrangement. Since the Trombe wall is now the source of heat within the space, massive furniture or built-in units that may obstruct heat flow should not be placed against it or directly in front of it. In this case, conversion to a thermal wall necessitates some reorganization in two of the four rooms directly on the heat storage wall. The kitchen, shown in the figure 11-2 floor plan, has built-in wall cabinets; the new plan, figure 11-7, moves them to the opposite wall with additional counter space along the new curved partition. In the master bedroom, figure 11-3, the partition wall enclosing a dressing room on the south wall is removed. If a dressing area is desired, it can be relocated on the north wall where it will serve as a buffer (see figure 11-8).

The next change can often be significant for occupants, especially in mild seasons. When the glazing for a heat storage wall is constructed, all windows on the wall are essentially closed in from direct outside airflow. Summertime exhaust vents at the top of the glazed wall do permit warmest air to escape; nevertheless, window openings can no longer function as before. If this condition is not desired, leaving various portions of the south wall unglazed will allow some window openings to be used for direct ventilation.

When a Trombe wall is used, the layout of interior spaces is an important design factor. The optimum spatial layout in a home with an indirect thermal storage wall is a linear one. The most-used spaces are located along the heat storage wall to receive direct thermal benefit. In new designs, the best shape for Trombe wall structures is slightly elongated on the east-west axis to increase southern exposure (elongation along the north-south axis enables the heat storage wall to heat only part of the interior spaces). Excessive elongation, however, dramatically increases exposed surface area as well as heat loss from the space, counteracting the benefits of the south exposure.

In retrofits, building shape is predetermined and may be a disadvantage to the performance of the system. The building shape in this case, however, is near optimum for cold and temperate climates. Because of the advantageous shape of the house its interior requires no significant layout changes. Major living spaces such as the living room, master bedroom, child's room, and kitchen are all along the thermal storage wall. The only room totally isolated from the wall is the second-story study, whose heating needs can be met by an individually controlled heater. Heat flow between the kitchen and dining area is encouraged by open planning

11-4. *With the addition of south-facing glazing, the existing masonry wall behaves like a Trombe-type thermal storage wall.*

Interior Changes

Although a thermal storage wall involves mostly exterior work, the interior of the spaces along the wall will require some changes as well.

11-5.   *Existing roof overhang. (Photo: Robert Stidolph)*

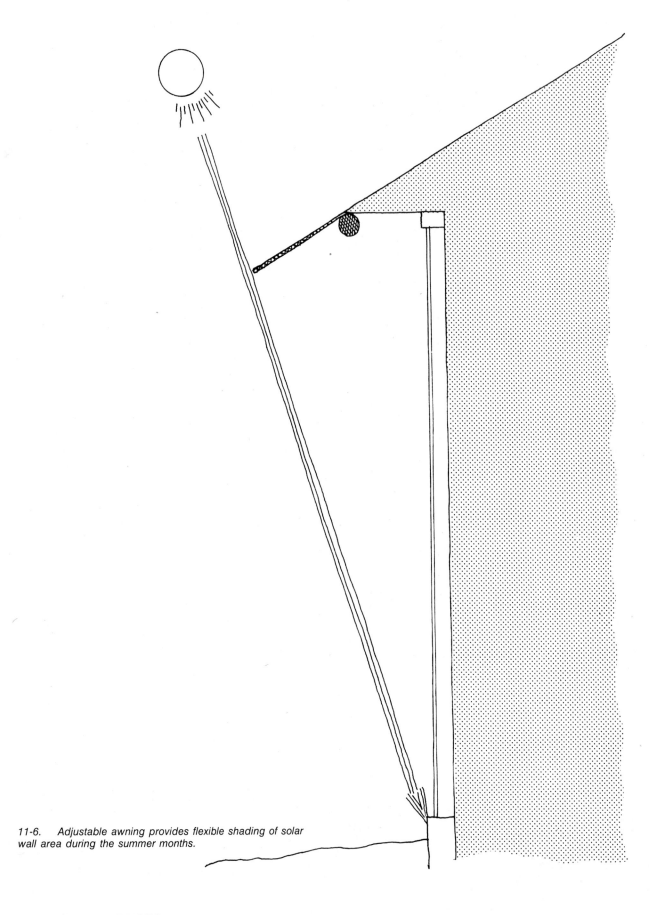

11-6.   Adjustable awning provides flexible shading of solar wall area during the summer months.

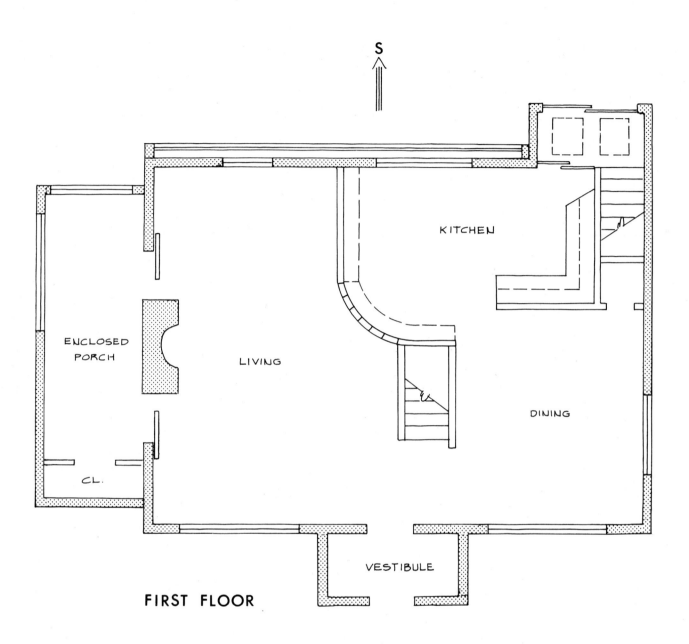

S

KITCHEN

ENCLOSED
PORCH

LIVING

CL.

DINING

VESTIBULE

FIRST FLOOR

11-7.   *Minor layout changes on the first floor assure efficient
heat distribution from the thermal storage wall.*

S

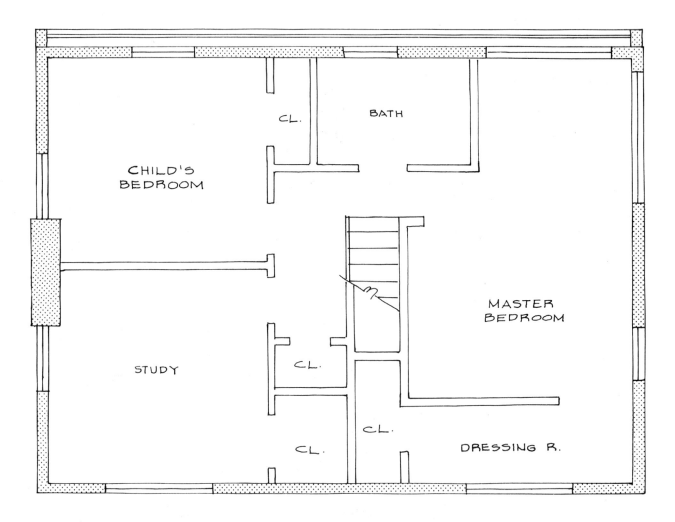

CHILD'S
BEDROOM

CL.

BATH

STUDY

CL.

CL.

CL.

MASTER
BEDROOM

DRESSING R.

SECOND FLOOR

11-8. Repositioning the second-floor dressing room area opens the master bedroom considerably to the benefits of south exposure.

11-9. *Double-story sunspace provides additional living space as well as supplementary heating.*

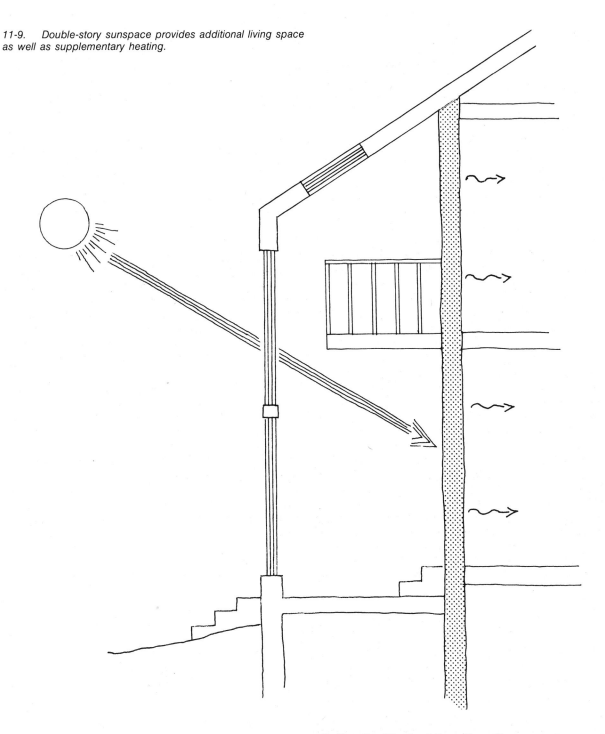

and operable vents at the top of the partition wall between the two spaces.

The remaining design changes, the closing off of north and east windows in the porch and the placement of a storage closet for a buffer space and of insulated sliding panels between the living room and porch, reduce the energy drain caused by the existing uninsulated porch, thus making the Trombe wall's efficiency greater. A glass block partition wall is used to increase the living room floor area while allowing diffused sunlight to enter from the kitchen.

Option 2—Attached Two-Story Sunspace

Adding a double-story sunspace in this house can satisfy the need for extra space and also provide a passive solar heat collector. The solid masonry exterior south wall supplies the thermal mass, working as a delayed heat provider for adjoining spaces (see figure 11-9). Daytime circulation of warm air from the sunspace takes place through open windows. When increased air circulation is needed or overheating of the sunspace occurs, a fan at the top of the masonry wall can pull air deeper into adjoining spaces.

In the summer, highly efficient exterior solar reflecting

shades shield sloped glazing and the top portion of the vertical glass from the hot sun. The bottom panels of the vertical glazing are replaced with solar screens for shading and natural ventilation. Operable glazing panels at the top of the sunspace provide efficient exhaust of warm air.

Interior Changes

Because the south wall is used for heat transfer, its interior surface should be stripped of all insulating materials as in the Trombe wall retrofit. The rearrangement of kitchen and bedroom furniture is also similar to the Trombe wall plan. With the sunspace addition, however, the solar vestibule on the lower level is replaced by the sunspace, which provides access to the outside through glass doors from the kitchen.

A sunspace works best as a heat collector when it can be closed off on cold winter nights. Although this practice produces large day-to-night temperature fluctuations in the sunspace, it eliminates the need for supplementary heating and insulating covers on its extensive glazing areas. Even after giving off the heat collected from the sun during the day, the closed-off sunspace is still useful as a buffer for adjacent living spaces.

If the double-story sunspace is intended for use on a regular basis, special design provisions are necessary. One problem, the rapid upward flow of warm air that leaves the occupied lower level uncomfortably cool on winter nights, can be solved by splitting the sunspace into two functioning living levels, thus doubling the usable floorspace. Operable floor vents on the second level can be used to regulate the upward flow of warm air and facilitate summertime ventilation.

Another problem, the large percentage of cold exterior surfaces such as windows provide, can be tackled by installing effective insulating covers on sunspace glazing. In this case the solar addition is converted into a study on the second level and a family room on the first level with furniture arranged to optimize comfort. Figure 11-10 shows

the first floor of the sunspace with the seating located near the thermal storage wall to increase its beneficial influence on the individuals within the space. The daytime problem of excessive sunlight and personal overheating is prevented by partial shading with dark, heat-absorbing blinds. This technique reduces glare without significant loss in heat-collecting efficiency.

Option 3—Direct Gain System—Passive Solar Panels (Thermosiphoning Air Panels)

A direct gain system can often be the simplest and least costly way to convert an interior into a passive solar space. When daytime overheating of the space is not a problem, large south-facing windows are the only ingredients necessary for direct solar heat gain. When large windows are present on the south wall of a space, a check for thermal efficiency can determine if they are suitable for direct solar gain. Double insulated glass, high solar transmission, and tight fit are some of the important qualities that direct gain windows should have. When existing window units are leaky and inefficient, energy-efficient windows should replace them. When south-facing windows are small, enlargement of the openings will be necessary. On a non-loadbearing wall, the structural work necessary to span new openings is relatively minor. On loadbearing walls, however, spanning large window openings can be a problem. In this case (see figure 11-11), windows on the south wall are replaced with energy-efficient units. Additional heat is brought into south-facing rooms through solar heat-collecting panels that visually extend the glazing on the south elevation. The panels are attached to the exterior of the wall, eliminating the need for spanning large window openings (see figure 11-12). These passive heat collectors trap heat between the glazing and the exterior wall which can be delivered into the house through top and bottom vents or mechanically.

Interior Changes

The new efficient window openings and heat-collecting

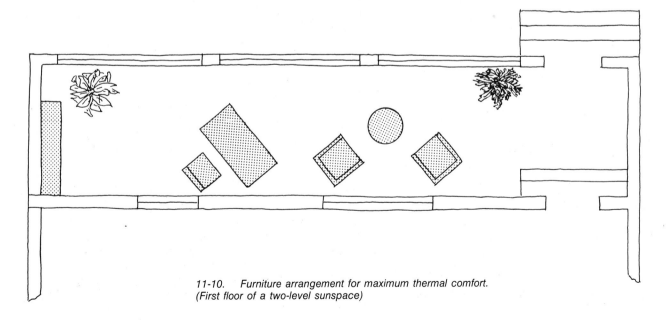

11-10.   *Furniture arrangement for maximum thermal comfort.*
(First floor of a two-level sunspace)

11-11.   Heat-collecting panels expand south facade glazing area without need for major structural changes.

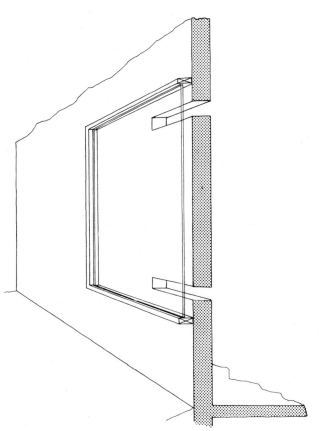

11-12.   Heat from panels circulates into living spaces through small upper and lower vents.

panels introduce more natural heat into south-facing spaces. Windows and panel vents, unobstructed during the day, are in the evening and on cloudy days securely sealed to prevent backflow of room air. Efficient window treatments on all glazing areas can further reduce energy requirements. Venting heat collectors to the outside during the summer months prevents heat buildup within the panels.

Case 2: Single-Family Residence

This second case is a single-family residence in a suburb in the northeast (figures 11-13, 11-14, 11-15). Wood-frame construction with the south facade close to the property line makes a passive solar retrofit somewhat more difficult than in Case 1.

Option 1—Direct Gain System

Before plans for a conversion can begin, a legal agreement with the neighbor is needed to assure present and future access to sunlight from the south. In areas without sunrights legislation, future sunlight blockage can be a serious problem.

Although this case has a number of south windows, they are insufficient in proportion to the size of the interior spaces. Enlarging window areas increases net heat gain.

11-13.   Case 2: Although south wall is too close to property line to accommodate a passive solar retrofit, exterior portion of chimney can be utilized as thermal mass. (Photo: Thomas Wieschenberg)

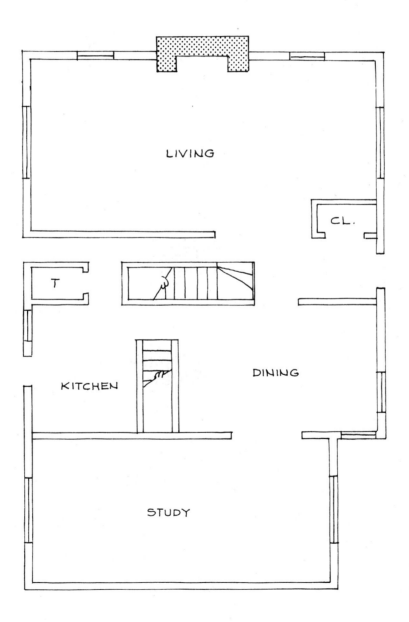

FIRST FLOOR

11-15.   Case 2: Second-floor plan.

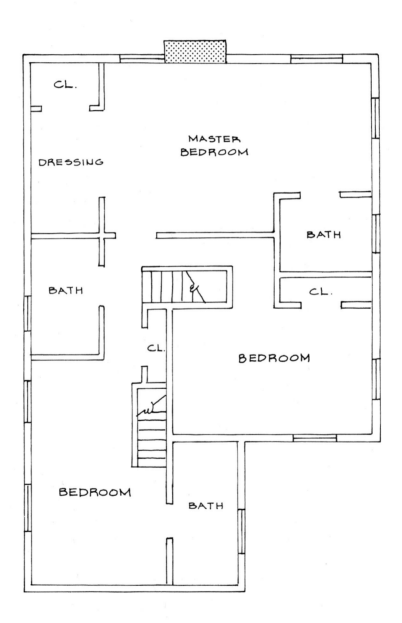

SECOND FLOOR

11-16 (below), 11-17.   A vertical glass enclosure of the chimney, with solar balconies on both levels, provides solarium space as well as supplementary heating for adjacent spaces.

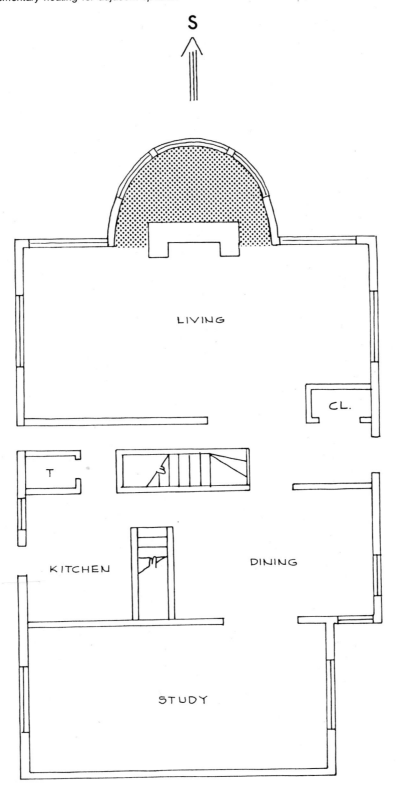

S

LIVING

CL.

T

KITCHEN

DINING

STUDY

FIRST FLOOR

S

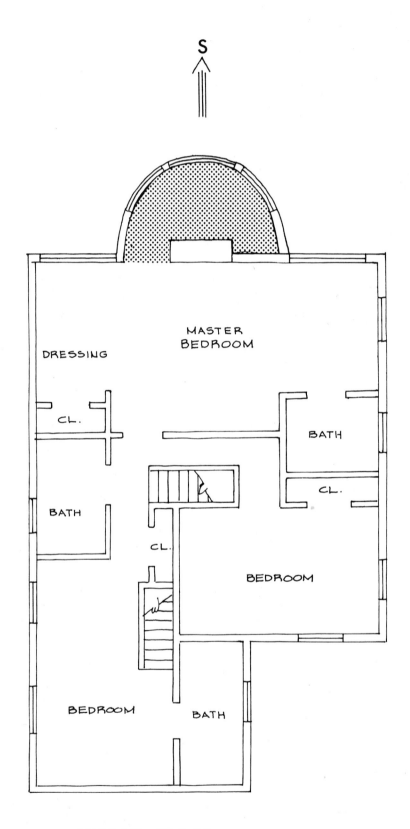

MASTER
BEDROOM

DRESSING

CL.

BATH

CL.

BATH

CL.

BEDROOM

BEDROOM

BATH

SECOND FLOOR

Although the south wall of the house is a side wall, two frequently used spaces are located along its surface and therefore receive direct benefits of the extra solar heat. When direct gain spaces become overheated, dark heat-collecting shades can be drawn, and overhead ducts can pull warm air into other spaces.

Interior Changes

Light-diffusing glazing was selected to disperse direct sunlight within the space to avoid fading of fabrics and carpets from excessive direct sunlight. Since the south wall is close to the property line, light-diffusing glazing provides the extra bonus of privacy.

Thermal floor-length drapes function as night insulation on both floors. A tall deciduous tree on the southeast corner of the house provides moderately dense summer shading of the south wall.

Option 2—Direct Gain with Solar Balconies

Although property limitations along the south wall make a solar addition impossible, a glass enclosure of the protruding brick fireplace chimney is an option. The vertical glass space (see figures 11-16, 11-17) contains two levels, with entrances from the living room and master bedroom.

During the daytime, the sun floods the balconies, giving them a tropical atmosphere while some of the solar heat is absorbed by and stored in the bricks. Excess heat from the balconies is mechanically vented into adjoining rooms.

Improvement of fireplace efficiency is a secondary benefit of the conversion. Since the masonry chimney is no longer exposed to the outside, the heat previously lost through the chimney by conduction can now be recaptured.

Interior Changes

The interior changes involved with adding the solar balcony to the direct gain system are the same as in option 1 with the thermal drapes now extending across the balcony entrance for night insulation. In addition, residents now have the benefits of a mini-solarium in the middle of winter.

Case 3: Single-Family Residence

This type of wood-frame structure has the limitation of being located in a higher-density urban neighborhood. Problems of present and future solar access along with high-density surroundings can limit possibilities for the solar conversion.

This case was selected to illustrate how the nature of

11-18.   Case 3: Wood-frame residence on narrow urban lot.

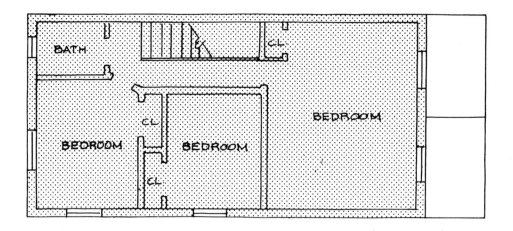

SECOND FLOOR

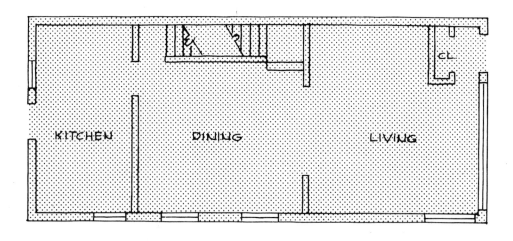

FIRST FLOOR

11-19.   Case 3: Floor plans for first and second stories. (For two possible orientations see figure 11-20)

city lots can create disadvantages in building shape and solar access. Two possible southern orientations of this type of house are investigated (s₁ and s₂ in figure 11-20) to suggest retrofit designs most suitable for each.

Option 1—Two-Story Sunspace Entrance

When the front, or street-facing, part of the house receives the south sun, a two-story sunspace entrance can work well. Although the walls in this case are not masonry, a concrete floor slab in the sunspace can function as the heat storage mass (figure 11-21).

Warm air circulation takes place through windows opening to the solar space. To balance heat throughout the house, mechanical circulation of warm air from the sunspace to the remote areas within may be desirable.

During the summer, deciduous street trees provide adequate shading. Operable windows along the top and at the bottom of the sunspace encourage airflow for ventilation.

Interior Changes

Because the sunspace faces the street, providing for privacy with translucent glazing may be desired.

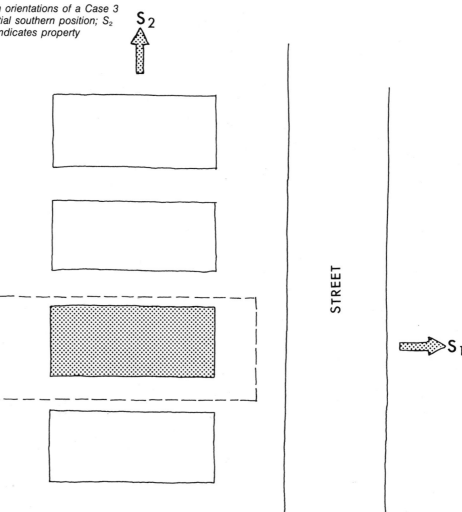

11-20. Two possible southern orientations of a Case 3 building. S_1 signifies one potential southern position; S_2 suggests another. Broken line indicates property boundaries.

S 2

PROPERTY LINE

STREET

S 1

To increase floor area, a second-story horizontal division of the sunspace as described on page 125 provides usable solar space on both levels.

Option 2—Skylights

When the south sun is on the long side of the house, the lower gambrel roof angle, which is near optimum for solar heat collection, can be utilized. A row of operable skylights along the lower portion of the roof provides a significant amount of solar heat. Night-insulating panels minimize heat loss through the glazing and reduce summer heat gain.

Interior Changes

When the attic is used as living space, heat collected by the system can be used directly. Heat storage, in the form of phase-change materials, can be placed in the space in direct sunlight. When excess heat accumulates in the attic, it can be mechanically ducted into spaces below.

Most often, an attic space functions as an unheated storage area. In these cases, a subdivision such as that shown in figure 11-23 can reflect and deflect incoming sunlight to the occupied areas below. Phase-change heat-storage modules mounted at the top of the wall receiving the sun can function as thermal mass to prevent excessive daytime temperatures.

The major interior change in this scheme is the creation of a "solar hallway" on the second floor. Because the hallway is purely a circulation and not living space, the usual problems of fabric fading and personal overheating are less critical.

Case 4: Three-Family Attached House

Attached two- and three-family structures offer a great thermal advantage over single-family detached units. Heat loss along the two attached side walls is eliminated, and one roof area serves three separate living units. In this case, an attached house with the street facade oriented toward the south is in an urban area with a temperate climate, masonry exterior walls make a thermal storage wall retrofit possible.

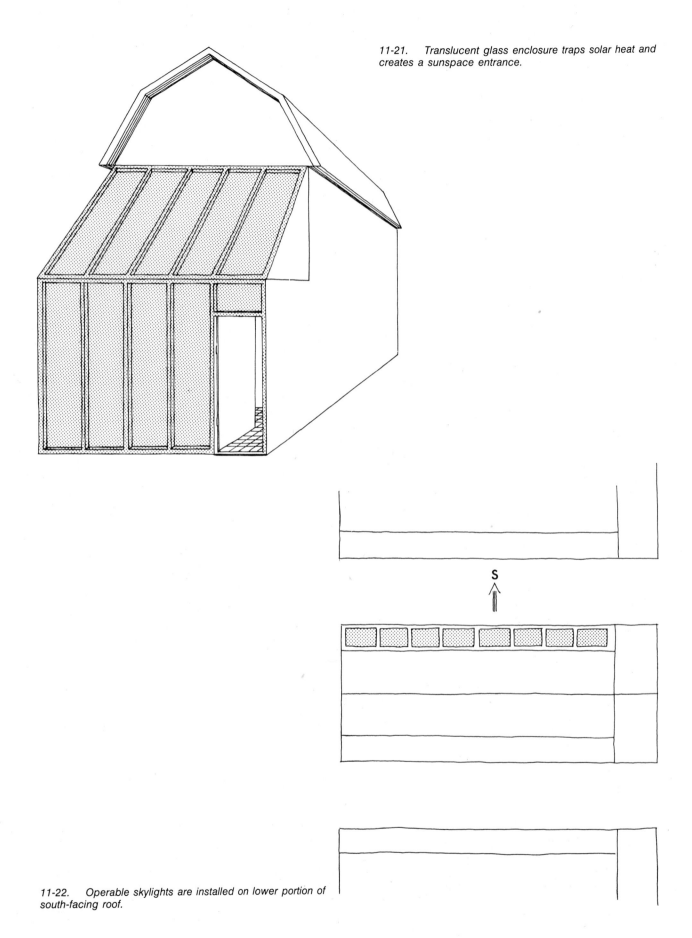

11-21.   Translucent glass enclosure traps solar heat and creates a sunspace entrance.

11-22.   Operable skylights are installed on lower portion of south-facing roof.

S

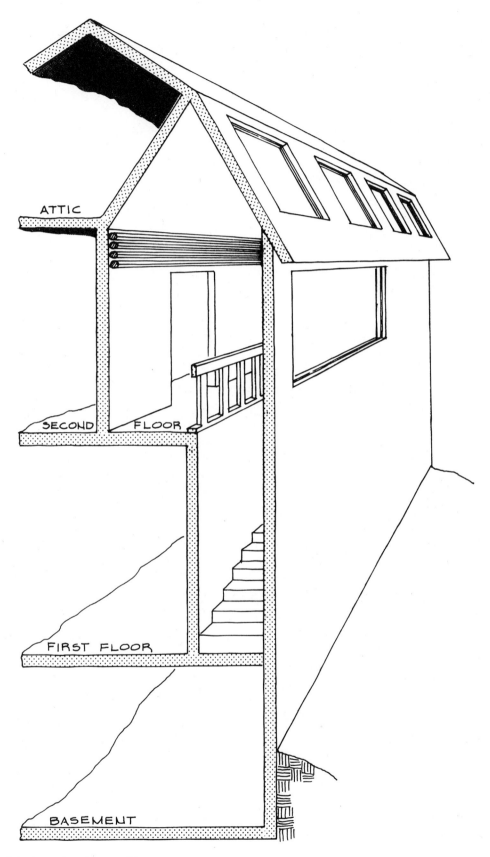

ATTIC

SECOND FLOOR

FIRST FLOOR

BASEMENT

11-23.   *South-facing skylights introduce wintertime sunshine into interior hallway.*

11-24. *Case 4: Typical three-family attached row house.*

Option 1—Indirect Thermal Storage Wall

Glazing attached to the south-facing wall of each house creates a Trombe wall effect in the interior spaces. The recessed entrances are glassed in as illustrated in figure 11-25 to form solar heat-collecting vestibules.

Interior Changes

Layout changes are not necessary, since living and dining areas are located along the street facing the thermal storage wall and both bedrooms face the back. As before, insulating interior finish on the south wall should be removed and obstructions to the flow of heat from the wall eliminated.

Case 5: Residential Multistory Apartment Unit

An individual apartment or condominium unit with unobstructed south access can benefit from a passive solar conversion. The design approach for these spaces, however, differs from that of single-family houses. The major difference stems from the lower heating requirements of the space: since most surfaces within the apartment are interior surfaces, the heat loss per square foot of floor area is greatly reduced, and therefore less glazing and less mass is needed to maintain comfortable temperatures. Second, since an apartment is only one part of an architectural element, any changes made will necessarily have an impact on the building as a whole. Last, because an apartment is often a rental unit, renters will want to keep the expense of a conversion to a minimum.

Case 5 involves a condominium apartment in a multistory residential structure in a large urban area with a cold climate. Non-loadbearing masonry walls and concrete slab floors are the thermal mass materials in the building.

Option 1—Direct Gain System

Existing window openings on the south wall are currently covered by drapes during the day even in the winter to prevent daytime overheating of the space, which occurs

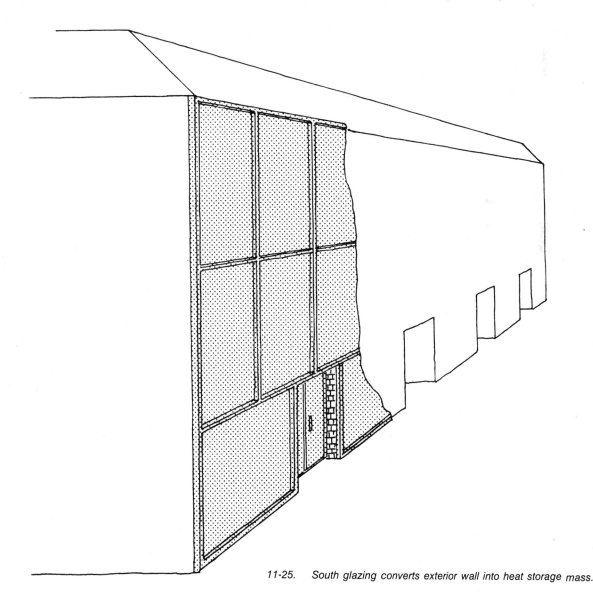

11-25. *South glazing converts exterior wall into heat storage mass.*

11-26. *Living room floor becomes a heat sink, while phase-change window panels store incoming solar heat in the bedroom.*

S

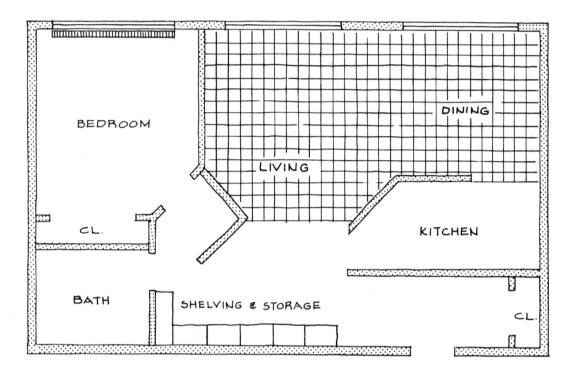

frequently. In the evening, the interior cools rapidly, and electrical heating elements, paid for by the owner of the condominium, are activated.

The conversion of this space to passive solar can make it thermally efficient by providing a heat sink for the incoming sunlight. Thermal mass is formulated by removing the wall-to-wall carpeting in the direct gain spaces, the living room and dining area. The bared concrete slab floor is then finished with moderately dark quarry tiles. With this design change, the concrete slab is transformed into a thermal storage floor, moderating both day and nighttime temperatures within the space (see figure 11-26).

Interior Changes

Existing drapes on south-facing windows are replaced by interior wooden thermal shutters. Opened during winter days, they allow unobstructed sun to enter the space. At night and during the summer, they function as insulation from undesired thermal effects.

Since maximum exposure of the floor to direct sunlight is essential to the effectiveness of this system, furniture in rooms with direct gain should not be bulky. Because of the beds and chests associated with bedrooms, a relatively high percentage of the floor may be shaded from direct

sun, therefore, an indirect heat gain is utilized within this space. Phase-change panels, made to fit into window openings, are installed in most of the bedroom windows. Translucent to allow some daylighting, these panels soak in sunlight directly before it enters the space.

Case 6: Apartment Unit with Balcony

A south-facing balcony or terrace can be retrofitted to function as a sunspace. Although individual balconies can be converted, the system works best when an entire vertical line of balconies is retrofitted so that each unit can benefit from those above and below it. The two side walls of each balcony can be constructed with insulating materials, and the front can be glazed as shown in figure 11-27. With this scheme, the floor and ceiling of each balcony becomes a heat sink, serving the spaces above and below. Excess heat collected on sunny days can be pulled into adjoining spaces mechanically or by natural gravity convection. When the wall between the balcony and the interior is solid masonry, it can be utilized for conductive heat transfer as described on page 126.

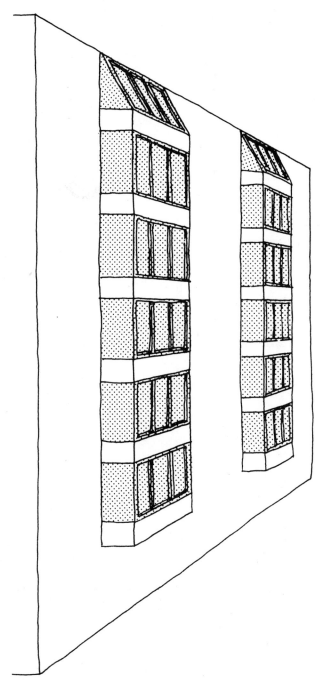

11-27. *Solar conversion uses balcony as floor space as well as increasing heat-collecting potential.*

Interior Changes

Because of the isolated nature of this type of heat gain, no major changes in the interior space are required. The conversion offers thermal benefits and adds more living space.

For summertime comfort, it is best to remove or replace some glass panels with solar screening. Vents on the side walls can encourage air movement.

Case 7: Nonresidential Space

In this case, an office space is examined within a high-rise building in a cold climate. The rented space takes up half of the floor, with access to both south and north exposures. The present subdivision of spaces represents inefficient use of available solar heat and causes overheating of small offices on the south side (see figure 11-28). The proposed conversion changes the layout and introduces usable thermal mass into the space (see figure 11-29).

Option 1—Combination Direct and Indirect Heat Gain

The major cause of solar heat waste is poor spatial layout, causing unbalanced thermal conditions within the office. Individuals working in small offices along the amply glazed south wall draw shades not only in the summer but also during most winter days to avoid overheating and glare.

Because the climate of the area can be a cold one, heating costs account for the largest overhead expenditure. A conversion of the space into a passive solar heat collector is therefore welcome.

Interior Changes

The office space is occupied by a large architectural and engineering firm, and requires small enclosed offices for engineers as well as large open drafting areas. Because of the type of work involved, good daylighting without glare is essential.

The layout scheme illustrated in figure 11-29 eliminates the small enclosed offices along the south wall and replaces them with large open drafting spaces. Solar radiation entering through the south-facing glass areas can now be dispersed through a larger area than before. The north side of the office space, where individual offices are located, is now zoned separately to assure comfortable conditions. Because the office is unoccupied at night, daytime heat utilization becomes top priority. Automatic temperature sensors in the direct gain spaces activate air circulation systems within the office when overheating occurs.

The problem of glare is solved by translucent light-diffusing interior window inserts to disperse incoming sunlight. The carpeting on the concrete floors is replaced by tiles in all areas except circulation paths where noise may be a problem. The thermal floors, while receiving little direct sunlight due to office furniture, will help moderate rapid temperature changes within the direct gain spaces.

Even with mechanical temperature controls, people in the north offices may experience discomfort from the large cold window surfaces. Special insulating translucent window shades can minimize this. The shades can be operated from the bottom up, stopping halfway, and from the top down. This method allows shades to be pulled up to head level, minimizing the direct adverse influence of the cold windows.

When the mild season begins, additional heat from the sun is no longer needed. Offices along the north wall may have brief direct sun and perhaps some indirect sunlight reflected from surrounding structures. On the south facade,

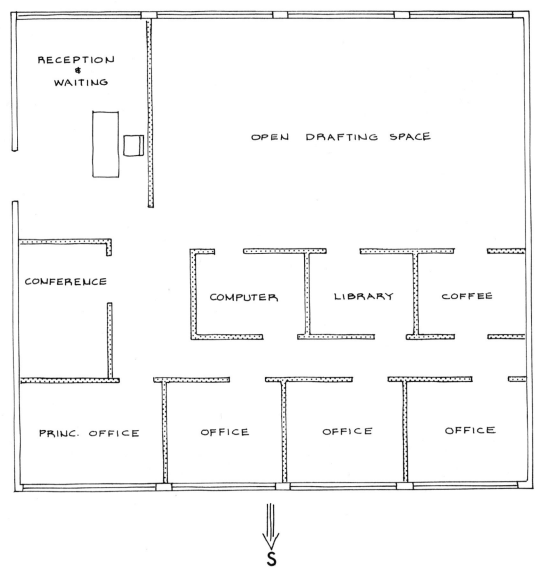

RECEPTION & WAITING

OPEN DRAFTING SPACE

CONFERENCE

COMPUTER   LIBRARY   COFFEE

PRINC. OFFICE   OFFICE   OFFICE   OFFICE

S

EXISTING OFFICE LAYOUT

11-28.   Existing plan necessitates rejection of available wintertime solar heat.

summertime heat gain is a greater concern. To avoid excessive cooling costs, energy-efficient exterior translucent shades should be installed on all south windows.

East and West Exposures

A space opening to the rising or setting sun can be beautiful. During the mild seasons of spring and fall, east and west orientations are at their best. The trouble starts in the summertime, when the hot sun shines in directly for a considerable length of time each day. In the winter, because of the short path of the sun, east and west receive little of the much-needed sunshine.

The amount of heat gained throughout the day on direct east exposures is equal to that gained on direct west exposures in all seasons. This fact may be surprising to those who have always referred to the hot west sun. Perhaps the misconception stems from the fact that during the summer, the air temperature is at its lowest in the morning, the peak temperature occurring sometime in the afternoon. The morning sun in the east, therefore, is easier to bear than the late afternoon sun in the west.

Wind pattern is another determinant of a favorable orientation. An exposure in the direction of prevailing summer breezes is preferred to one oriented toward winter winds. Prevailing winds differ in various parts of the world, although north is often the source of cold winds. In the temperate climate of the northeast United States, for instance, the general direction of winter winds is north-northwest, and the summer breeze originates from the southwest. In these regions, therefore, the east exposures are associated with

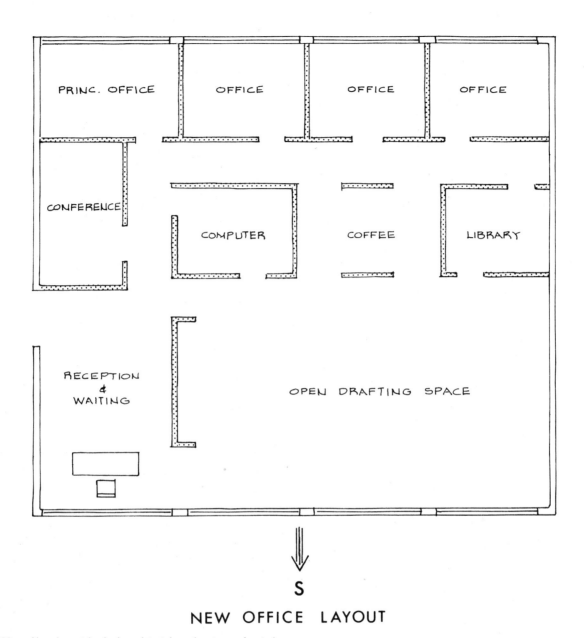

PRINC. OFFICE OFFICE OFFICE OFFICE

CONFERENCE COMPUTER COFFEE LIBRARY

RECEPTION & WAITING OPEN DRAFTING SPACE

S

NEW OFFICE LAYOUT

11-29.   New layout is designed to take advantage of entering solar radiation.

less adverse thermal influences than are direct west orientations. In the northwest United States and the western part of Europe, winter winds originate from the southwest and summer breezes from west-northwest, still making east exposure preferable to west.

Although east and west directions have no substantial wintertime heat gain in temperate climates, design techniques to increase cold-season solar heat gain are often possible. The case studies that follow analyze options that decrease the adverse effects of east and west exposures and increase possible benefits.

Case 8: Attached Two-Family Brick Homes with East-West Exposure

Although neighborhood zoning limits heights of adjacent

buildings, access to the south is often minimized because of poor planning. The north-south axis of a street with the row of attached residences parallel to the street axis makes the south wall of each structure a party wall. A design retrofit that increases the amount of winter sun entering the interior is desired.

Option 1—Clerestory Windows along the East-West Axis

Solar access through a row of 3-foot-high (.9 m) clerestory windows across the roof of each building introduces heat and light into each top floor apartment. Heat storage, in the form of phase-change materials, is located in an enclosed clerestory loft shown in figure 11-31. Metal ceiling panels below the thermal storage loft permit efficient radiation of

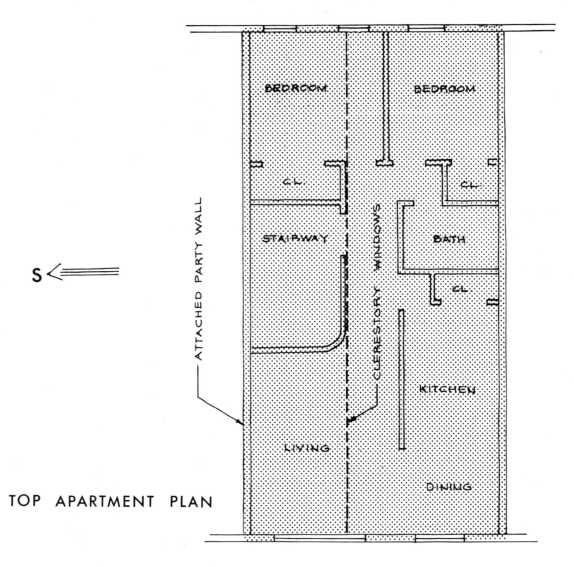

S ⟸

TOP APARTMENT PLAN

11-30. *Case 8: Exterior walls have access only to east or west. A row of south-facing clerestory windows adds natural wintertime heating.*

stored heat to the living spaces below.

An architectural overhang at clerestory windows shades these glazing areas from the summer sun. To further facilitate summer cooling, windows are operable for efficient exhaust of warmest air.

Interior Changes

Although the top apartment receives most of the direct solar advantage in this option, the heating costs of the building as a whole are significantly reduced.

Now that adequate daylight and solar radiation enters the upper apartment through the clerestory glass, some energy-wasting windows can be closed off. West windows in the master bedroom are now eliminated, and east windows in the living room and dining area are replaced with smaller energy-efficient units. Insulating shades, operated from below, are installed on the clerestory windows to minimize nighttime heat loss and to regulate incoming daylight.

Because the winter sunlight enters above head-level and its heat is stored in the clerestory loft, it has little direct impact on human comfort. In addition, problems such as furniture shading the mass or fabrics fading do not occur.

Option 2—Isolated Heat Gain

When direct light from clerestory windows is not desired, an isolated heat storage loft can be constructed. The clerestory rooftop addition shown in figure 11-32 is a well-insulated thermal storage space that contains phase-change materials to absorb direct sunlight. Solar heat is distributed through both apartments by thermostatically controlled

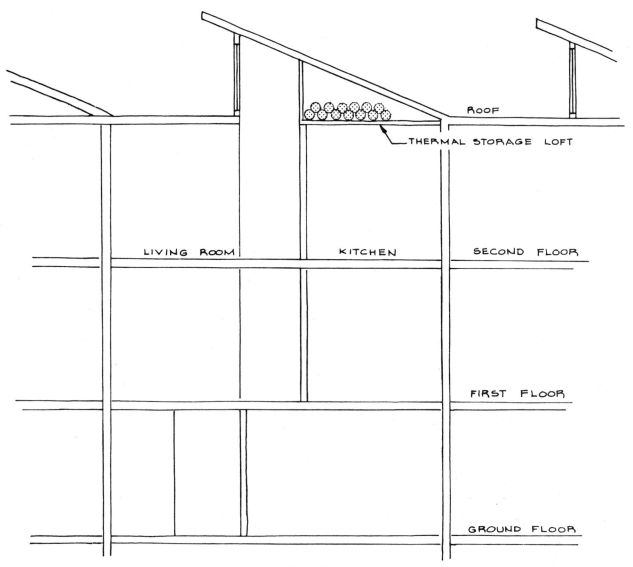

11-31.   *Solar radiation from south-facing windows adds light and heat to existing interior.*

forced-air systems.

Interior Changes

Due to the isolated nature of this option, major design changes in the interior spaces are not required. Since the conversion does not add direct sunlight to the interior spaces, however, windows on adverse exposures cannot be eliminated. To improve the thermal behavior of the existing windows, roll-down exterior insulating shutters provide shade in the summer and insulation in the winter.

Case 9: Multistory Apartment Building with East Exposure

This fire-damaged apartment building, located in a temperate climate, is currently being reconstructed and renovated. Situated on a tight building lot, the street frontage is due east, with buildings of similar height on either side of the property line (see figure 11-33).

Because of the afternoon shading of the building, con-

version to a passive solar system is infeasible. Window orientation changes, however, bring considerably more wintertime solar heat and light into each apartment than did the previous east windows.

A quick comparison of before-noon solar heat gain for 40° north latitude, that of Denver, Colorado, on direct east exposure and southeast exposure reveals the thermal advantage of the southeast over east. The two existing 3-by-5-foot (.9 by 1.5 m) east-facing windows provide a total of 13,470 Btu's in solar heat on a sunny mid-winter day. To create a more favorable orientation, these windows are replaced with the new southeast glazing shown in figure 11-34. The new windows, 10 by 5 feet (3 by 1.4 m) high, now allow approximately 45,150 Btu's of solar heat into each apartment on a sunny mid-winter day (see figure 11-35).

Interior Changes

With the east-facing windows in the old arrangement,

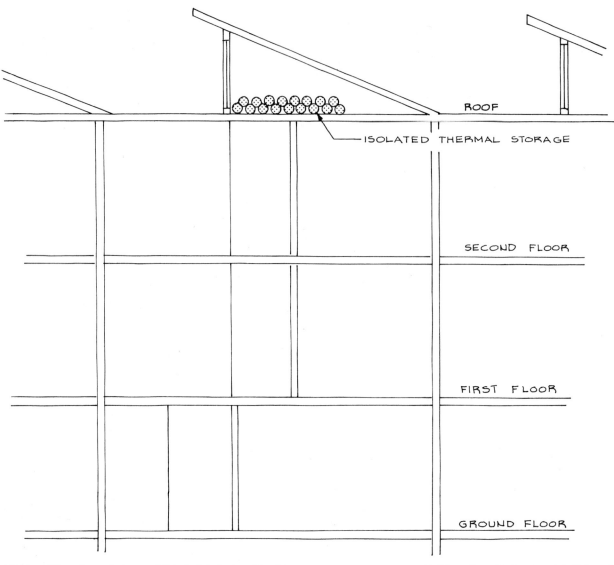

ROOF

ISOLATED THERMAL STORAGE

SECOND FLOOR

FIRST FLOOR

GROUND FLOOR

11-32.   When thermal storage loft is isolated, stored heat is
mechanically distributed throughout the building.

11-33.   Case 9: Apartment building site.

S

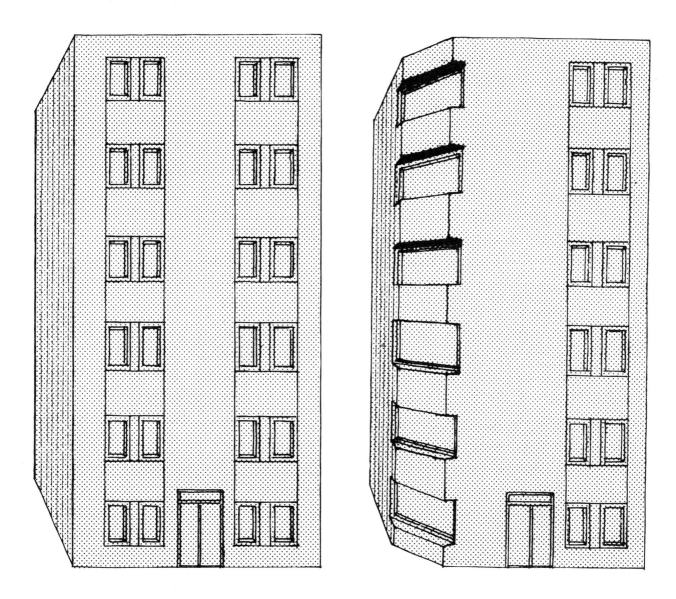

EXISTING EAST FACADE   NEW SOUTHEAST WINDOWS

11-34. Old and new window orientations.

winter sun entered the interior for only a brief period in the morning. After the addition of southeast exposures, significant direct sunlight now enters until noon. Although on an overall daily basis the heat gained on an unobstructed southeast exposure is less than that on direct south orientations, the morning heat gain on the southeast is greater than on direct south. To distribute the morning heat more evenly throughout the day, therefore, the massive brick fireplace, located opposite the southeast window, serves as a heat sink.

Insulating louvers on all windows are used to reduce heat loss after the sun goes down and for shading and daylight regulation. Highly reflective insulating exterior shades are selected for bedroom windows.

Interior layout is such that the most used spaces receive the benefit of the favorable exposure. Open planning of

living room/dining area along with glass-block kitchen partition allows daylight deep into the interior.

Case 10: Office Space on an East Exposure

A direct east orientation in an office can produce a heat and glare problem in the summer. In winter, the small amount of solar heat is welcome, but the direct glare of the sun between 9:00 and 10:00 AM may be annoying to workers. Window treatments can solve both problems.

Energy-efficient exterior translucent shading devices that lower automatically with direct sunlight reduce summer heat gain while letting in some daylight. In winter, the shades are activated during the night by a central control system to reduce conductive heat loss from office spaces.

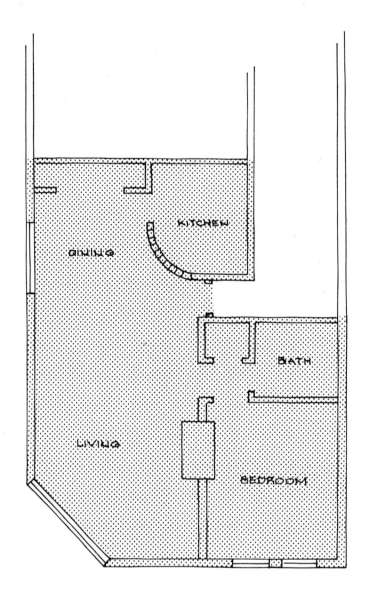

NEW LAYOUT OF EAST APARTMENTS

11-35.   Southeast windows create warmer and sunnier apartments.

Interior Changes

Tight-fitting sheer curtains on the inside surface of glazing areas form an insulating air space between the glass and the interior and lessen the direct adverse effect of the cold window surface on individuals. Open planning of the interior with low partitions allows daylight to penetrate deep within the space. Carpeting is installed for its thermal benefits and for noise reduction.

Case 11: Multistory Apartment Building with West Exposure

Window orientation changes made on west-facing apart-ments are similar to those for east orientations. In this case, however, the new orientation is toward the southwest, with solar radiation entering the space in the afternoon.

Interior Changes

The amount of heat gained from the southwest is identical to that gained from the southeast, but the interior space is different in its thermal behavior. Because sunlight enters later in the day, more solar heat remains in the space in the evening when living spaces are most utilized. Additionally, interior thermal mass surfaces warmed by the afternoon sun stay warmer in the evening than on southeast orientations where surfaces lose most of their stored heat by late afternoon.

Insulating louvers again provide window insulation and sunlight reflection for summertime efficiency.

Case 12: Office Space on a West Exposure

A west-facing office has problems similar to an east-oriented one with one major difference. As noted before, outdoor summertime temperature conditions make the west sun appear to be a greater heat burden than the east sun. In addition, the cooling load of air conditioning systems is usually lower in the morning. As the outdoor temperature rises, more people come and go, operating more lights and equipment, all of which cause the mounting Btu's to become a strain on the building's cooling system by late afternoon.

A study comparing heating and cooling costs can determine if permanent shading is appropriate. When cooling costs far outweigh heating expenditures, light-reflective film can be mounted on west-facing glazing areas. When heating is the greatest expense, translucent exterior shades are more suitable.

Interior Changes

Because the cold winter winds originate from the northwest, the west exposure has a more serious draft problem than the east windows. To reduce cold air infiltration, existing windows are caulked and thermally reinforced with clear interior glazing units.

The office layout is dictated by functional requirements necessitating enclosed divisions along the window wall. Each private office is designed to avoid adverse thermal effects of large glass surfaces by locating seating near interior partitions.

North Exposures

North light is associated with a pleasant uniform illumination. Nevertheless, the amount of daylight available from a direct north exposure (figure 11-36) is considerably less than from any other orientation. For this reason, a space on the north is much darker than a similar space on a different orientation.

Another characteristic typical of north exposures is rapid loss of heat. The heat loss in Btu/square foot through a window or solid wall facing north is significantly higher than losses through surfaces facing east, west, or south. Spaces on north exposures, therefore, or any other orientation totally obstructed from the sun, often have two problems; inadequate daylight and cold, sunless conditions throughout most of the year.

The task of the designer of nonsolar interiors, therefore, will be to increase natural lighting and shelter occupants from cold drafts and surfaces.

Case 13: Loft to Be Converted into Living Spaces

The loft in this case opens into a north-facing courtyard. The courtyard is shaded most of the day by the building itself and nearby structures. With no prospects for a solar conversion, techniques to increase daylighting and reduce heat loss from the space must be investigated.

11-36.   Approximate relative noontime clear-day sky illumination on vertical surfaces facing east, west, north, and south compared to lighting levels on horizontal surfaces at 40° north latitude. (Values represent skylight alone without the effect of direct solar radiation.)

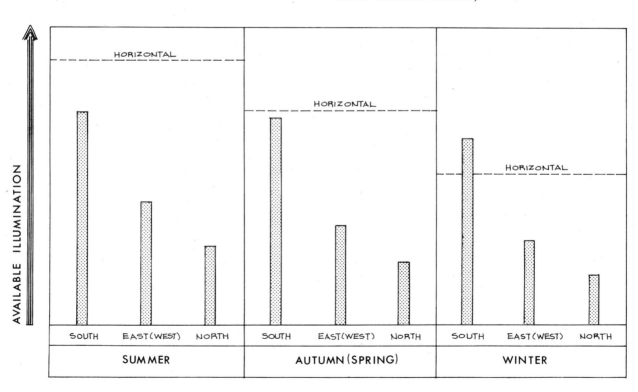

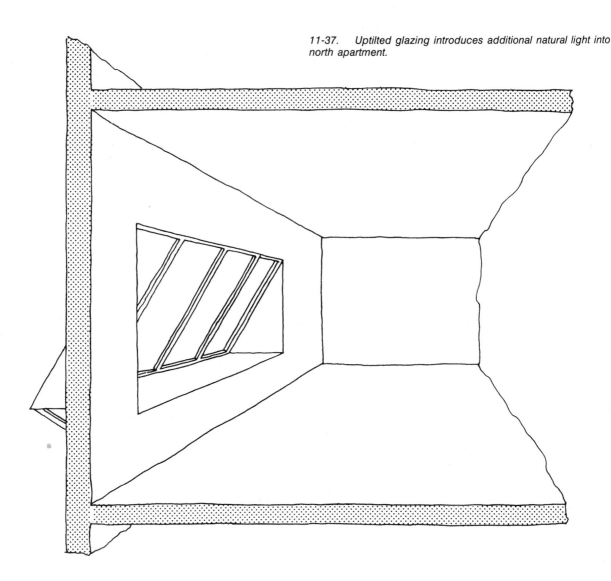

11-37. *Uptilted glazing introduces additional natural light into north apartment.*

The three single-pane windows in the space measure 4 by 7 feet (1.2 by 2.1 m) and are extremely inefficient thermally.

The first step is to improve window areas. Although energy-wasting north windows must be reduced in size, the daylight they admit is essential. An uptilted window angle will increase the incoming daylight while reducing the actual glass area. The previous overall glass area of 84 square feet (7.8 m²) is now reduced to 50 square feet (4.6 m²), yet it provides more natural illumination than before (see figure 11-37). A 3½-foot (1.1 m) cantilever provides structural support of the new window. The new windows are double-glazed reinforced plastic fiberglass panels tilted 45° from the horizontal.

Interior Changes

The new window extension provides natural light and becomes the focal point of the room during the day. The sill area, painted a glossy white, further enhances natural daylighting within the room. At night, tight-fitting thermal shutters are pulled across the entire opening.

Because of the lack of abundant daylight, all major surfaces are painted white. The 11-foot (3.3 m) ceiling is lowered by 2 feet for thermal and lighting advantages. Care is taken to select furniture, carpets, and fabrics with relatively high light-reflecting qualities. Darker accent colors are used to balance the overall color scheme.

Since winter cold is a greater problem than summer heat, attention is given to occupants' "contact comfort." Highly textured and plush fabrics are good selections for seating and floor covering. Thermodecor wallpaper with thermal-reflecting capabilities is effective on the north exterior wall for lowering heat loss and increasing individual comfort.

The interior of the loft studio is laid out so that most daytime activities receive natural illumination (see figure 11-38). Bathroom, kitchen, and sleeping areas are moved farther back within the space.

Case 14: Low-Rise Building with Obstructed Exposure

Although both facades of this two-story residential struc-

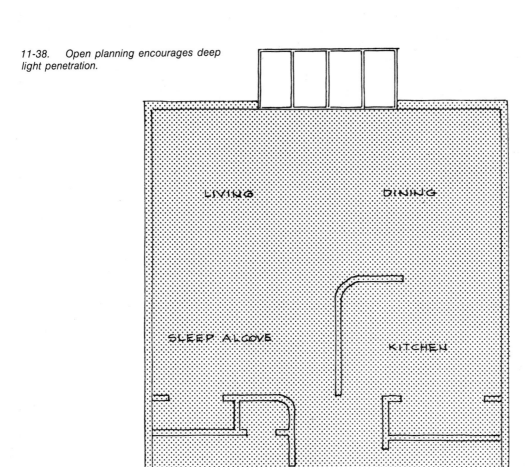

11-38. *Open planning encourages deep light penetration.*

ture are obstructed from direct sunlight, the roof has clear access to the sun. To increase lighting and introduce sun into the top apartment, four south-facing skylights are recommended. With skylight glazing at 60° with the horizontal, maximum winter sun is captured and reflected down into the spaces below. Although the typical skylight area is only 12 square feet (1.1 m²), the additional light provided is several times the light available from existing vertical windows.

Interior Changes

To minimize heat loss through the new skylights, a quilted fabric is drawn over the shaft during the night. On hot summer days, the fabric can be used for shading the spaces below. In the late afternoon, when direct solar radiation through the skylight is minimal, skylight can be opened for efficient exhaust of accumulated heat.

Case 15: Company Dining Area on the North Wall

The dining room in this case is located in a cold climate within an old building with high ceilings. All windows are single glazed and oriented to the north with a minimum of

reflected sun passing through them.

The objective of the design is to minimize some of the adverse effects of the window orientation.

Interior Changes

Because good daylighting in the dining room is desired, existing window areas are not reduced. To slow the transfer of heat, an extra layer of clear glazing is applied to all windows from the inside. In addition, light-filtering fabric shades that can be pulled up from the bottom further reduce adverse thermal effects of cold window surfaces.

The layout of the dining area separates circulation space from eating space with a 1½-foot (.46 m) elevation change (see figure 11-40). Individuals seated at the elevated dining level have the advantage of daylight without direct draft from nearby window surfaces.

Case 16: Private House with Unobstructed Exposures and Scenic View Toward the North

When a private house has a clear access to the south, a passive solar conversion is feasible. Along with the con-

11-39. Skyshaft-type skylights brighten upper level.

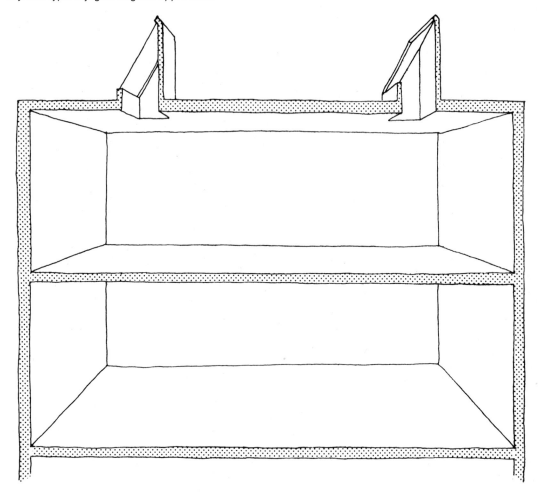

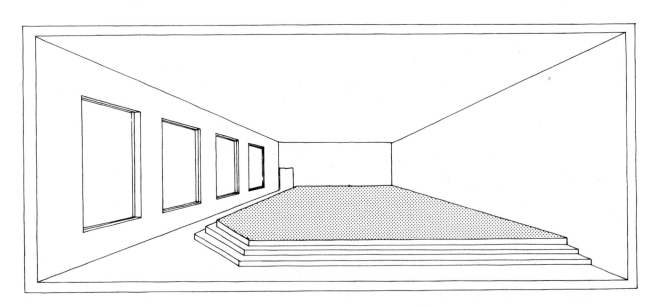

11-40. Elevation differential divides dining and circulation space and offers increased thermal comfort to those seated.

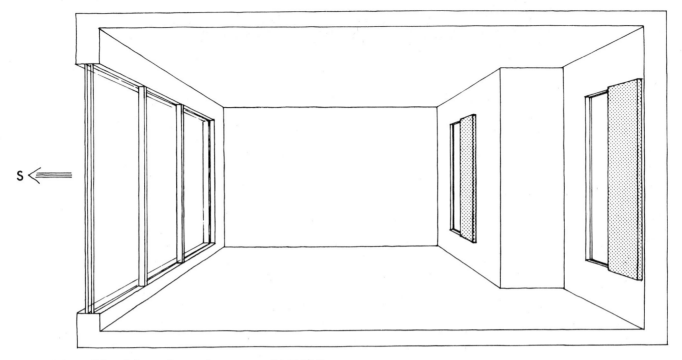

S ⟸

11-41.   *Although large glass surfaces are on the south to capture solar radiation and provide daylight, narrow, triple-glazed windows with hinged thermal shutters on the north give visual access to the view with a minimum of heat loss.*

version, excess windows on north and west orientations are usually eliminated for maximum efficiency. In this case, however, the view of a lake makes windows on the north highly desirable. One of the design objectives therefore is to solve the conflict between thermal efficiency and aesthetics.

Interior Changes

Since the passive solar conversion produces a direct gain system, daylight and sun enters living and dining space through south windows. Although existing windows on the north are no longer needed, they are desirable because of the lake view.

An ideal design will preserve the view while reducing heat loss through north-facing glass. The two existing large north-wall windows are removed and replaced by three

triple-glazed energy-efficient units totalling one-third the original glazing area. These smaller windows, occurring at various intervals along the north wall, provide a subtle visual access to the view. Night-insulating hinged shutters further reduce heat loss through north windows (see figure 11-41).

Solar Interiors–Nonsolar Interiors

Individuals can improve their interior space by weighing options against personal priorities. Existing spaces can often be converted to solar interiors. Even when solar heating is not possible, interiors can be designed to take maximum advantage of the benefits available. Solar interior planning can make a sunny exposure sunnier in the winter, a dark interior brighter, a cold space warmer, and an overheated room more comfortable.

APPENDIX: MANUFACTURERS

Window Insulation and Shading

Bali Duotone Venetian Blinds, available at Marathon, Carey, McFall, 1107 Broadway, New York, NY 10010

The Hopper and Company Heatkeeper™ (movable insulation rolls up from the bottom of the window), Hopper and Company Inc., Box 689, Blue Hills Road, Durham, CT 06422

Insulating Curtain Wall™ (multilayer reflective shade), Thermal Technology Corporation, P.O. Box 130, Snowmass, CO 81654

Insulating Shade-High R Shade (multilayer shades), Insulating Shade Company Inc., P.O. Box 282, Branford, CT 06405

Insul Shutter (insulating skylight shutter), distributed by Sunsitive Systems Inc., 365 East Park Avenue, Long Beach, NY 11561

NRG Shade (see-through reflective shade), Sun Control Products Inc., 431 Fourth Avenue SE, Rochester, MN 55901

Pella Slimshade^R (interglazing miniblinds), Pella/Rolscreen Company, 102 Main Street, Pella, IA 50219

Plastic-View Shade (see-through high-quality reflective shade), Plastic-View Transparent Shades Inc., P.O. Box 25, Van Nuys, CA 91408

Roldoor Systems (roll-down exterior insulation), One Design, Inc., Mountain Falls Route, Winchester, VA 22601

RIB Reflective Insulating Blind (experimental wood insulating blinds), for information contact Oak Ridge National Laboratory, Energy Division, P.O. Box X, Oak Ridge, TN 37830

Rolladen, American German Industries, Inc., 14601 North Scottsdale Road, Scottsdale, AZ 85260

Skylids (insulating skylight shutters), Zomeworks Corporation, P.O. Box 25805, Albuquerque, NM 87125

Sol-R-Veil, Sol-R-Veil Inc., 635 West 23rd Street, New York, NY 10011

Sun Mover, Solar Technology Corporation (SOLTEC), 2160 Clay Street, Denver, CO 80211

Sun Quilt (quilted shades), Sun Quilt Corporation, P.O. Box 374, Newport, NH 03773

Sun Saver™ (insulating interior shutters), Homesworth Corporation, 18 Main Street, Yarmouth, ME 04096

Thermafold Shutters (interior insulating shutters), Shutters Inc., 110 East Fifth Street, Hastings, MN 55033

Thermanel (insulating shutters), Neilson Company, Route 1, Foreside Mall, Falmouth, Foreside, ME

Thermo-Shades™ (interlocking slatted shade system), Systems for Energy Conservation, 251 Welsh Pool Road, Lionville, PA 19353

Window Blankets (quilted insulating fabric), Window Blanket

Company, 107 Kingston Street, Lenoir City, TN 37771

Window Quilt™ (quilted insulating shade), Appropriate Technology Corporation, P.O. Box 975, Brattleboro, VT 05301

Drapery Liners

Warm-In Drapery Liner, Conservation Concepts Ltd., Box 376, Stratton Mountain, VT 05155

Wind-N-Sun Shield (drapery liners), Wind-N-Sun Shield Inc., P.O. Box 2504, Indian Harbor Beach, FL 32937

Wall Coverings

Fabri Trak (frame for installing padded wall covers), Unique Concepts, Inc., 59 Willet Street, Bloomfield, NJ 07003

Thermodecor, Enertec Systems, Inc., P.O. Box 127, 101 South Hough, Barrington, IL 60010

Fabrics

Foylon (insulating fabric), Duracote Corporation, 350 North Diamond Street, Ravenna, OH 44266

Simtrac fabrics (used in shading for greenhouses), Simtrac Inc., 8243 North Christiana, Skokie, IL 60076

Glazing Materials for Solar Transmission

Solakleer, General Glass International, 270 North Avenue, New Rochelle, NY 10801

Sunadex™ and Lo-iron™, ASG Industries, P.O. Box 929, Kingsport, TN 37662

SunGain, 3M Company, Bldg. 223-2, 3M Center, Saint Paul, MN 55101

Glazing Materials for Insulation

Defender 1™ (interior storm windows), Defender Energy Corporation, P.O. Box L, Dept. S, Mahopac, NY 10541

Flexigard (insulating window kits), Energy Control Products, 3M Company, Bldg. 220-E, SE 223-2W, 3M Center, Saint Paul, MN 55144

Temp-Rite, Solar Usage Now, Inc., Box 306, Bascom, OH 44809

Wind-O-Gard (acrylic panels), Hadco Home Improvements, 9 East Street, Boston, MA 02111

Sun Shade Screens

Kool Shade, Kool Shade Corporation, 722 Genevieve Street, P.O. Box 210, Solana Beach, CA 92075

Shade Screen, Kaiser Aluminum, 300 Lakeshore Drive, Oakland, CA 94643

Shading Films

Kool-Vue, Solar Screen, 53-11 105th Street, Corona, NY 11368

Reflecto-Shield, Reflecto-Shade, Madico, 64 Industrial Parkway, Woburn, MA 01801

Sungard, Metallized Products, 224 Terminal Drive, Saint Petersburg, FL 33712

Heat Exchangers

Echo Changer (air to air heat exchanger), Mephremagog Heat Exchangers, Inc., P.O. Box 456, Newport, VT 05855

Mitsubishi-Lossnay, available from BTU Systems Inc., 451 Fulton Avenue, Hempstead, NY 11550

Human Comfort Instrument

Comfort Meters (measures human comfort by the combined effects of air temperature, air movement, and the radiant temperatures of the surrounding surfaces), Solarware Inc., IA Solar Park, Pawlet, VT 05761

Thermal Storage: Water

Heat Wall™, Suncraft, 5001 East 59th Street, Kansas City, MO 64130

Kallwall™ Storage Tubes, Kallwall Corporation, Solar Components Division, P.O. Box 237, Manchester, NH 03105

Stud Space Module™, One Design, Inc., Mountain Falls Route, Winchester, VA 22601

Tubewall™, Tankwall™, Waterwall Engineering, Route 1, Box 6, New Paris, OH 45347

Thermal Storage: Phase Change Materials

Enerphase, Dow Chemical Company, FP&S Department, 2020 Dow Center, Midland, MI 48640

Heat Pac™, Colloridal Materials, Inc., P.O. Box 696, Andover, MA 01810

Kallwall Solar Pod™, Kallwall Corporation, Solar Components Division, P.O. Box 237, Manchester, NH 03105

SCM Energy Rod™, Certified Energy Systems Inc., 24147 Juanita, San Jacinto, CA 92383

Sol-Ar-Tile™ (floor tile), Architectural Research Corporation, 13030 Wayne Road, Livonia, MI 48150

Texxor Heat Cells™, Texxor Corporation, 9910 North 48th Street, Omaha, NE 68152

Thermalrod-27, Energy Materials, Inc., 2622 South Zuni Street, Englewood, CO 80110

Thermol 81–The Energy Rod™, PSI Energy Systems Inc., 15331 Fen Park Drive, St. Louis, MO 63026

Sunspaces and Greenhouses

Four Seasons Solar Products, 910 Route 110, Farmingdale,

NY 11735

Garden Way Solar Greenhouse, Garden Way Research, Charlotte, VT 05445

Solar Room Kit, Solar Resources Inc., P.O. Box 1848, Taos, NM 87571

Soltec Greenroom™, Solar Technology Corporation, 2160 Clay Street, Denver, CO 80211

Sunglo Solar Greenhouses, Sunglo Greenhouses, 4441 26th Avenue, West Seattle, WA 98199

The Sunspace, Northern Sun, 21705 Highway 99, Lynnwood, WA 98036

Sunwrights Sun-Kit, Sunwrights, 1798 Massachusetts Avenue, Cambridge, MA 02140

Thermosiphoning Air Panels

Free Heat BTU Bank™ (installation under south facing window), Solar Bank Inc., 5600 Roswell Road NE, Suite 290, Prado East, Atlanta, GA 30342

Heliopass™ 100 (passive thermosiphoning air panel), Independent Energies, Inc., Route 131, Box 398, Schoolcraft, MI 49087

Passive Solar Heat Wall™ (thermosiphoning air panel with thermal storage), Crimsco, Inc., 5001 East 59th Street, Kansas City, MO 64130

Sunway Wall Collector™ (fan assisted thermosiphoning air panel), Sunway Corporation, P.O. Box 9723, Pittsburgh, PA 15229

BIBLIOGRAPHY

Passive Solar Design

Alternologies, *Passive Solar Sizing Guide*™, Fort Collins, CO: Alternologies, 1982.

Anderson, Bruce and Wells, Malcolm. *Passive Solar Energy*. Andover, MA: Brick House Publishing Company, 1981.

Balcomb, J. Douglas, et al. (Los Alamos Scientific Laboratory). *Passive Solar Design Analysis*. Passive Solar Design Handbook, vol. 2. Washington, DC: U.S. Department of Energy, 1980.

Cassiday, Bruce. *The Complete Solar House*. New York: Dodd, Mead, 1977.

Crowther, Richard L. *Sun/Earth*. New York: Van Nostrand Reinhold Company, 1983.

Gropp, Louis. *Solar Houses, 48 Energy Saving Designs*, New York: Pantheon Books, 1978.

Keyes, John. *Harnessing the Sun*. Denver, CO: Conestoga Graphics, 1974.

Langdon, William K. *Movable Insulation*. Emmaus, PA: Rodale Press, 1980.

Mazria, Edward. *The Passive Solar Energy Book*. Emmaus, PA: Rodale Press, 1979.

Shurcliff, William A. *Super Insulated Houses and Double Envelope Houses*. Andover, MA: Brick House Publishing Company, 1981.

Skurka, Norma, and Naar, Jon. *Design for a Limited Planet*. New York: Ballantine Books, 1976.

Strickler, Darryl J. *Passive Solar Retrofit*. New York: Van Nostrand Reinhold Company, 1982.

Wright, David. *Natural Solar Architecture*. New York: Van Nostrand Reinhold Company, 1978.

Wright, David, and Andrejko, Dennis. *Passive Solar Architecture*. New York: Van Nostrand Reinhold Company, 1982.

Wright, Rodney, et al. (The Hawkweed Group). *Passive Solar House Book*. Chicago: Rand McNally & Company, 1980.

Technical

The American Society of Heating, Refrigerating and Air-conditioning Engineers (ASHRAE), *Handbook of Fundamentals*. New York: 1982.

Dolan, Winthrop W. *A Choice of Sundials*. Brattleboro, VT: The Stephen Greene Press, 1975.

Kreider, Jan F., and Kreith, Frank. *Solar Energy Handbook*. New York: McGraw-Hill Book Company, 1981.

Kreider, Jan F., and Kreith, Frank. *Solar Heating and Cooling: Engineering, Practical Design and Economics*. Washington, DC: Hemisphere Publishing, 1975.

McGuiness, William J., and Stein, Benjamin. *Mechanical and Electrical Equipment for Buildings*. New York: John Wiley & Sons, 1971.

Mott-Smith, Morton. *The Concept of Heat and Its Workings Simply Explained*. New York: Dover Publications, 1962.

Waugh, Albert E. *Sundials, Their Theory and Construction*. New York: Dover Publications, 1973.

The Environment and Energy

Flynn, John E., and Segil, Arthur W. *Architectural Interior Systems*. New York: Van Nostrand Reinhold Company, 1970.

Givoni, B. *Man, Climate and Architecture*. New York: Van Nostrand Reinhold Company, 1981.

Halacy, D. S., Jr. *Earth, Water, Wind, and Sun: Our Energy Alternatives*. New York: Harper & Row, 1977.

Olgyay, Victor. *Design with Climate*. Princeton, NJ: Princeton University Press, 1963.

Stein, Richard G. *Architecture and Energy*. Garden City, NY: Anchor Press/Doubleday, 1977.

Energy Conservation

Dubin, Fred S., and Long, Chalmers G., Jr. *Energy Conservation Standards for Building Design, Construction and Operation*. New York: McGraw-Hill Book Company, 1978.

Jarmul, Seymour. *The Architect's Guide to Energy Conservation*. New York: McGraw-Hill Book Company, 1980.

The Residential Energy Audit Manual. Prepared by the U.S. Department of Energy with Oak Ridge National Laboratory, the University of Massachusetts Cooperative Extensive Service Energy Education Center, and the Solar Energy Research Institute, Atlanta, GA: The Fairmont Press Inc., 1981.

Human Comfort

Huntington, Ellsworth. *Principles of Human Geography*, 6th ed. New York: John Wiley & Sons, 1951.

Periodicals

New Shelter. Published by Rodale Press, 33 East Minor Street, Emmaus, PA 18049.

Popular Science. Published by Times Mirror Magazines, Inc., P.O. Box 2871, Boulder, CO 80302.

Solar Age. Published monthly by SolarVision, Inc., Church Hill, Harrisville, NH 03454.

Studies

Airborne Radionuclides and Radiation in Buildings: A Review. A. V. Nero, University of California, Lawrence Berkeley Laboratory Report, 1981.

Influence of Color on Heat Absorption. Faye C. Jones, University of Arizona Agricultural Experiment Station, Report No. 244, 1968.

Passive Solar Buildings: A Compilation of Data and Results. Sandia Laboratories, Los Alamos, NM, 1978.

Predicting the Performance of Passive Solar Heated Buildings. E. Mazria, M. S. Baker, and F. C. Wessling. University of Oregon, 1976.

Saving Energy, The New Gold. Results of a two-year study in Automatic Thermostat Setback and Setup. Edmond, OK: Honeywell, Inc., 1980.

INDEX

About the Author

Katherine Panchyk is a free-lance energy consultant and designer of solar spaces. Since 1977 she has been a member of the faculty of the Parsons School of Design, where she teaches courses on energy-consciousness. Most recently affiliated with Paul Weidlinger Associates in New York, she has lectured to community groups and is a member of the Alliance of Women in Architecture.